Alien Chic

Why have we fallen in love with aliens?

Alien Chic provides a cultural history of the alien since the 1950s, asking why our attitudes to aliens have shifted from fear to affection, and what this can tell us about how we now see ourselves and others.

Neil Badmington begins by exploring how our relationship with aliens is inscribed in films such as *The War of the Worlds*, *Mars Attacks!*, *Mission to Mars*, and *Independence Day*. He then considers how thinkers such as Descartes, Barthes, Freud, Lyotard and Derrida have conceptualised what it means to be human (and post-human).

The book then examines the concept of posthumanism in an age in which the lines between what is human and what is non-human are increasingly blurred by advances in science and technology, for example cloning and genetic engineering, and the development of AI and cyborgs. This leads to the question of whether or not our current embracing of all things 'alien' – in the form of extraterrestrial gadgets or abduction narratives, for instance – stems from a desire to reaffirm ourselves as 'human' at a moment of radical uncertainty.

Written in a clear and engaging style, *Alien Chic* is an original and thought-provoking contribution to the study of posthumanism.

Neil Badmington is Lecturer in Cultural Criticism and English Literature at the Centre for Critical and Cultural Theory, Cardiff University. He is the editor of *Posthumanism* (2000).

Alien Chic

Posthumanism and the Other Within

Neil Badmington

LONDON AND NEW YORK

First published 2004
by Routledge
2 Park Square, Milton Park, Abingdon, Oxon, OX14 4RN

Simultaneously published in the USA and Canada
by Routledge
270 Madison Avenue, New York, NY 10016

Routledge is an imprint of the Taylor & Francis Group

Transferred to Digital Printing 2005

Typeset in Galliard by M Rules

British Library Cataloguing in Publication Data
A catalogue record for this book is available from the British Library

Library of Congress Cataloging in Publication Data
Badmington, Neil, 1971–
Alien chic: posthumanism and the other within / Neil Badmington.
p. cm.
1. Human-alien encounters—Public opinion—History. 2. Martians—Public opinion—History. 3. Humanism—History. 4. Science fiction films—History and criticism. I. Title.
BF2050.B33 2004
001.942—dc22
2004002290

ISBN 0-415-31022-9 (hbk)
ISBN 0-415-31023-7 (pbk)

For Maria

Chic, but no alien

Contents

Acknowledgements

Close encounters of various kinds made the writing of *Alien Chic* infinitely easier. I owe special thanks to the following (although, needless to say, any remaining errors are entirely the work of alien beings):

James Annesley; The Badmingtons and the Prossers, for years of tirelessly watching the skies; Rebecca Barden and Lesley Riddle, for editorial guidance; Catherine Belsey, for leading the way, and for committed conspiring over watery sandwiches; Catherine Bernard; Clare Birchall; Fred Botting, for a whisky that put things in context; Noel Castree; Claire Connolly; Tom Dawkes and the staff of the Arts and Social Sciences Library at Cardiff University; Jill Didur; Mary Dortch, for her meticulous copy-editing; Diane Elam, for gin, vermouth, and a twist of Roswell; Ruth Evans; Elaine L. Graham, for support; Terence Hawkes, for lending crucial support at an early stage; Teresa Heffernan; Matthew Herbert, for showing me how humans can sound like aliens; Claire Joubert; Martin A. Kayman, for discussion and, in the criminal absence of a common room, for turning his office into the Kayman-room; Jean-Jacques Lecercle; Wendy Lewis, for help with figures; Emma Mason, for disagreeing like a true friend; Hannah Mayled, for *Manic Martians*; Laurent Milesi; Jessica Mordsley, for making me think, and for introducing me to the Raëlians long before the tabloids took an interest; Iain Morland; Jürgen Pieters and other members of the University of Ghent's Department of Dutch and Comparative Literature, for an illuminating day of discussion; Maria Prosser, for putting up with what no other human being (or alien) could; Bart Simon; David Skilton, for support and for not (as far as I could tell) batting an eyelid when I talked to the incoming Vice-Chancellor about inflatable aliens; Jonathan Smith and the members of the Temple Society at Rugby School; Julia Thomas, for sanity and monster chic; Mike Thomas, for interrupting his duties as father of the bride to talk about the nature of the universe; Miles Thompson; Sara Thornton, for objects; Ailbhe Thunder; Thomas Vargish; Richard Vine, for inside information, for reading the whole thing, and for kindly observing a UFO with me from a hot-tub in Santa Cruz.

I first discussed some of the ideas contained in this book with the students of my Alien Chic module in the Cultural Criticism programme at Cardiff University. I thank them all for their patience, enthusiasm, and remarkable ability to find examples of Alien Chic on the streets of Cathays.

Sections of *Alien Chic* were presented as papers at the following institutions: University of Birmingham, Cardiff University, University of Exeter, University of Ghent, Kingston University, University of Oxford, University of Paris VII, Rugby School, Marc Bloch University of Strasbourg, and University of Warwick. I should like to thank all those who commented.

Some of the material in chapter 4 first appeared as 'Theorizing posthumanism', *Cultural Critique*, 2003, vol. 53, pp. 10–27. Chapter 5 consists in part of material published as 'Pod Almighty! Or, humanism, posthumanism, and the strange case of *Invasion of the Body Snatchers*', *Textual Practice*, 2001, vol. 15.1, pp. 5–22 (http://www.tandf.co.uk/journals/routledge/0950236X.html), and '*Roswell High*, Alien Chic and the in/human', in Glyn Davis and Kay Dickinson (eds) *Teen TV: Genre, Consumption and Identity*, London: British Film Institute, 2004, pp. 166–76. I gratefully acknowledge permission to reprint from these sources.

Alien Chic could not have been written without the year of research leave generously awarded to me by Cardiff University and the Arts and Humanities Research Board (http://www.ahrb.ac.uk).

NB

Penarth, South Wales, December 2003

Introduction: They all laughed

> Ho, Ho, Ho!
> Who's got the last laugh?
> Hee, Hee, Hee!
> Let's at the past laugh
> Ha, Ha, Ha!
> Who's got the last laugh now?
>
> ELLA FITZGERALD,
> 'They all laughed'[1]

Between the baby and the weightlifter

I began with a desire to stop my students laughing.

As part of an undergraduate course on post-war American culture, I had decided to show a brief clip from *Invasion of the Body Snatchers* (dir. Don Siegel, 1956), one of the best-known alien invasion narratives of the period.[2] After some deliberation, I chose the sequence in which Miles and Becky, the central characters, tragically learn that one of their close friends, Jack Bellicec, has been captured by the extraterrestrial invaders. I need not have worried, in fact, about finding a suitable moment in the film, for it was impossible to hear the dialogue over the students' uncontrollable laughter.

I was, however, somewhat prepared for such a response. Nancy Steffen-Fluhr describes, in a fine essay written many years ago, a similar reaction by a group of her students.[3] And, if really pressed on this point, I would probably admit that many of the science fiction films of the 1950s never fail to bring a smile to my face. In the case of *Invasion of the Body Snatchers*, however, the students' laughter carried with it a certain irony, for, much to the annoyance of Don Siegel, Allied Artists had set out to remove all traces of humour from the film. Science fiction, the studio executives believed, was no laughing matter.[4] In the mid-1950s, that is to say, *Invasion of the Body Snatchers* was not meant to be funny; almost half a century later, it provokes howls of laughter.

Walter Benjamin once remarked that 'there is no better starting point for thought than laughter'.[5] And, as I struggled on with the lecture, I began to think somewhat obsessively about the students' response to the film. Why, I wondered, had they reacted in such a manner? Why had a once-serious text become something wildly amusing? Why laugh *now*, but not *then*? That wondering would eventually lead to the writing of this book.

The past, of course, often seems comically different from the present. Even tragedy, as Marx once pointed out,[6] can all too easily become farce. And the more I thought about my students' amusement, the more I began to wonder if difference *itself* was at stake in their response. Perhaps *Invasion of the Body Snatchers* struck them as ridiculous because it seeks to inscribe a set of values that are quite different from those currently recognized as 'normal'. Maybe, above all, the film approaches the relationship between humans and aliens in a manner that is laughably alien to the present. Perhaps, I thought, things have changed. Perhaps aliens are not what they once were: enemies, others, monsters. These thoughts continued to run through my head until the end of the lecture, when I suddenly realized that I was on the right track. As the students stood to leave the room, I noticed that one of them was carrying a backpack that bore the face of an extraterrestrial. Two words had been added by hand: 'Alien Love'.

That same week, I was correcting the proofs to a book on posthumanism.[7] Although it was too late to add anything to the volume, I nonetheless began to wonder if there might be a connection between what I had experienced in the lecture theatre and a more general cultural shift from humanism to posthumanism. Like other alien invasion narratives of the 1950s (several of which will figure in the following chapter), *Invasion of the Body Snatchers* depends upon a set of simple binary oppositions – above all, human versus inhuman, us versus them, and real versus fake – that are as hierarchical as they are absolute. Aliens are not just entirely different from humans; they are at once an enemy to be feared, hated, and destroyed. The film, it might be said, inscribes 'alien hatred', a clear sense of 'versus'.

The student's backpack, of course, declared the apparent opposite to 'alien hatred', and I began to wonder if a phenomenon that might be named 'alien love' had emerged from the contemporary crisis in humanist discourse that I was considering in *Posthumanism.* If the human and the inhuman no longer stand in binary opposition to each other, aliens might well be expected to find themselves welcomed, *loved*, displayed and celebrated as precious treasures. The 'versus' of the past might have given way to what Jacques Derrida calls a 'Crisis of *versus*'.[8] 'Alien love', that is to say, might be read as proof of the end of humanism.

I would not base a sustained piece of cultural criticism upon a single backpack, however, and began looking around for other examples of 'alien love'. I started, as usual, by shopping, and the more I browsed, the more I found: alien key rings and T-shirts, badges and socks, stationery and inflatable sofas, snacks and baby clothes, jigsaw puzzles and guitar picks, doormats and bottles of spring water, garden gnomes and zipper pulls, clocks and watches, mugs and hats, stickers and contact lenses,[9] and, perhaps for the city-dwelling alien lover, a large metal sign that reads 'Reserved Parking – Aliens Only'. Much of this idle browsing took place on the internet, and as I typed my way through contemporary cyberculture, I could not fail to notice that Microsoft had included a familiar face among the 'Webdings' symbols. Between the baby and the weightlifter, there lies an alien.

At about this time, a religious group called the International Raëlian Movement published a book entitled *Let's Welcome the Extra-Terrestrials: They Genetically Engineered All Life on Earth – Including Us!*[10] In a philosophy that recalls the argument developed in von Däniken's *Chariots of the Gods?*,[11] the Raëlians claim that human beings should be opening their arms to aliens because humans were, as the subtitle of the book suggests, created by extraterrestrials. The leader of the movement – a former racing driver who changed his name from Claude Vorilhon to Raël – has argued that key sections of the Bible have consistently been mistranslated, thus distorting the truth about life on Earth.[12] 'Elohim', he claims, does not mean 'God', but 'those who came from the sky', and this should be taken absolutely literally. By 1997, the group had raised around 7 million dollars towards the cost of building a huge 'embassy' that will be used to welcome the Elohim back to Earth.[13] With this moment of contact in mind, collective attempts to communicate telepathically with extraterrestrials are strongly encouraged, and another Raëlian publication, *The True Face of God*, contains a helpful little section entitled 'Technique for attempting telepathic contact with the Elohim'.[14]

Everywhere I looked, I found examples of 'alien love'. The market appeared to be endless. As Jodi Dean put it, referring to a visit to Roswell in 1997, 'You could buy alien *everything*'.[15] And, as is so often the case, love leads to sex. When I recently asked a group of students to bring examples of 'alien love' to a seminar, one woman drew our attention to the 'alien love doll', an inflatable vinyl object advertised in the 'Animal/Alien' section of an adult-themed website.[16] 'The invasion has begun. Make love not war!', runs the description, and for less than 40 dollars, the 'life size' doll, which 'has open mouth and inflates by blowing in crotch', can be discreetly acquired.

I have looked long and hard for similar items that would have been available in the 1950s. There were various children's toys that involved outer space and extraterrestrials, but none of these celebrated aliens with quite the passion of the present. And contemporary alien-themed commodities are often aimed, moreover, exclusively at adults (I am not merely thinking of the alien love doll). Things have clearly changed; a difference divides the present from the past. If the 1950s inclined towards 'alien hatred', the current moment would seem to be one of widespread 'alien love'. That was then, this is now.

Why 'Alien Chic'?

'Alien Love' might well have been the title of this book. I eventually settled upon *Alien Chic*, however, out of deference to Tom Wolfe. In a scathing essay first published in 1970, Wolfe set out to expose the hollowness, 'the essential double-track mentality',[17] of what he termed 'Radical Chic', the phenomenon that saw wealthy residents of New York's more privileged neighbourhoods throwing spectacular soirées for poor and oppressed revolutionaries. Behind the apparent radicalism of Leonard and Felicia Bernstein's courting of the Black Panthers, for instance, Wolfe detected a more reactionary impulse.

There was, he argued, a sense in which the rich and powerful confirmed themselves as such in the very act of giving space and (non-tax-deductible) donations to worthy causes. Contrary to first appearances, the presence of the Panthers in the Bernsteins' 'thirteen-room penthouse duplex on Park Avenue'[18] merely reinforced the traditional distinction between what Wolfe explicitly identified as '*them* and *us*'.[19] While the basic impulse of Radical Chic might, Wolfe admits, have been sincere, 'there seemed to be some double-track thinking going on'.[20] The excessively *public*[21] display of support for groups such as the Panthers was, he concluded, a way for the wealthy actually to 'legitimiz[e] their wealth',[22] implicitly to show their standing to the world. The 'season'[23] of Radical Chic was simply that: a passing moment, 'a trend, a fashion'[24] that offered the upper classes a touch of seasoning, exoticism, 'Soul, as it were'.[25] While it appeared at first glance to upset the traditional American social formation, Radical Chic in fact reaffirmed traditional values, reinscribed borders between 'them' and 'us'. Rather than making a difference, it marked difference:

> Radical Chic, after all, is only radical in style; in its heart it is part of Society and its traditions. Politics, like Rock, Pop, and Camp, has its uses; but to put one's whole status on the line for *nostalgie de la boue* in any of its forms would be unprincipled.[26]

Little, in other words, had really changed.

I think that the same applies to what I am calling 'Alien Chic'. It seems to me that there is a sense in which 'alien love' ends up, perhaps against all odds, reinforcing the traditional humanist binary opposition between the human and the extraterrestrial. While texts such as *Invasion of the Body Snatchers* seem laughably outdated in certain respects, their fundamental assumption that there is an absolute difference between human beings and aliens haunts the culture of 'alien love'. The present secretes the past. 'Alien love', that is to say, could be better understood as 'Alien Chic', in that – like Radical Chic – it quietly reaffirms a traditional border between 'them' and 'us'.

I should perhaps explain what I mean by the term 'humanism'. Like many other 'isms', its meaning has a habit of wandering with usage. As Tony Davies puts it, in his useful introduction to the subject:

> Humanism is a word with a very complex history and an unusually wide range of possible meanings and contexts; and for anyone attempting to offer an account of those meanings, the attraction of Humpty Dumpty's approach to the problems of definition is obvious.[27]

Rather than simply providing a long and abstract list of characteristics, therefore, I want to turn to a concrete example of humanist thinking.

When René Descartes writes about what it means to be human, his words exude certainty, security and mastery. Near the beginning of the *Discourse on the Method*, which was first published in 1637, reason is held aloft as 'the only thing that makes us men [sic] and distinguishes us from the beasts'.[28] This essential 'power of judging well and distinguishing the true from the false . . . is naturally equal in all men',[29] and it is precisely this ability to determine the truth that convinces Descartes of his human being: '*I think, therefore I am*'.[30]

In the Cartesian model, the essence of the human lies in the rational mind, or soul,[31] which is entirely distinct from the body:

> Next, examining attentively what I was, and seeing that I could pretend that I had no body and that there was neither world nor place where I was; but that I could not for all that pretend that I did not exist; and that on the contrary, simply because I was thinking about doubting the truth of other things, it followed quite evidently and certainly that I existed; whereas, if I had merely ceased thinking, even if everything else I had imagined had been true, I should have had no reason to believe that I existed; I knew from there that I was a substance whose whole essence or nature is solely to think, and who, in order to exist, does not require any place, or depend on any material thing. So much so that this 'I', that is to say the soul, by which I am what I am, is entirely distinct from the body . . .[32]

Although the *Meditations*, published four years after the *Discourse on the Method*, initially concede that there is some kind of link between the mind and the body, the fundamental dualism is soon reaffirmed:

> [W]hen I consider the mind, or myself in so far as I am merely a thinking thing, I am unable to distinguish any parts within myself; I understand myself to be something quite single and complete. Although the whole mind seems to be united to the whole body, I recognize that if a foot or arm or any other part of the body is cut off, nothing has thereby been taken away from the mind.[33]

For Descartes, the human being is known, knowable and present to the very being that is engaged in the meditation upon what it means to be human: 'I understand myself', he insists, 'to be something quite single and complete'. It is, moreover, absolutely distinct from the inhuman, for only human beings are capable of rational thought. And reason, which 'distinguishes us from the beasts', also confers upon the human being the power to tell the difference between itself and its non-human others. *I think, therefore I am.*

Descartes often seeks to win his reader over by telling stories, and there is a passage in the *Discourse on the Method* that reads to me like an early example of science fiction (in fact, not being a philosopher, I tend to read Descartes as if he were a novelist). If, the argument runs, there were a machine that looked like a monkey, it would not be possible to distinguish between a real monkey and the fake – at the level of essence – because the fact that neither the animal nor the machine could ever exercise rational thought means that there would be no essential difference. Both figures are, in Descartes's eyes, ultimately and absolutely inhuman. If, however, machines were to attempt to simulate humans, it would, for two simple reasons, always be easy to tell the difference between the true and the false human being:

> The first of these is that they could never use words or other signs, composing them as we do in order to declare our thoughts to others. For we can certainly conceive of a machine so constructed that it utters words, and even utters some regarding the bodily actions that cause certain changes in its organs, for instance if you touch it in one spot it asks what you want to say to it; if in another, it cries out that you are hurting it, and so on; but not that it arranges them [the words] diversely to respond to the meaning of everything said in its presence, as even the most stupid [*hébétés*] of men are capable of doing. Secondly, even though they might do some things as well as or even better than we do them, they would inevitably fail in others, through which would we would discover that they were acting not through understanding [*connaissance*] but only from the disposition of

> their organs. For whereas reason is a universal instrument which can be of use in all kinds of situations, these organs need some particular disposition for each particular action; hence it is impossible to conceive that there would be enough of them in a machine to make it act in all the occurrences of life in the way in which our reason makes us act.[34]

The real human is wholly distinct from the fake human, the inhuman, over which it towers in a position of natural supremacy: *I think, therefore I cannot possibly be an automaton.* While machines and animals can certainly emit signs, they can never truly reply, and it is upon this inability that a binary opposition between the human and the inhuman is constructed. The difference naturally tells itself.

I will return to this remarkable passage at a later moment in *Alien Chic*. At this stage, however, I merely wish to note that Descartes offers an early and extremely influential version of humanism, according to which the figure of 'Man'[35] is at the very centre of things, is entirely present to itself, is sure of itself, is absolutely distinct from the inhuman, and shares with all other humans beings a unique essence. On the one hand, there is the human; on the other hand, there is the alien, and the two remain distinct, pure, opposed, unlinked. It is precisely this way of understanding the world that I want to trace in the culture of Alien Chic.

I should stress at this point that I am not offering an encyclopaedia of aliens or Alien Chic. I have, rather, merely isolated selected examples for closer attention. This, of course, involved making choices, and I have often deliberately wandered away from some of the more familiar instances of Alien Chic. I have, for example, very little to say about *The X-Files* and the *Alien* films,[36] and not even a sentence devoted to the various incarnations of *Star Trek*. This is not because I find these texts uninteresting or irrelevant (although *Star Trek* does bore me); it is, rather, simply a matter of wanting to look elsewhere in a crowded field. In the case of these three particular examples, moreover, a considerable amount of academic work has already been undertaken, and I have no desire to retread such pathways.[37]

I am similarly uninterested in providing a precise date for the arrival on Earth of Alien Chic. In the realm of cinema, the invasion narratives of the 1950s were notably rewritten in the late 1970s and early 1980s by the hugely popular *Close Encounters of the Third Kind* (dir. Steven Spielberg, 1977)[38] and *E.T.: The Extra-terrestrial* (dir. Steven Spielberg, 1982). Although the working title of the former, *Watch the Skies*,[39] alluded to the final lines of *The Thing from Another World* (dir. Christian Nyby, 1951), both of Spielberg's films suggested that contact with aliens might actually be something to cherish: *E.T.* is the perfect friend for a lonely boy, and close encounters with an extended extraterrestrial family offer an escape from a chaotic and unhappy terrestrial counterpart. And, as *Close Encounters of the Third Kind* and *E.T.* were so readily and widely embraced, it might be tempting to locate the genesis of Alien Chic somewhere between 1977 and 1982. This, however, would be to ignore earlier examples, such as *2001: A Space Odyssey* (dir. Stanley Kubrick, 1968), a film which, as I will discuss in more detail in the following chapter, also radically revised the invasion narratives of the 1950s. Where, then, is the true beginning? The apparent moment of pure origin can easily recede beyond the event horizon.

There is a further reason for refusing to establish a simple genesis, for one of the projects of *Alien Chic* is to trace how the assumptions of the past have never quite disappeared, have never been eclipsed by an entirely new way of seeing and being. On the contrary, it seems to me that the recent 'alien love' and the older 'alien hatred' are constructed upon precisely the same foundations. *Plus ça change, plus c'est la même chose* from another world.

While working on this book, I have often been asked why I decided to devote several years of my life to aliens. What could possibly be the point of such an activity? Could I not have chosen something more scholarly, worthwhile, becoming? Was I serious? Had I been abducted by little green men? Was I secretly one of them? First, of course, there is the simple fact that extraterrestrials have invaded contemporary western culture. They signify, they are part of everyday life, and it is my responsibility as a cultural critic not to ignore their presence. Culture is not '*a study of perfection*';[40] it is, rather, as Clifford Geertz has argued,[41] simply what has meaning. Cultural criticism, that is to say, is not concerned with 'sweetness and light',[42] with sorting out the good from the bad, or with training gatekeepers.[43] It involves, rather, the study of *meanings*. But second, and perhaps more important, I am interested in what aliens might reveal about how human beings see themselves and their others at the beginning of the twenty-first century. What if to read the extraterrestrial were also to read 'us'?

Chapter 1 establishes the general space of the book by comparing the 'alien hatred' of the past to the 'alien love' of the present. Considering a series of Hollywood films that revolve around the planet Mars and its little green inhabitants, I map how, with time, the meaning of Mars appears to change, as monstrous invaders become either comical, insignificant, or friendly ancestors. Martians, the archetypal aliens, do not seem to be what they once were.

Without wanting to erase this shift, chapter 2 traces how the aliens of the past nonetheless continue to haunt recent cinematic production. There are still monsters on the loose, and 'Man' continues to be threatened by 'his' alien others. Humanism has not entirely disappeared, and the present moment, it follows, is one of contradiction: 'alien love' exists alongside 'alien hatred'. But why?

Chapter 3 addresses this question by turning to the phenomenon of alien abduction, focusing in particular upon the recent work of John E. Mack, a psychiatrist who believes that abduction is something to be welcomed and celebrated. Through a close reading of Mack's theories and case histories, I argue that his 'alien love' is, in fact, structurally similar to 'alien hatred' in its implicit insistence upon the opposition between the human and the alien. 'Alien love' is a kind of humanism; 'alien love' is Alien Chic.

In chapter 4, I examine a selection of the many alien-themed objects and gadgets that are available in the present moment. These objects of desire, I suggest, effectively confirm the human subject *as a subject*. To own is to be your own person; while the extraterrestrial is explicitly celebrated, it is implicitly celebrated only as an *object*. The chapter concludes by proposing a response to the impasse sketched out in the previous chapters. If the binary opposition between the human and the alien continues to inform the culture of Alien Chic, it is nonetheless possible to challenge the rule of humanism. Drawing upon the work of Jacques Derrida, I propose a posthumanism that sets its sights upon the moments at which humanism begins to deconstruct itself.

The fifth chapter asks what difference such an approach might make to a reading of texts that depend upon an opposition between the human and the inhuman. On closer inspection, it transpires that Alien Chic both underlines and undermines the principles of humanism. Things are not what they seem. And the troubles are not confined to the present, for even the most apparently humanist texts of the past exhibit a similar tendency to pull themselves apart. Humanism is always becoming posthumanism.

1

Reading the red planet; or, little green men at work

It's not easy bein' green.

VAN MORRISON,
'Bein' green'[1]

Why Mars?

I wrote a great deal of this book at a window that overlooks the house from which, on 13 March 1781, William Herschel discovered the planet Uranus. Today, the unassuming Bath townhouse is a popular museum devoted to Herschel's life and work. For a modest fee, visitors can study his letters and books, inspect a replica of the telescope used to make the discovery, and wander around the garden from which he would have watched the skies.[2]

While working on early drafts of *Alien Chic*, I was always aware that the history of the street in which I was living orbits around that of another planet. At the same time, however, I was slightly uneasy about the fact that I still know very little about the reality of the worlds that I so happily study on screen or page. My knowledge of Mars, for instance, is fairly basic: the encyclopaedia tells me that it is the fourth planet from the sun, around which it orbits at a distance of some 141 million miles, but I have consistently failed to commit this information to memory. I am, moreover, somewhat ashamed to admit that I have never even glanced at the planet through a telescope. Fortunately, just as I was rewriting the present chapter for the final time, the red planet found itself at its closest point to Earth in some 60,000 years. Although it was still around 34.6 million miles away, its distinctive light could now be seen with the naked eye.[3] On 4 September 2003, from a friend's garden in Orpington, I finally saw Mars.

I could not, therefore, possibly hope to write about the planet itself; that remains the field of astronomy. As a cultural critic, however, I do have access to the *meaning* of Mars as it is inscribed in signifying practices at different moments in history. I can, that is to say, read Mars and, moreover, read the changes in its meaning. With this in mind, the present chapter offers a brief and resolutely selective account of the relationship between humans and Martians in Hollywood cinema since the 1950s. I am not for one moment claiming to have written an exhaustive, masterful history. I have, rather, selected several representative films from different moments for analysis. Above all, I want to tell a story about an apparent shift in the meaning of the red planet and its inhabitants.

Why Mars? My choice perhaps requires some explanation: this is, after all, a book about aliens in general. I give Mars special attention here simply because it seems to me that western culture has always done so. This may be little more than an accident of history, or it may have something to do with the fact that, more than any other planet, Mars was long thought to be 'a likely habitat for intelligent life'.[4] And this fascination, which dates in its present form back at least as far as the nineteenth-century interest in Martian 'canals', is by no means dead, for, while I was writing *Alien Chic*, Mars regularly featured in the British daily news, particularly when the *Beagle 2* spacecraft set off on its historic (and ill-fated) journey.

When Hollywood needed a convenient home for the monsters that cast their alien shadows over the invasion narratives of the 1950s, it regularly turned – perhaps unsurprisingly – to Mars. The planet does not, of course, figure in every such text, but I think that there is a real sense in which Martians stand, and perhaps continue to stand, as the archetypal, most obvious, most *alien* aliens. While it is certainly possible to talk of 'Venusians' or 'Uranians', these terms seem slightly awkward, uncommon, forced. 'Martians', on the other hand, is a decidedly familiar signifier. The inhabitants of Mars have a name, if not a face, that fits.

'They're them, we're us'; or, Martians? No, thanks!

On the evening of 30 October 1938, the United States of America was invaded by Orson Welles. Or, to be more precise, by his notorious radio adaptation of *The War of the Worlds*.[5] The story, by now, is somewhat familiar.[6] What is less well known, however, is that the CBS network did not set out to fool its listeners into believing that the breaking news reports about a Martian invasion of Earth were authentic. The artifice, in fact, was perfectly clear, for the transmission was prefaced by an announcement that stated that 'The Columbia Broadcasting System and its affiliated stations present Orson Welles and the Mercury Theatre on the Air in *War of the Worlds* by H. G. Wells'.[7] This was followed by Welles's own introduction to the performance, and several further explicit reminders of the fictional nature of the events being described occurred during the broadcast.[8]

But many listeners – some of whom had apparently tuned in some way into proceedings – took the fiction for terrible fact. Panic erupted across the nation:

> In Harlem, a black congregation fell to its knees; in Indianapolis a woman ran screaming into a church where evening service was being held and shouted 'New York has been destroyed. It's the end of the world. Go home and prepare to die.' A woman gave premature birth, and another fell down a whole flight of stairs (her husband, according to Norman Corwin, called CBS to thank them for the broadcast. 'Geez, it was a wonderful programme!'). In Newark, New Jersey, all the occupants of a block of flats left their homes with wet towels round their heads as improvised gas

> masks. In Staten Island, Connie Casamassina was just about to get married. Latecomers to the reception took the microphone from the singing waiter and announced the invasion. 'Everyone ran to get their coats. I took the microphone and started to cry – "Please don't spoil my wedding day" – and then my husband started singing hymns, and I decided I was going to dance the Charleston. And I did, for 15 minutes straight. I did every step there is in the Charleston.'[9]

Before long, the moving news sign in New York's Times Square was reporting 'Orson Welles frightens the nation'. CBS, meanwhile, took to issuing hourly disclaimers, assuring its millions of listeners that what they had been hearing was fiction. One outraged individual threatened to bomb the network's building, which soon found itself besieged by reporters.

Orson Welles was shocked and annoyed by the whole affair, which was widely covered in American and European newspapers. He is even rumoured to have fired a Mercury employee for eating a Mars bar in his presence on the day following the broadcast.[10] But, as one of his biographers has pointed out, '[f]or Welles in October 1938, the immediate result of the broadcast was notoriety'.[11] Three years before the release of *Citizen Kane*, the text for which he is now most readily remembered, Orson Welles had become something of a household name.

Terror is difficult to repeat; surprise is its closest ally. Indeed, fifteen years to the very month later,[12] Byron Haskin's cinematic adaptation of *The War of the Worlds* failed to provoke the same kind of mass hysteria. The newspapers reported no cases of deaths, premature births, interrupted nuptials, or even dampened towels. Cinema audiences, in fact, had been well prepared for this particular invasion of H. G. Wells's tale by a spectacular trailer that had announced 'It's coming!'. And yet, even without the element of surprise at its disposal, there remained a fundamental sense in which Haskin's film set out to terrify its viewers.

Unlike many of the alien invasion B-movies of the period, *The War of the Worlds* was a decidedly polished product. Paramount Studios had spent both time and money on the film, which, after more than a year in development, boasted state-of-the-art special effects and a distinctive use of Technicolor.[13] The result was the creation of an army of eerie, memorably malevolent aliens. The terrible extent of the invaders' power becomes apparent soon after one of their spaceships lands on the outskirts of a small town that lies not too far from Los Angeles. When three amiable local men set out to investigate, they witness a strange object emerging from the craft. Wanting only to be friendly, to establish peaceful interplanetary contact, the men advance, bearing a makeshift symbol of peace. 'Everybody understands when you wave the white flag,' one of them confidently reasons, 'you want to be friends'. They are, however, instantly evaporated by a Martian energy beam. If this were not enough to convince the audience of the sheer evil facing the human race, the scene is echoed later in the narrative, when Pastor Collins – who has convinced himself, in a strange piece of theological deduction, that the aliens are closer than humans to God – advances towards the Martian stronghold. 'We should try to make them understand we mean them no harm', he says, clutching a copy of the Bible and reciting Psalm 23. He is quickly destroyed. Goodness and mercy seem not to be concepts recognized by the alien invaders.

'They seem to murder everything that moves', remarks one of the human characters, and the film duly relays images of mass destruction from around the world. 'It was', as the solemn voice-over puts it, 'the beginning of the rout of civilization, the massacre of humanity.' Those lucky enough to escape death have been driven from their houses. Humans are no longer at home in the world, *their* world, and no amount of military might can halt the Martians' advance. 'They haven't even been touched!', cries one of the soldiers, shortly after an atom bomb, ten times stronger than any previously used, has been dropped on the invaders.

In order to tell its tale, the film sets up a clear opposition between an 'Us' and a 'Them'. One of the ways in which this 'versus' is established is with an insistence upon groups and crowds of human beings. Throughout the film, Haskin tends to frame humans in numbers, often creating a noticeably cluttered *mise en scène.* There are, in fact, just 82 shots that feature a sole and uninterrupted human presence, and many of these occur in sequences that deliberately emphasize individual characters for dramatic effect.[14] In *The War of the Worlds*, humans come together in order to fight for their future (or, as one reporter puts it, 'future history'). More precisely, the sudden invasion of the other brings human beings together, and this unity, this creation of an 'Us' to resist the terrible 'Them', is played out even at the level of filmic composition. The age of conflict *between* races and nations is, as the text's prologue suggests, a thing of the past. Every human being now stands with every other human being, and the enemy is precisely that which is not human. And even if the mobs that appear towards the end of the movie have descended into atomistic selfishness, there nonetheless remains a clear sense of representable humanity, opposed, of course, to the monstrous invaders.

Those riotous crowds are, in fact, quickly transcended. As mob rule descends upon the city, Forester takes refuge in a church, hoping to be reunited with Sylvia. But, as the death of Pastor Collins has already suggested, the Martians have little respect for Christianity, and the building is soon under attack. Suddenly, however, the destruction ceases and the alien machines crash to the ground. The hatch of one of the fallen craft opens, and a slimy hand reaches out, only to fall limp. 'We were all praying for a miracle', says Forester, and, as he looks towards the heavens, church bells begin to ring.[15] The invaders have, it transpires, been defeated by ordinary human bacteria, to which they had no resistance. 'After all that *men* could do had failed', concludes the narrator, 'the Martians were destroyed and humanity was saved by the littlest things which God, in His wisdom, had put upon this Earth.' The war of the worlds is over, the aliens have been eradicated, and humans will live on. To the choral sound of 'Amen', the credits begin to roll.

Earlier that year, however, God was nowhere to be found. In *Invaders from Mars* (dir. William Cameron Menzies, 1953), the struggle between the human and the alien is allowed to run its course without interference from above. There is only an 'Us' versus a 'Them'. In spite of this textual difference, *Invaders from Mars* nonetheless shares with *The War of the Worlds* a belief in an ordinary (which is to say, human) order of things, which is disturbed by hostile and unexpected alien invaders. The film begins in the safe space of the family home, where, as Patrick Lucanio points out, '[b]y avoiding open spaces and allusions to vastness (and preferring tight shots), Menzies visualizes the closeness of the family'.[16] But this peaceful existence is soon shattered when David – the young hero of the film – witnesses the crash landing of an alien spacecraft near his family's home. His parents dismiss his story as merely a dream (an irony upon which the whole film will eventually turn), but before long, families across the small town are falling apart as humans are captured and converted into soulless workers for the Martian cause. The 'warmth and security with which Menzies opened the film is', Lucanio concludes, 'in shambles'.[17]

The absolute difference between the Martians, their 'mutant' slaves, and the besieged humans is repeatedly asserted. It is both physical (the aliens leave a strange mark on the back of their victims necks) and metaphysical (as soon as a human has been captured by the invaders, he or she changes in manner, in 'spirit'). 'That's the coldest pair I ever saw', remarks one of the policemen upon encountering David's alienated parents, and elsewhere the film shows characters both before and after their brush with the invaders, in order to stress the difference of the alien: David's father, once a loving husband, now happily leads his wife into the arms of the invaders, for instance, while a small girl torches her family home with a horrifyingly cold smile.

As in *The War of the Worlds*, the human originally has its own space and its own way of being, both of which are subsequently violated by an alien presence. An entirely different order of being crashes, quite literally, into the human world, and the consequences are terrifying. Contact with the extraterrestrial is a source of horror, for it destroys everything that precedes it. Having established this disturbance, the film can proceed to tell its tale of 'Us' versus 'Them'. The lines are clearly drawn, the camps determined, and the struggle to which *Invaders from Mars* devotes most of its narrative is the struggle of the 'Us' to conquer and negate the 'Them'.

Mars itself is entirely absent from Menzies's film. The effects of its inhabitants upon everyday human life are enough to tell the tale. Menzies was renowned within the industry for his visual flair; 'it was said of him', reports Christopher Frayling, 'that he had been born with a two-inch lens instead of eyes'.[18] And, as in his earlier science fiction film, *Things to Come* (1936), he wonderfully shows how the once-familiar landscape of Earth can suddenly become startlingly different, strikingly uncanny: a house is no longer a home, a child no longer innocent, a husband no longer a lover. In *It! The Terror from Beyond Space* (dir. Edward L. Cahn, 1958), however, there is, as in *The War of the Worlds*, a brief glimpse of the terrible red planet. This, in fact, is precisely where the film begins. As the opening credits come to an end, the camera tracks across the Martian scenery that had been visible beneath the text, and comes to rest upon a gleaming spacecraft which is poised to return to Earth, having rescued the sole survivor of a doomed mission to the planet. But the survivor – Colonel Carruthers – is no hero; he is, rather, due to stand trial for the deaths of his fellow crew members, and although he claims that his colleagues were 'killed by *something*, not me', the rescue party refuses to believe his story about a 'mysterious creature'. Until, that is, yet more deaths occur during the return flight, for the monster of which Carruthers spoke is stowed away on the spaceship, and, being a 'terror from beyond space', it is intent on killing everything in its path.[19] 'There's enough voltage in these lines to kill thirty human beings', remarks one of the crew as he inspects yet another trap set for the creature. 'The only drawback is,' he continues, 'the thing isn't human'.

The realization that Carruthers's fantastic story is terrifyingly true marks a turning point in the narrative, and serves to establish the same binary opposition between the human and the inhuman that informs *Invaders from Mars* and *The War of the Worlds*. Once again, the sudden presence of the alien creates a coherent sense of the human (the film's trailer notes, for instance, that 'the "Thing" from space threatens all mankind!', and that, 'In the silent void of space, puny man matches his cunning against a monster from Mars running rampant'). If there is an

'It',[20] there must be something that is not an 'It', and this, of course, is 'Us'. The monster, in fact, is so utterly other that it does not even come from outer space, a field partially mapped by humans. 'It' comes, rather, as the film's title somewhat bafflingly declares, from *beyond* space, from beyond the infinite expanse that human beings have at least begun to explore, to know, to conquer.

The formation of the human 'Us' is matched by a change in the composition of the *mise en scène* itself. At the very beginning of the film, before the creature has made its presence felt, the viewer is introduced to the crew members as they prepare to fire the ship's engines. As each person speaks his or her name directly to camera, the film cuts, framing every character separately (even the disgraced Carruthers, who plays no part in the technical procedures, is pictured individually at this point). Later, however, as the struggle against the monster intensifies, shots are frequently composed to show several, if not all, of the human group in the same frame. To wander off alone, moreover, leads to death. As in *The War of the Worlds*, human unity is visible, formal.

Colonel Carruthers, once shunned by the crew, now becomes part of the 'Us', brought back to the human fold by the irruption of the other. So much so, in fact, that a romance with Ann seems to be blossoming, and, in the depiction of this development, the film further underscores the solidarity of the human against the alien. At one point, approximately forty minutes into the narrative (by which time the monster has undertaken a considerable amount of rampaging), Carruthers is pictured alone in the ship's makeshift infirmary. Suddenly, Ann's hand reaches into the frame to touch his shoulder. Without cutting, the camera pulls back, reframing the shot now to embrace both human figures. Something of an obstacle remains, however, for a vertical line (part of the background) now separates them. While Carruthers's nose and face occasionally cross fractionally to Ann's side of the divide, it is not until she speaks that the barrier is overcome. 'You were right and we were all wrong', she says, gazing into his eyes. 'It's taken this to prove it.' As she finishes speaking, he grasps her hand, finally breaking the line that had been dividing them.[21] Two become one.

But if the movie hints at love, it is more noticeably haunted by loss: Carruthers's opening monologue mentions nine fatalities and describes the planet as 'alive with something we came to know only as death'; the struggle with the monster leads to several more losses of life; and the film's final line concludes that 'another name for Mars is death'. As in *The War of the Worlds* and *Invaders from Mars*, if there is life on the red planet, it can only bring about the end of the human. When worlds collide – whether on Earth, on Mars itself, or even in outer space – human beings die. This is a sentiment echoed in *The War of the Worlds* and *Invaders from Mars.* Textual differences notwithstanding, the three films' texts share an inscription of the alien – or, to be more precise, the Martian – as absolutely other, absolutely malevolent, absolutely opposed to the interests of human beings. And with this comes an appeal to a united human race that sets aside its superficial differences to fight against the monstrous aliens.[22] In this respect, the films are entirely typical alien invasion narratives of the period. Like *The Thing from Another World*, *Earth vs. the Flying Saucers* (dir. Fred F. Sears, 1956), *Invasion of the Body Snatchers*, *Invasion of the Saucer Men* (dir. Edward L. Cahn, 1957), *The Blob* (dir. Irwin S. Yeaworth Jr., 1958), and many other similar texts, *The War of the Worlds*, *Invaders from Mars*, and *It! The Terror from Beyond Space* orbit around a set of related binary oppositions: human/alien; good/evil; Us/Them; real/fake; life/death. It precisely this sense of opposition that becomes troubled with time.

'They're us . . . we're them'; or, Martians? Yes, please!

I do not know if the students who laughed at *Invasion of the Body Snatchers* had seen *Mars Attacks!* (dir. Tim Burton, 1996), a mischievous parody of the invasion narratives of the 1950s. Burton's film clearly acknowledges its debt to the past. At times, in fact, it appears to be a hymn to *The War of the Worlds.* As in Haskin's film, nothing appears to be able to halt the invaders' gradual destruction of the planet: once again, for instance, a nuclear attack is useless (here, in a scene to which the written word cannot possibly hope to do justice, it is a nothing but a source of entertainment for the Martians), and major cities of the world are soon reduced to ruins. But, as in *The War of the Worlds*, the smallest detail eventually saves the human race. This time, however, it is not God, but Slim Whitman. The aliens, it transpires, have no immunity to country music, and their little green heads explode upon exposure to the sound of yodelling.

As this brief description might suggest, the solemn tone of the earlier narratives has been replaced with an overwhelming sense of the comic. *Mars Attacks!*, in short, is played for laughs, and the film consistently revels in the absurdity of its own narrative: Martians pose for a quick 'holiday' photograph before the doomed Taj Mahal; Mount Rushmore is neatly remodelled in the image of the invaders; and the disembodied heads of Pierce Brosnan and Sarah Jessica Parker flirt coyly with each other. 'Oh Natalie,' he sighs, 'I wish that I could hold you in my arms.' Meanwhile, the future of the human race appears to lie in the hands and voice of Tom Jones (I must confess, however, that, as a Welshman, I am tempted simply to read this as good old-fashioned utopian thinking).

Mars Attacks! implies that the approach to the alien articulated in the invasion narratives of the 1950s can no longer be taken entirely seriously. The motifs and the meanings of the past circulate only as comedy in the 1990s; when Mars attacks, it does so with a knowing smile. And while the film does not actively rewrite the rhetoric of the earlier texts with quite the same vigour as *Red Planet* (dir. Antony Hoffman, 2000) and *Mission to Mars* (dir. Brian De Palma, 2000) – texts to which I will turn in a moment – it does, through this explicit use of comedy, comment upon the current status of the humanism that underpinned the films of the past. Through an insistence upon the familiar formula, *Mars Attacks!* exposes the absurdity of that very formula in the 1990s. The film, that is to say, hints that things have changed: to approach Martians in the manner of the 1950s is, quite simply, laughable. The aliens of the past are alien to the present. Tragedy repeats itself as farce.

Henri Bergson's well-known account of laughter is, in many ways, comical in its humanism. The comic, he insists near the beginning of his essay, 'does not exist outside the pale of what is strictly ***human***', and if someone laughs at an inanimate or inhuman thing, this is merely because he or she has 'detected in it some human attitude or expression'.[23] For Bergson, writing in 1900, laughter marks and makes the human. I have no desire to 'save' Bergson, either from himself or from humanist discourse, but it seems to me that his essay, however problematic, does offer a theory of laughter that at least begins to account for what is at stake in *Mars Attacks!*

Bergson repeatedly claims that the comic arises when a sense of the mechanical is imposed upon the living, vital human being. '***The attitudes, gestures and movements of the human body***', he argues at one point, '***are laughable in exact proportion as that body reminds us of a mere machine.***'[24] By the same token, any attempt by the inhuman to mimic the human, 'to follow its lines and counterfeit its suppleness',[25] can only provoke laughter. Because, for Bergson, everyday human life requires that individuals remain thoroughly vital and adaptable, society has come 'to dread . . . that each one of us, content with paying attention to what affects the essentials of life, will, so far as the rest is concerned, give way to the easy automatism of acquired habits'.[26] In the face of this anxiety, laughter stands as a corrective, 'a sort of *social gesture*':[27]

> By the fear which it inspires, it restrains eccentricity, keeps constantly awake and in mutual contact certain activities of a secondary order which might retire into their shell and go to sleep, and in short, softens down whatever the surface of the social body may retain of mechanical inelasticity.[28]

A little later in the text, Bergson asks himself why items of clothing occasionally provoke laughter:

> It might almost be said that every fashion is laughable in some respect. Only, when we are dealing with the fashion of the day, we are so accustomed to it that the garment seems, in our mind, to form one with the individual wearing it. We

> do not separate them in imagination. The idea no longer occurs to us to contrast the inert rigidity of the covering with the living suppleness of the object covered: consequently, the comic here remains in a latent condition . . . Suppose, however, some eccentric individual dresses himself [sic] in the fashion of former times our attention is immediately drawn to the clothes themselves; we absolutely distinguish them from the individual, we say that the latter *is disguising himself* – as though every article of clothing were not a disguise! – and the laughable aspect of fashion comes out of the shadow into the light.[29]

Laughter emerges when something has come to seem eccentric, when it no longer goes without saying, no longer passes as transparent, no longer means in quite the same way. The fashion of the past becomes amusing when its artifice, its lack of vitality, becomes evident. This laughter, I think, echoes in the emergence of a different understanding of Mars within recent Hollywood cinema. One of the reasons that *Mars Attacks!* – like, to return to my point of departure, *Invasion of the Body Snatchers* – strikes contemporary audiences as amusing is that its scenarios are now eccentric, outdated, alien. Times have changed, and meanings with them. And if the simple formula of 'Us versus Them' is no longer entirely credible, perhaps a new approach is required.

Several years after the appearance of *Mars Attacks!*, in fact, two films with similar storylines challenged in a more direct manner the meaning of Mars found in the films of the 1950s. In *Red Planet* and *Mission to Mars*, there is absolutely no sign of the terrestrial invasion that had driven texts like *The War of the Worlds*, *Invaders from Mars*, and *It! The Terror from Beyond Space*. In fact, it is now Mars that finds itself invaded by humans. The theme of the colonization of Mars is nothing new. Ray Bradbury's *Martian Chronicles*[30] famously explored the question in 1950, Kim Stanley Robinson's *Mars* trilogy has returned to the subject in more recent times,[31] and it is even now possible to purchase a one-acre plot of land on Mars.[32] But I think that *Red Planet* and *Mission to*

Mars construct the relationship between the human and the alien in a manner that departs significantly from the invasion films of the 1950s.

Set in the mid-twenty-first century, *Red Planet* narrates the difficulties encountered during 'the first manned mission to Mars'. Earth has been devastated by overpopulation and ecological neglect, and a new home is needed for the human race. Algae samples have already been sent to the surface of Mars, but their initial success at producing oxygen is now overshadowed by doubt. A team is sent to investigate. 'It's another giant leap for mankind,' as Commander Bowman puts it, 'and if we don't figure out what's wrong on Mars, it could be our last.' While the exploration of the planet is extremely difficult and dangerous – all but one of the landing party is eventually killed – the threat has nothing to do with Martians, and little to do with the terrain itself. There are no rampaging Martians to be found on Mars, and the famously hostile climate is, even when it produces an ice storm, fairly amenable to human existence. The danger, rather, comes in the form of a robot named AMEE (Autonomous Mapping, Exploration and Evasion), which has been brought to the planet by the explorers themselves.

The autonomous nature of the machine, in fact, proves to be the true problem, the heart of the threat. AMEE is not answerable to humans; 'her' actions are not limited by anything resembling Asimov's well-known laws of robotics.[33] 'She' does, rather, whatever 'she' wants, and when the crew casually mentions the possibility of deactivation and dismantlement, 'she' switches to military mode and becomes a ruthless killer. The subsequent struggle between AMEE and the humans is, in short, what drives the narrative. Against all odds, Mars sustains human life. What threatens human existence and, moreover, the future of the human race itself, is an object *created and brought to Mars by human beings.* Humans, in effect, endanger themselves. Having already ruined their own planet, they now look set to play out their self-destruction on the surface of Mars.

Things, quite clearly, have changed. As *Mars Attacks!* had already hinted, the meaning of the red planet and its inhabitants is no longer the same as it was in the 1950s. Martians are no longer the ultimate threat to humanity, for humanity itself has now taken on this role. The certainty of the binary opposition between 'Us' and 'Them', between the human and the alien, no longer holds in quite the same way. In *Red Planet*, the 'Them' (AMEE) is evidently a product of the 'Us', and the absolutely other 'Them' of the 1950s is notably absent. Earth no longer needs the eruption of an outside force to place it and its inhabitants on the point of extinction; the circumstances, rather, are already present within. The 'Them' has invaded the 'Us'.

There is, however, a swarm of mysterious alien bugs on the surface of Mars. Briefly glimpsed at one point, they eventually make a spectacular appearance towards the end of the film, bursting from the corpse of Pettengil to devour the wounded Burchenal. But, horrific as these strange creatures are – their *modus operandi* recalls, among other things, the monsters of the *Alien* quartet and *Starship Troopers*[34] – they are not, it would seem, to be viewed as a genuine enemy. While the struggle against AMEE occupies a large part of the narrative, the encounter with the insects is both slight and singular. And, moreover, it transpires that their very presence accounts for the oxygen in the Martian atmosphere. They, in short, guarantee the future of the human race in its new home. 'Hard to believe they're the good guys', remarks Gallagher at the end of the film, implying that evil now resides elsewhere.

But if the human-made AMEE represents the real threat, *Red Planet* at once narrates a more benign side to technology. Throughout the different crises faced by the crew, there is a marked reliance upon the technological, particularly the ship's central computer, Lucille. Without Lucille, for instance, Gallagher would not have been able to escape from Mars, for the computer both relays vital information from Earth and, at the crucial moment, guides the Commander towards Gallagher's floating pod. AMEE and Lucille are, in short, very different entities. Whereas the former is autonomous (a fact incorporated into her very name), Lucille remains entirely under human control. In *Red Planet*, it seems that the problems begin when humans are no longer able to dominate their machines, for the autonomous AMEE uses her freedom to wound and kill members of the crew. Subservient technology sustains life; autonomous technology leads only to death.

This is nothing new. The characterization of autonomous technology as malevolent is common in western culture. But I think that in the history of cinematic depictions of Mars, *Red Planet* nonetheless marks an important shift, a certain change of spirit. Whereas the films of the 1950s located the threat to humans in Mars and Martians, Hoffman's film suggests that the threat lies elsewhere, *within the human itself*. Mars is no longer to be feared, for human creations are now far more terrifying. Earth and the human race are endangered not by invaders from Mars or an 'It' from beyond space, but by the activities of the human race itself.

In the same year that Warner Brothers released *Red Planet*, Touchstone unveiled its rival, *Mission to Mars*. The two films share many thematic features – a rescue mission to the surface of Mars; near disaster on board the main spaceship; a vaguely mystical undercurrent – but it seems to me that *Mission to Mars* is even more radical than *Red Planet* in its rethinking of the relationship between the human and the alien. As a director, De Palma has always played with cinema's past, and *Mission to Mars* continues this trend.[35] But, unlike Tim Burton, De Palma does not look to the 1950s for inspiration; the main point of reference, rather, appears to be *2001*.

Kubrick's ghost haunts *Mission to Mars* in many ways. Perhaps most memorably, the giant set that spins to the sounds of Van Halen recalls *2001*'s remarkable visual experiments with revolving scenery. Meanwhile, both films feature a strange extraterrestrial monument that emits a mysterious signal for humans to interpret, a troublesome central computer, and a fatal space-walk. Even the suits worn by the astronauts in *Mission to Mars* recall those of *2001*. But this recycling is not undertaken in the name of parody; De Palma approaches the past in a very different manner from Tim Burton. He does so, I think, because to refer specifically to *2001* is to refer to something of a turning point in Hollywood's long relationship with extraterrestrials.

Although Kubrick's film was released just ten years after *It! The Terror from Beyond Space*, its approach to alien beings was strikingly different.[36] The simple binary opposition that had motivated so many of the films of the 1950s was now called into question, as an emphasis of the roots of the human race in simian culture found itself married to the suggestion that extraterrestrial beings want merely to communicate and share their vastly superior technology, knowledge and wisdom. Indeed, Kubrick's slightly awkward simians are aped in *Mission to Mars*'s brief retelling of the story of evolution. Both films, that is to say, address the origin of (the human) species. And in *Mission to Mars* the origin, when finally revealed, is somewhat startling.

When Luke, Teri and Jim crack the code that allows them to access the mysterious extraterrestrial monument, they are greeted by an alien who presents them with a living history of Mars. This reveals that when the original Martian race departed the planet, a genetic sample was sent to Earth, where it subsequently formed the basis of life. This radically different story of genesis is not entirely unfamiliar. Some scientists have come to believe in its narrative, inspired in part by the announcement in 1996 that a Martian meteorite – rock ALH 84001 – discovered in Antarctica some twelve years earlier contained possible traces of life.[37] Meanwhile, later episodes of *The X-Files* repeatedly appealed to the non-terrestrial beginnings of the human race. As Agent Skinner put it, in the very last episode (which was broadcast in 2002), 'Life, human life, is extraterrestrial by definition.' In *Mission to Mars*, Luke comes to the precisely the same conclusion when he notes: 'They seeded Earth.' 'They're us,' says Jim, finally figuring out the film's central puzzle, 'we're them'. The strange monument discovered by the first humans to set foot upon Mars is not, after all, a weapon or a warning; it is, rather, in Jim's words, 'an invitation for us to follow them home'.

Home, quite clearly, is not what it used to be. The familiar picture of picket fences and the nuclear family is now absent. More importantly, as in *Red Planet* (where Mars becomes the new dwelling place of the human race), home is no longer the singular location identified in films like *Invaders from Mars*, *The War of the Worlds*, and *It! The Terror from Beyond Space*. On the contrary, there are two irreconcilable notions of home in circulation at the end of *Mission to Mars*, and there appears to be no hierarchy, no discourse of authenticity in place: Teri, Luke and

Phil are returning to the Earth shown in the opening scenes (which centre, notably, around a traditional family house), but Jim is 'returning' to a (non-terrestrial) home he has never actually known, but which he feels he 'was born for'. In De Palma's film, humans no longer have *a* home, a unique space that is entirely distinguished from that of the alien other. If 'they're us' and 'we're them', the opposition between the homely and the unfamiliar can no longer hold, for the alien is no longer the wholly other.

Contact with the extraterrestrial is, accordingly, nothing to fear. Whereas a close encounter brought death and destruction in the 1950s, in *Mission to Mars* it brings life, knowledge, pleasure and new opportunities. Aliens can be touched without terror, as De Palma makes particularly clear in a scene that occurs towards the end of the film. Having just revealed that life on Earth has alien origins, the serene extraterrestrial being reaches out to the three humans, who readily accept its hand and form a circle. It is at this precise moment that Jim speaks the line: 'They're us . . . we're them.' In the 1950s, however, the same gesture elicited a very different response, for, when one of the Martians of *The War of the Worlds* extends its slimy hand and touches Sylvia's shoulder, she recoils in horror. Exclusion becomes inclusion; terror gives way to friendship. What was once outside is now inside.

The confident humanism of the past seems not to apply at the beginning of the twenty-first century. The line that once absolutely divided and distinguished human from alien has become blurred. There is no invasion and, more strikingly, no apparent enemy. Earth no longer needs to be defended against invaders from Mars or an 'It' from beyond space, and there is no call for a war of the worlds. More significantly, traces of the inhuman are now within the human, as a brief discussion of genetics in *Mission to Mars* notably implies. Still struggling to understand the meaning of the alien signal, Phil, Luke, Jim and Teri decide to study the DNA pattern, the 'signature . . . [the] self-portrait of whatever created the face' on the surface of the planet. A wide shot captures all four characters in focus, and a subsequent shot shows the DNA simulation on the screen of the computer. As Teri remarks that 'the difference between man and ape is less than 3 per cent genetic material', the film cuts to reframe her in a close-up. Phil remains visible, but is now out of focus, further back in the frame. Teri continues by saying: 'But that 3 per cent gives you Einstein, Mozart . . .', but is suddenly interrupted by Phil, who adds: '. . . Jack the Ripper'. As he says these words, the focus pulls to him, rendering Teri a blur in the foreground. Four quick shots follow, in which Jim, Phil, Jim again, and then Luke are shown in isolated close-ups. The scene ends with another image of the DNA pattern. The filmic practice here is unusual for *Mission to Mars*, which habitually uses long shots[38] and deep focus to maintain clarity and consistency within the frame and across different planes. The scene, that is to say, stands out from the main body of the film, and I want to suggest that in this moment of emphasis the film lays bare its difference from the humanist invasion narratives of the 1950s.

Developments in genetics have prompted something of a shift in the way that the human race understands and represents itself. The common assumption that genes contain the fundamental truth – or, as *Mission to Mars* has it, the 'signature' – of human life tends to render the 'essence' of the human little more than a piece of readable, communicable, and malleable information.[39] The intangible mystery – the Cartesian 'soul' or 'mind' – upon which humanism traditionally depended evaporates into a concrete code (or, as Elaine L. Graham puts it, the 'code of codes'[40]). Suddenly, the secret is all-too-readable and all-too-writable; the 'signature' can be copied, forged. There is a curious paradox here: while the Genome Project set out to provide the human being with unprecedented knowledge of itself, and was a major step in controlling its elements, the actual mapping of human genetic patterns – a process that reached the stage of 'first draft' in June 2000, shortly after *Mission to Mars* had been released[41] – effectively undermines the sovereignty of the traditional subject of humanism. Mastery undoes the mastering.

Always willing to take matters one step further, Jean Baudrillard proceeds to ask:

> [I]s there even a *genetic* definition of the human? And if it does exist, does a species have rights to its own genome and to its own eventual genetic transformation? We share 98 percent of our genes with apes and fully 90 percent of them with mice. Based on this common inheritance, what rights shall revert to the apes and the mice? Furthermore, it appears that some 90 percent of the genes making up our genome serve no purpose at all. What right do these genes have to exist? This is a critical question: if we describe them as useless, we arrogate to ourselves the right to destroy them.
>
> The same thing goes for any given aspect of humanity itself: once the human is no longer defined in terms of transcendence and liberty, but in terms of functions and of biological equilibrium, the definition of the human itself begins to fade, along with that of humanism. Occidental humanism was already challenged by the irruption of other cultures as early as the sixteenth century. Now the assault is not only against a particular culture but against the whole species: *anthropological* deregulation, along with the deregulation of all the moral, juridical, and symbolic codes that founded humanism.[42]

Or, to put things in a slightly different manner: 'Is a species that succeeds in synthesizing its own immortality, and that seeks to transform itself into pure information, still particularly a human species?'[43] The desire to master the human with science, to make it finally and fully present, actually has the effect of destabilizing the human being's position at the centre of things. What once was sacred, untouchable, unique and absolutely distinct from other living things begins to lose its preciousness in the face of reproducibility, malleability and the 'common inheritance' of which Baudrillard writes. How can humanism possibly hope to survive?

It is precisely this moment of uncertainty, inscribed even in Baudrillard's questioning mode of address, from which *Mars Attacks!*, *Red Planet* and *Mission to Mars* emerge. This is not to claim that Tim Burton, Philip Hoffman and Brian De Palma are avid readers of the work of Jean Baudrillard, N. Katherine Hayles or Elaine L. Graham; I have no way of knowing such things. It is, rather, a question of culture in general, a question of an uncertainty that circulates widely at an everyday level. The three films arise at a historical moment in which the meaning of the human (and, by extension, its relationship with the inhuman or the alien) is being rethought and reconfigured.

The knowledge of DNA is, of course, nothing new; it was, in fact, discovered in 1953, the year of *The War of the Worlds* and *Invaders from Mars.* But the actual *mapping* of the genome, and the related move to frame the truth of the human in genetic terms, are more recent developments. I think that it would be possible to understand the second half of the twentieth century as a gradual movement away from a traditionally humanist understanding of who 'we' are, and towards what Baudrillard uneasily calls a '*genetic* definition of the human'. Anthropocentrism, accordingly, trembles, and it seems to me that this unsettling has made its mark upon Hollywood's portrayal of Mars. The simple 'versus' that informed films such as *The War of the Worlds*, *Invaders from Mars*, and *It! The Terror from Beyond Space* no longer seems to hold. The traditional binary opposition between 'Us' and 'Them' becomes what Derrida calls a 'Crisis of *versus*'. As *Mission to Mars* suggests: 'They're us . . . we're them.'

With this crisis comes the waning of a hatred of the alien. Suspicion no longer has a trusted target. Martians no longer need to be resisted, feared and destroyed, for the other is far closer to home than the films of the 1950s suggested. And the beliefs of such movies are, as *Mars Attacks!* implies, now laughably outdated. To read the 1950s alongside the present moment is to read difference, change, departure. Cultural criticism asks what such a difference might mean, what kind of story it might sanction, and it seems to me that the change with which this chapter has been concerned announces a movement from 'alien hatred' towards what my student's backpack named 'alien love'. What was once repelled is now embraced. What was once a 'Them' is now part of 'Us'. To give Freud an alien twist, where 'It' was, there *eros* shall be.[44]

2

It lives; or, the persistence of humanism

What strikes me as odd is not that everything is falling apart, but that so much continues to be there.

PAUL AUSTER, *In the Country of Last Things*[1]

They came from Paris; or, invasion of the anti-humanists

A cultural critic looking only for quick and easy answers might conclude that the shift from 'alien hatred' to 'alien love' outlined in the previous chapter marks the absolute end of humanism. The argument would run as follows: if the binary opposition between 'Us' and 'Them' no longer holds, if the alien invasion films of the 1950s now seem laughably absurd, if contemporary culture suggests nothing short of a 'Crisis of *versus*', then we cannot possibly still be in the orbit of anthropocentrism. 'Man' must surely have died, and with that passing comes the birth of 'alien love'.

Such reports would be exaggerations. They would also be nothing new, for the end of humanism has been reported at various moments in the past. And yet, that end never quite seems to come. In the middle of the twentieth century, for instance, a series of French thinkers issued, as Kate Soper neatly puts it, 'a warrant for the death of Man'.[2] In 1957, one year before the invasion of *It! The Terror from Beyond Space*, the young Roland Barthes published what would go on to be his most famous book. 'The starting point of this reflection', he noted in the original preface to *Mythologies*:

> was usually a feeling of impatience in the face of [*devant*] the 'naturalness' with which the press, art and common sense constantly dress up a reality which, even though it is the one we live in, is none the less historical through and through. In short, in the account given of our contemporary circumstances, I resented seeing Nature and History confused at every turn, and I wanted to rediscover, in the decorative display of *what-goes-without-saying*, the ideological imposition which, in my view, is hidden there.[3]

The book, which brought together more than 50 short pieces that had originally appeared in popular publications such as *France-Observateur* and *Les Lettres nouvelles*, scratched the surface of Nature until it exposed the irreducible History of contemporary French culture. And Barthes's gaze was dazzlingly promiscuous, for *Mythologies* discusses, among many other things: the Eiffel Tower, steak and chips, washing powder, Michelin guide books, the Citroën DS, wrestling, striptease, Billy Graham, and the Tour de France.[4] Humanism – which relies, of course, upon a sense of the natural – was repeatedly attacked, and this was perhaps nowhere more clear than in Barthes's devastating critique of the popular photography exhibition, 'La Grande Famille des hommes'.

The Family of Man, as it was originally known, was a remarkable exhibition of photographs that was first shown in 1955. Its curator, Edward Steichen, had begun work on the project three years earlier, hoping to make 'a positive statement on what a wonderful thing life was, how marvelous people were, and, above all, how alike people were in all parts of the world'.[5] Eric J. Sandeen, who has written the definitive history of the exhibition, takes up the story:

> Steichen issued calls for photographs to professionals and amateurs. In 1952, with Robert Frank as his interpreter, he had journeyed to Europe, where he met with hundreds of photographers in eleven countries . . . [Wayne] Miller also

> traveled to Washington to examine some files at the National Archives and the Library of Congress, including the photographs of the Farm Security Administration. *Look* magazine opened its files . . . Finally, Miller solicited photographic services such as Black Star and Magnum, as well as the SovFoto collection, which yielded a few 35mm shots of the Soviet Union during the war years. In all, more than 6 million photographs were surveyed for *The Family of Man*.[6]

It was never going to be easy to narrow that staggering figure down to something more practical, but Steichen and his team eventually settled upon just 503 images. A press release issued in January 1954 by New York City's Museum of Modern Art revealed the criteria for selection: 'It is essential', Steichen wrote, 'to keep in mind the universal elements and aspects of human relations and the experiences common to all mankind rather than situations that represented conditions exclusively related or peculiar to a race, an event, a time or place.'[7] The project was not, in other words, concerned with the local, the particular, or the historically-specific; it was, rather, intended to be 'a mirror of the universal elements and emotions in the everydayness of life – as a mirror of the essential oneness of mankind throughout the world'.[8]

The Family of Man was finally unveiled to the public on 26 January 1955. That morning, 'long before the Museum of Modern Art opened, a crowd began waiting in line, soon flooding the long crosstown block in front of the building. People came and kept on coming in record-breaking numbers.'[9] Before long, the exhibition began to travel around the world, where it continued to enjoy remarkable success (by 1963 more than 9 million people in 69 countries had encountered *The Family of Man*).[10] In Paris, it was seen by Roland Barthes, who found it guilty of a reactionary appeal to universal human Nature. 'Everything here,' he wrote, 'the content and photogenic nature of the images, the discourse which justifies them, aims to suppress the determining weight of History.'[11] This denial of History went hand in hand with an honouring of humanism:

> [F]irst the difference between human morphologies is asserted, exoticism is insistently stressed, the infinite variations of the species, the diversity in skins, skulls and customs are made manifest, the image of Babel is complacently projected over that of the world. Then, from this pluralism, a type of unity is magically produced: man is born, works, laughs and dies everywhere in the same way; and if there still remains in these actions some ethnic peculiarity, at least one hints that there is underlying each one an identical 'nature', that their diversity is only formal and does not belie the existence of a common mould. Of course this means postulating a human essence . . .[12]

Humanism, for Barthes, is to be resisted on the grounds that it inhibits change, difference, and knowledge. Like all myths, it bestows upon the established order of things 'a natural and eternal justification'[13] that grants normalized practices the status of 'inevitability'[14] (a signifier that makes three appearances in the penultimate paragraph of Barthes's essay alone). Nature renders otherness unnatural, impossible, unthinkable. 'Man' rests upon a bland, complacent, unjust sameness.

This was not only true of texts that dealt with human subjects; it also applied to aliens, as Barthes noted in another of his *petites mythologies du mois*. Popular fictions of Mars, he observes, consistently fail to do justice to the radical otherness of the red planet; the extraterrestrial is always overwhelmingly terrestrial. 'Probably if we were to land in our turn on the Mars we have constructed', he mischievously concludes, 'we should merely find Earth itself, and between these two products of a same History we would not know how to disentangle our own.'[15] Humanism cannot think difference, cannot think differently:

> For one of the constant features of all petit-bourgeois mythology is this impotence to imagine the Other. Otherness is the concept most antipathetic to 'common sense'. Every myth tends fatally to a narrow anthropomorphism and, worse

> still, to what might be called an anthropomorphism of class. Mars is not only Earth, it is petit-bourgeois Earth, it is the little district of mentality cultivated (or expressed) by the great [*grande*] illustrated press. No sooner has it taken form in the sky than Mars is thus *aligned* by the most powerful of appropriations, that of identity.[16]

In 1957, however, Barthes was not quite willing to abandon anthropocentric discourse altogether, for the essay on *The Family of Man* makes a clear distinction between 'traditional humanism' and 'progressive humanism'. The former, of which Edward Steichen is guilty, 'postulates that in scratching the history of men a little, the relativity of their institutions or the superficial diversity of their skins . . . one very quickly reaches the solid rock of a universal human nature'.[17] Progressive humanism, on the other hand – knowing that 'it is when History is denied that it is most unmistakably at work',[18] as Barthes puts it elsewhere – 'must always remember to reverse the terms of this very old imposture, constantly to scour nature, its "laws" and its "limits" in order to discover History there, and at last to establish Nature itself as historical'.[19] In this respect, Barthes's book is probably best understood as a playful exercise in progressive humanism.[20] In 1962, however, an anthropologist who would later be one of Barthes's colleagues at the Collège de France took the challenge to humanist discourse one step further.

Claude Lévi-Strauss might have recognized a trace of himself in *Mythologies*. As an anthropologist, he had written extensively about what he explicitly identified as the myths of other cultures, and he would even go on to write a vast work entitled *Mythologiques*.[21] While Barthes was not an anthropologist, there was a sense, I think, in which he turned the anthropologist's gaze away from the other, and towards the self, towards his own culture. Above all, both figures were greatly influenced by the radical rethinking of meaning proposed in Ferdinand de Saussure's *Course in General Linguistics*.[22] In the preface to the 1970 edition of *Mythologies*, for instance, Barthes recalls that he 'had just read Saussure'[23] when he began to write his *petites mythologies du mois*, and the arbitrariness of the relationship between signifier and signified informs the entire book (and, indeed, the rest of his career). Meanwhile, a section of *Tristes Tropiques* entitled 'The making of an anthropologist' sees Lévi-Strauss criticizing his teachers 'because they were more intent on Bergson's *Essai sur les données immédiates de la conscience* than on F. de Saussure's *Cours de linguistique générale*'.[24]

Five years after the publication of *Mythologies*, Lévi-Strauss used the final chapter of *The Savage Mind* to dismiss the humanism of existentialism, a philosophical movement that, largely under the guidance of Jean-Paul Sartre, had come to dominate post-war French thought.[25] In 1953, Roland Barthes had implicitly devoted a great deal of *Writing Degree Zero*, his first book, to taking issue with Sartre's understanding of the literary. In typically mischievous manner, Barthes began his text – like Sartre's *What is Literature?*[26] – with a chapter entitled 'What is writing?', but proceeded to make no explicit reference whatever to Sartre's book.[27] Lévi-Strauss, meanwhile, openly admitted that he had permitted himself 'to borrow a certain amount of Sartre's vocabulary'[28] in *The Savage Mind*, but proceeded to challenge existentialism's faith in the figure of 'Man'. 'I believe', he declared, 'the ultimate goal of the human sciences to be not to constitute, but to dissolve man. The pre-eminent value of anthropology is that it represents the first step in a procedure which involves others.'[29] Barthes's circumspection is nowhere to be found; dissolving 'Man' is, it seems to me, a more roundly radical gesture than appealing to something called 'progressive humanism'. While *Mythologies* and *The Savage Mind* both recognize that any appeal to universal human identity can only savage difference, force the other into a version of the same, Lévi-Strauss is even more suspicious than Barthes of what *Tristes Tropiques* calls an 'over-indulgent attitude towards the illusions of subjectivity'.[30] 'Man' must be dissolved, not given resolve.

If *The Savage Mind* identified what it names 'the first step' beyond humanism, the work of Louis Althusser would soon propose nothing short of a giant leap. *For Marx*, which first appeared three years after Lévi-Strauss's book, contained a bold essay entitled 'Marxism and humanism', in which anthropocentric interpretations of Marx's work were forcefully denounced. While the influence of Hegel[31] upon his early writings meant that Marx once subscribed to the dominant principles of humanism, there was, Althusser insisted, a moment of maturity at which Marx suddenly came to see things very differently:

> Beginning in 1845, Marx breaks radically with all theory that founds history and politics on an essence of man. This unique rupture consists of three indissociable theoretical aspects:
>
> (1) The formation of a theory of history and politics founded on radically new concepts: concepts of social formation, productive forces, relations of production, superstructure, ideologies, determination in the last instance by the economy, specific determination of the other levels, etc.
>
> (2) A radical critique of the *theoretical* pretensions of all philosophical humanism.
>
> (3) The definition of humanism as *ideology*.
>
> In this new conception, everything also takes place with rigour, but it is a new rigour: the essence of man criticized (2) is defined as ideology (3), a category belonging to the new theory of society and history (1).
>
> The rupture with all *philosophical* anthropology or humanism is not a secondary detail; it is Marx's scientific discovery.
>
> It signifies that, in one and the same act, Marx rejects the problematic of the earlier philosophy and adopts a new problematic. The earlier idealist ('bourgeois') philosophy rested, in all its domains and developments, . . . upon a problematic of *human nature* (or of the essence of man). This problematic was, for whole [*entiers*] centuries, obviousness itself [*l'évidence même*], and no one had dreamed of calling it into question, even in its internal reshufflings [*remaniements*].[32]

When Marx refused to accept humanism as 'obviousness itself', he founded 'a new problematic, a new systematic way of asking questions of the world, new principles and a new method':[33]

> Strictly from the point of view of theory, therefore, one can and must speak openly of a *theoretical anti-humanism of Marx*, and see in this *theoretical anti-humanism* the absolute (negative) condition of possibility of (positive) knowledge of the human world itself, and of its practical transformation. One can only *know* something about men [sic] on the absolute condition of reducing to ashes the philosophical (theoretical) myth of man.[34]

In this respect, Althusser's essay was a work of fire. As such, it makes frequent appeal to novelty: Marx offers a 'new conception' with 'new rigour'; a 'new problematic' replaces that of 'the earlier philosophy'; and again, Marx 'established a new problematic, a new systematic way of asking questions of the world, new principles and a new method'. In short, Althusser identifies what he sees as something 'radically new'.[35] In rereading Marx, he seeks to rediscover the forgotten novelty of historical materialism, to reclaim Marx's 'theoretical anti-humanism' from 'socialist humanism' (a phrase that Althusser feels to be nothing short of a 'theoretical disparity'[36]). It is time, Althusser insists, to reject humanism, to 'rid the domain of Marxist philosophy of all the "Humanist" rubbish that is brazenly being dumped into it',[37] to move on to a new order of things.

Historical materialism makes such a break possible; 'Man' can be reduced to ashes by Marx's 'scientific discovery' of 1845. A new beginning, a genuine beginning, can finally occur:

> One thing is certain: one cannot *begin* with man, because that would be to begin with a bourgeois idea of 'man', and because the idea of *beginning with* man, in other words the idea of an absolute point of departure (= of an essence)

> belongs to bourgeois philosophy. This idea of 'man' as a starting-point, an absolute point of departure, is the basis of all bourgeois ideology; it is the soul of the great Classical Political Economy itself. 'Man' is a myth of bourgeois ideology: Marxism-Leninism cannot *start* from 'man'. It starts 'from the economically given social period'; and, at the end of its analysis, when it 'arrives', it *may find real men.* These men are thus the *point of arrival* of an analysis which starts from the social relations of the existing mode of production, from class relations, and from the class struggle. These men are quite different men from the 'man' of bourgeois ideology.[38]

He also came from Paris; or, Derrida's difference

Novelty implies a certain apocalypse: the old is razed and the new is raised. 'Man' dissolves, disrobes, disappears. Jean Baudrillard once asked, in fact, 'what are the writings of Barthes, Lacan, Foucault (and even Althusser) but a philosophy of disappearance? The obliteration of the human, of ideology.'[39] And with this disappearance, something 'quite different', as Althusser puts it, comes to take the place of humanism. It was precisely this apocalyptic aspect of anti-humanism that worried Jacques Derrida. Although he moved in the same Parisian intellectual circles as Barthes, Althusser, and Lévi-Strauss, Derrida took a somewhat different approach to the question of 'Man'. While he was not for one moment interested in defending humanism, he did have doubts about absolute breaks from tradition, about the speed and ease with which 'Man' could be dissolved, about the inescapably apocalyptic tone of anti-humanism.

On 4 March 1963, those doubts were made public, when Derrida gave a lecture at the Collège Philosophique. The theme of his talk was *Folie et déraison: Histoire de la folie à l'âge classique*,[40] Michel Foucault's influential book on madness, which had been published two years earlier. Perhaps knowing that Foucault was in the audience, Derrida chose to begin with words of praise, noting that 'having formerly had the good fortune to study under Michel Foucault, I retain the consciousness of an admiring and grateful disciple'.[41] But, as David Macey has pointed out, this was nonetheless the moment at which Derrida stepped boldly out of Foucault's shadow and 'consolidate[d] his growing reputation as a master and not a disciple'.[42] The 'eulogy', it transpired, was merely the preface to a 'savagely critical reading of *Histoire de la folie*'.[43]

Most of Derrida's essay consists of a detailed reading of a passage from Descartes's *Meditations* to which just three pages of the 693-page *Folie et déraison* had been devoted. Foucault, Derrida insists, has not read Descartes closely enough. But while this aspect of Derrida's text is something of a tour de force, I am more interested here in the opening pages, where Foucault's general approach to the issue of insanity is called into question. 'In writing a history of madness', Derrida begins:

> Foucault has attempted – and this is the greatest merit, but also the very infeasibility of his book – to write a history of madness *itself. Itself.* Of madness itself. That is, by letting madness speak for itself. Foucault wanted madness to be the *subject* of his book in every sense of the word: its theme and its first-person narrator, its author, madness speaking about itself. Foucault wanted to write a history of madness *itself*, that is madness speaking on the basis of its own experience and under its own authority, and not a history of madness described from within the language of reason, the language of psychiatry *on* madness . . . on madness already crushed beneath psychiatry, dominated, beaten to the ground, interned, that is to say, madness made into an object and exiled as the other of a language and a historical meaning which have been confused with logos itself.[44]

Foucault positions his book beyond the humanist tradition of reason, which habitually exiles madness, makes it nothing but a silent object, an other, an outside. If *Folie et déraison* is not operating 'from within the language of reason', it must be without. This, remarks Derrida, is 'the most audacious and seductive aspect of his venture, producing its admirable tension'. 'But', he solemnly adds, 'it is also, in all seriousness, the *maddest* aspect of his project.'[45]

Foucault claims that he is offering 'an archaeology of silence'. But, asks Derrida:

> is not an archaeology, even of silence, a logic, that is, an organized language, a project, an order, a sentence, a syntax, a work? Would not the archaeology of silence be the most efficacious and subtle restoration, the *repetition*, in the most irreducibly ambiguous meaning of the word, of the act perpetrated against madness – and be so at the very moment when this act is denounced?[46]

Folie et déraison repeats precisely what it claims to repeal: the book is perfectly reasonable, logical, ordered, coherent. Its '*histoire*' is both story and history. The book, that is to say, quietly subscribes to the principles of humanism. The accuser stands accused of the crime against which he speaks with such passion. The outside sides with the inside. Just as an absolute break with humanism is announced, humanism affirms its presence. In a devastating final blow, Derrida concludes that Foucault 'has already passed over to the side of the enemy, the side of order'[47] as soon as he begins to write.

It is probably fair to say that a 'symbolic murder of the master'[48] occurred on 4 March 1963. And, for a while, it seemed that Foucault had accepted his death sentence: he kept his silence during the lecture, when the talk was published the following year in *Révue de métaphysique et de morale*, and when the text was reprinted in *Writing and Difference* in 1967.[49] Finally, in 1972, he struck back. In 'My body, this paper, this fire',[50] Derrida was denounced as 'the most decisive modern representative' of a system that habitually practised 'the reduction of discursive practices to textual traces; the elision of the events produced therein and the retention only of marks for a reading; the invention of voices behind texts to avoid having to analyse the modes of implication of the subject in discourses'.[51] And the close reading of Descartes was not, it seemed, quite close enough, for Foucault claimed that Derrida had failed at a crucial moment to consult the original Latin text of the *Meditations*, to which the French translation was not entirely faithful.[52] The errant pupil was guilty of 'so many omissions . . . displacements, interversions and substitutions'.[53] The penultimate paragraph pulled no punches:

> I will not say that it is a metaphysics, metaphysics itself or its closure which is hiding in this 'textualisation' of discursive practices. I'll go much further than that: I shall say that what can be seen here so visibly is a historically well-determined little pedagogy. A pedagogy which teaches the pupil that there is nothing outside the text, but that in it, in its gaps, its blanks and its silences, there reigns the reserve of the origin; that it is therefore unnecessary to search elsewhere, but that here, not in the words, certainly, but in the words as erasures, in their *grid*, the 'sense of being' is said. A pedagogy which gives conversely to the master's voice the limitless sovereignty which allows it to restate the text indefinitely.[54]

While Foucault's counter-attack was furious, it confined its focus to Derrida's reading of (his reading of) Descartes. 'My body, this paper, this fire' had very little to say about the critique of the way in which *Folie et déraison* positioned itself outside and beyond the humanist legacy of reason. Derrida had perhaps touched a nerve.

The critique of Foucault's project signals, I think, the emergence of a somewhat different approach to the question of 'Man'. There is, in Derrida's text, a reluctance to be seduced – he writes, after all, of the 'seductive' quality of *Folie et déraison*[55] – by anti-humanism's appeal to a pure outside. As he has insisted on numerous subsequent occasions, a pure, apocalyptic break with the past is simply not feasible.[56] Thought is only possible, only meaningful, only takes place because of a certain tradition, a certain culture. And thought, therefore, must bear some trace of that tradition, even when it sets itself against the established order of things in the name of the new. Because every aspect of western thought is touched in some way by the legacy of humanism, any claim to be marking the end of 'Man' is bound to be marked with the language of 'Man'. What Baudrillard calls the 'philosophy of disappearance' secretes the apparition of anthropocentric discourse, and it seems to me that there is a sense in which Derrida might be called a philosopher of *reappearance.*

There is no pure outside to which the knowing critic can simply step. Each 'transgressive gesture reencloses us'[57] because every such gesture will have been unconsciously choreographed by humanism. Foucault's memorable image of the figure of 'Man' being erased from the sand by an incoming tide[58] finds itself beached, for every new order of things harbours traces of the old. The relationship between sand and water, it transpires, is not unlike the situation that Freud encountered with the 'mystic writing-pad'.[59] Just as the well-known toy offers a convenient analogy for the way in which the unconscious continues to bear meaningful marks of what had once been present to the conscious mind, it might also be used to illustrate how the scores of humanism linger in the wax – waiting to be settled, ready to unsettle – even when they appear to have been wiped out and silenced to history.

It does not follow, however, that humanism is inevitable or insurmountable, and Derrida goes on to develop a convincingly different way to resist its hegemony. I will return to this in chapter 4 of *Alien Chic*, however. I have invoked his critique of anti-humanism at this early stage in order to problematize an account that would conclude that the narrative traced in the previous chapter signals the absolute end of humanism. Anthropocentric assumptions, in fact, are alive and well in Hollywood science fiction, for, while *Mission to Mars*, *Red Planet* and *Mars Attacks!* are strikingly different from the invasion narratives of the 1950s, more recent years have witnessed a simultaneous fidelity to the patterns – the humanist patterns – of the past.

Signs of the times

'It's like *War of the Worlds.*' These words are spoken by Merrill Hess, one of the central characters in *Signs* (dir. M. Night Shyamalan, 2002), and refer to the alien invasion of Earth which is unfolding before his eyes on a television screen. They are, however, also a good description of the film itself.[60] At the most fundamental level, this is a simple question of plot: *Signs* is an old-fashioned tale of invasion from the skies. The rewriting with which *Mission to Mars* and *Red Planet* concerned themselves has been completely abandoned. And, as in *The War of the Worlds*, although the geographical focus of the narrative is somewhat confined, it soon becomes clear that a certain metonymy is at work, for the entire planet, as the news reports watched by Merrill confirm, is under attack.

As invaders, the film's aliens are unequivocally hostile; gone is the soft, serene, benevolent figure of *Mission to Mars.* While De Palma's film allows the extraterrestrial to open up new spaces for humans, to expand their knowledge and horizons, *Signs* turns the clock back to the 1950s in its equation of a close encounter with desperate enclosure. Although the Hess family lives in a large farmhouse which is surrounded by open land, the space available to its members becomes increasingly limited as the plot unfolds. Before the invasion, the family roams the open fields and takes a leisurely trip to a nearby town, but as soon as the aliens arrive, the humans are driven inside, and the doors and windows of the house are quickly boarded up. When the invaders find a way to enter the building, the Hesses find themselves confined to the small, dark, dirty basement.[61]

And still the aliens advance. As Morgan sits with his back to the wall, an extraterrestrial hand reaches through a vent to grab his shoulder, and the subsequent panic results in the boy suffering from an asthma attack. The touch of the alien has brought only imprisonment and the threat of death. In *Mission to Mars*, the extraterrestrial extended a hand in friendship, and the astronauts willingly took it to form a circle; in *Signs*, however, as in *The War of the Worlds* (where Sylvia felt a slimy hand upon her shoulder), the touch of the alien is to be avoided.

No hand is held, no circle is formed. The only circle involving aliens, in fact, is a crop circle, and this is to be found outside (a space to which the humans no longer have access), where it is a sign of aggression, a hint of things to come.

This distancing, this repulsion of the other, is matched – as in the narratives of the 1950s – by a coming-together of the human characters. One particular scene, which occurs approximately 70 minutes into the film, neatly encapsulates this reactive solidarity. Having boarded up their windows and doors, the Hesses gather for what might well be their last supper together. The meal is prepared, and the family sits to eat. Almost immediately, however, an argument breaks out when Graham refuses to allow grace to be said. 'I'm not wasting one more minute of my life on prayer', he declares. 'Not one more minute, understand?' Before long, three of the four people present at the table are in tears. 'I hate you . . .', Morgan tells his father. 'You let mom die.' But the division is quickly overcome, as Morgan, Bo and Merrill leave their seats to embrace Graham. From this point onwards, the Hesses stand united against the invaders.

The movement from antagonism to human unity is actually matched, as in *The War of the Worlds* and *It! The Terror from Beyond Space*, by the composition of the film. The scene begins with a long shot, which frames the whole family at the table. However, as the argument develops, the film progresses through a sequence of eleven close-ups, in each of which only one character is ever visible. Division has set in. The twelfth shot is essentially of Morgan alone, but begins with Graham violently reaching into the frame to snatch food from his son's plate; although the two characters are present, they are at odds with each other. Four more isolated close-ups follow, and it is only on the subsequent shot of Graham that Morgan and Bo move into picture to hug their father. The bonding is not yet complete, however: Merrill is shown alone in the following shot, but Graham's arm reaches in from the left of the frame to grab his brother. Finally, the twentieth shot in the sequence brings all four characters together again, as Graham's arms encircle the rest of his family. The differences have been set aside;

the cutting has come to an end. The journey from long shot to long shot is complete. Things have come full circle.

As in *The War of the Worlds*, *It! The Terror from Beyond Space* and *Invaders from Mars*, the threat of the other shores up the human. And, as if to underscore this, *Signs* allows the alien to make its presence felt at the very end of the dining scene. As the Hesses embrace each other, the camera tracks back across the table until the baby monitor (which has been receiving signals from the extraterrestrials) is seen in the foreground. Suddenly, as it crackles into life, the film pulls focus to isolate the alien element within the frame. The humans are now a blur, set apart from the sign of the other. When they are returned to focus, the baby monitor loses its distinction. The Hesses, in other words, are not only physically distant (to reach the trace of the alien, the camera has moved away from them); they are once again visually distinguished by the filmic practice. The human is focused, consolidated, rendered distinct by the otherness of the other. The humans make a circle, and the aliens make a circle (in the field), but the two never overlap. It is, indeed, 'like *War of the Worlds*'.

But while *Signs* readily calls up the ghost of the 1950s, it refuses to reproduce the relentless solemnity of the earlier invasion narratives. On the contrary, there are some unmistakably comical moments in the film: Graham's speech to the alien that is trapped in Ray Reddy's pantry is delightfully clichéd ('We already took some of your friends downtown in a paddywagon . . . Don't throw your life away, son'); Bo and Morgan, and later Merrill, fashion ludicrous pointed hats from aluminium foil ('So the aliens can't read our minds'); and all that Graham can find to say in response to the rising panic is: 'Everybody in this house needs to calm down and eat some fruit or something.'

It seems to me, however, that the humour does not function in the same manner as it does in *Mars Attacks!* Whereas Burton's film is a sustained parody of the invasion narratives of the past, *Signs* seeks out the small moments of absurdity that haunt an otherwise terrifying situation. While the odd remark or gesture is undoubtedly amusing, the invasion itself – the arrival of alien beings – is deadly serious. Whereas the killings in *Mars Attacks!* are played purely for laughs, the attempt on Morgan's life in *Signs* is, by comparison, a moment of extreme tension and pathos. There is, in short, a difference of tone and balance that distinguishes *Signs* from *Mars Attacks!* In Shyamalan's film, the laughs are not at the expense of the 1950s; they are, rather, brief moments of relief from a familiar scene of terror.

'Just a little anxious to get up there and whoop E.T.'s ass . . .'

Signs was one of the box-office successes of the summer of 2002. I happened to be in Las Vegas at the time of its release, and even though the Strip had countless other distractions to offer, every screening of the film seemed to sell out. Six years earlier, a movie that owed even more to the invasion narratives of the 1950s achieved the highest opening week ticket sales ever recorded, and even found itself on the covers of both *Time* and *Newsweek* magazines.[62] *Independence Day* (dir. Roland Emmerich, 1996) would go on to be 'the top-grossing movie of 1996 in the United States, the United Kingdom, Germany and around the world, [and subsequently become] the sixth top domestic-grosser of all time'.[63] More unusually, perhaps, as the American presidential elections loomed, it received support from both Republican and Democrat candidates. 'I recommend it', declared Bill Clinton, who was treated to a special screening at the White House.[64] 'I liked it', countered Bob Dole, before adding: 'Bring your family too. You'll be proud of it. Diversity. America. Leadership. Good over Evil.'[65] On the last count, Dole was, for once in his life, absolutely right.

Independence Day does not take long to establish its principal point of reference. Indeed, before the first ten minutes have elapsed, there have been two explicit references to the era of Eisenhower. Marty is the first to make the connection, saying of the media's response to the appearance of alien spacecraft in the skies that 'every station's making like it's the 1950s'. And, just in case the allusion were not clear enough, the following scene opens with a group of characters watching *The*

Day the Earth Stood Still (dir. Robert Wise, 1951), an alien invasion film of the period. The past is on screen, visibly present.

Building upon these early moments, the film proceeds to approach extraterrestrials, in short, 'like it's the 1950s'. This dependence upon the invasion narratives of the past is, I think, more straightforward than Vivian Sobchack believes. 'In *Independence Day*', she argues:

> alien flying saucers blow up the White House and the Empire State Building, visibly reducing the USA's major cities to rubble. Nonetheless, while there is panic in the streets, there is no Cold War fear and anxiety here to inform and historically ground it – merely cinematic nostalgia and the imperatives of the latest special effects. And, while one might want to link the urban destruction in *Independence Day* and the films that follow it with recent and explosive acts of urban terrorism in New York and Oklahoma City, there seems to be no human affect or real consequence attached to it.[66]

While I accept that the paranoia of the Cold War is largely absent from the film, it seems to me that Sobchack overlooks the humanism that confirms a direct line of continuity between *Independence Day* and the invasion narratives of the 1950s. When the aliens strike at American monuments, they at once strike – within the textual economy – at the entire human race. To group Emmerich's film with *Mars Attacks!*, as Sobchack does on two separate occasions within the space of one page,[67] is to elide a fundamental difference between the texts: Tim Burton mocks the humanism of the past, but *Independence Day* remains faithful to the traditional understanding of aliens as malevolent invaders. While the two films were released within several months of each other,[68] and even used the same set for interior shots of the White House,[69] their textual politics and approach to history were radically different.

If *Independence Day* is a fine example of 'alien hatred', it is not, however, unaware of the phenomenon of 'alien love'. Quite the opposite, in fact, for not long after the first sighting of the huge spacecraft, a report from the *Entertainment Tonight* programme (the familiar acronym of which now takes on new significance) announces that 'hundreds of UFO fanatics . . . have gathered on rooftops here in downtown Los Angeles to welcome the new arrivals'. Some of these revellers are actually dressed as aliens, while others carry signs that bear phrases such as: 'Please take me away', 'Welcome – make yourselves at home', and 'Remember me? June 21, 1977'. Meanwhile, a group of demonstrators has gathered outside the White House to protest against the mobilization of the military in response to the aliens' appearance.

It would be easy to dismiss these marginal moments as a light-hearted mockery of 'New Age' beliefs and practices, but I think that the place and, moreover, the fate of the 'alien lovers' are central to the film's project, for 'alien love' is soon exposed as pure *naïveté*. Having failed to obey a police order to leave the roof, the group in Los Angeles finally finds itself facing the spacecraft. The jubilant atmosphere reaches fever pitch, and the ship slowly opens, revealing a brilliant blue light. The group waves its arms and holds up its signs in anticipation . . . and the building is instantly destroyed. The very first strike at the surface of the Earth,[70] that is to say, is at those who have explicitly signalled their love of aliens. In *Independence Day*, to welcome the other is to welcome only death. When aliens take up the offer to make themselves 'at home', human beings, as in *The War of the Worlds* and *Invaders from Mars*, are left without. The monsters of the 1950s have made a terrible return, and it would seem that the only true 'welcome' should be of the type offered by Captain Steven Hiller. Having already declared that he is 'just a little anxious to get up there and whoop E.T.'s ass', Hiller is delighted when he manages to shoot down an alien craft. Opening its hatch, he finds himself facing a slimy alien being. 'Welcome to Earth', he says, punching the creature unconscious.

The destruction of the 'alien lovers' recalls, of course, the two moments in *The War of the Worlds* at which welcoming parties are obliterated as they attempt to make peaceful contact with the invaders. And the connection between the two films has been openly acknowledged by Dean Devlin, the producer of *Independence Day*, who has suggested that 'this film could not exist without *War of the Worlds*'.[71] Picking up on Devlin's comment, Michael Rogin goes on to outline further similarities between the two films. '*Independence Day*', he notes, 'repeats two battle scenes from the earlier movie, one in which the alien force field repels our combat weapons, the other in which an atomic bomb fails to harm the aliens' presence on the ground.'[72] Elsewhere, Rogin continues, *Independence Day* borrows but updates key tropes from *The War of the Worlds*. In Haskin's film, for instance, everyday germs eventually save the day, defeating the helpless Martian invaders. In *Independence Day*, the theme of infection has, in a contemporary twist, spread from the literal to the virtual:

> The human germs that fell 1950s aliens in *War of the Worlds* enter *Independence Day* by way of Jewish hypochondria, for when David's father nags him about getting a cold, David gets the idea of giving the aliens one. Experimentally demonstrating how to disable an invisible shield, David explains, 'I gave it a cold. I gave it a virus.'[73]

David is referring, of course, to a computer virus that, when introduced to the central computer of the mothership, disables the aliens' defence shield and allows the humans to strike the victorious blow. 'As in *War of the Worlds*', concludes Rogin, 'the "littlest things . . . upon this Earth" . . . destroy the invaders.'[74]

What distinguishes these borrowings from those found in *Mars Attacks!* (and even *Signs*) is a certain nostalgia, which, I think, runs far deeper than the 'mer[e] cinematic nostalgia' identified by Vivian Sobchack. While Tim Burton's film invokes the past *as* past, exploiting for comedy the anachronism of the traditional invasion narrative, *Independence Day* does not in any way set out to mock the fundamental anthropocentrism of texts like *The War of the Worlds*. There are, as in the case of *Signs*, incidental moments of humour in Emmerich's film, but these do nothing to unsettle its reactionary humanism. Jodi Dean is right, I think, to read the film as little more than a simple 'remake'[75] of *The War of the Worlds*, for it seems to me that *Independence Day* hangs dearly on to Haskin's humanism, shores up the binary opposition between the human and the alien. While *Mars Attacks!* laughs, *Independence Day* longs; where *Mission to Mars* deconstructs, *Independence Day* reconstructs.

This is not to say that Emmerich's film is unaware of the 'Crisis of *versus*' with which a text like *Mission to Mars* is concerned. As Michael Rogin has acutely observed, there are, in fact, several scenes in which *Independence Day* hints at the possible instability of the opposition between the human and the inhuman. The film, he suggests, 'capitalises on a popular distrust of government so strong in the years leading up to [1996] that the *New York Times Magazine* mused in 1994, "People talk as if our political system had been taken over by aliens."'[76] In *Independence Day*, there is no clear sense of a United States entirely united against tyranny and evil, for – as in the various conspiracy theories surrounding the Roswell incident,[77] and television series such as *The X-Files*, *Dark Skies*,[78] and *Taken*[79] – the American government keeps secrets about extraterrestrials from its people. Even the President, it transpires, has no knowledge of the work being undertaken in Area 51. 'Two words, Mr President', replies the Secretary of Defense when questioned about the cover-up. 'Plausible deniability.'

The real-life American military, in fact, withdrew its support for the making of the film when the producers refused to remove all reference to the 'non-existent' installation that allegedly lies in the Nevada desert.[80] Perhaps in response, the film hides some of its more dramatic secrets deep within Area 51. Not only does the underground base house an alien spacecraft and a collection of extraterrestrials neatly preserved in large glass tanks, but the principal scientist – Dr Brakish Okun – has made a startling discovery. 'They're not', he announces, 'all that dissimilar from us. Breathes [*sic*] oxygen, comparable tolerances to heat, cold – probably why they're interested in our planet.' The human and the alien, in other words, partially occupy a common biological ground, and while the invaders appear to be entirely unstoppable, their bodies, when removed from their tough bio-mechanical shells, are, according to Okun, 'just as frail as ours'.

This similarity is not even unsettled by the fact that the aliens enjoy, as in *The War of the Worlds*, a degree of technological supremacy. On the contrary, as Michael Rogin has pointed out, technology translates remarkably well:

> The alien flying saucer has the shape of the earth communication satellites that replace it on screen [in the opening sequence] . . . Preserved in bottles, [the aliens'] vulnerable, oxygen-breathing bodies could pass for human foetuses. At the other end of the biology-technology interface, the aliens' technological competence is so interchangeable with ours that our pilot can fly their aircraft and our computer whiz can penetrate their software.[81]

But, having hinted at ways in which the opposition between the human and the alien might be unstable, *Independence Day* retreats from this possibility, quickly replacing it with a traditionally humanist perspective. While *Mission to Mars* explores an unsettling of the binary opposition, *Independence Day* deplores such a condition, seeking instead to 'pu[t] on screen widely-shared worries about the breakdown of difference in order to re-establish the contrast between us and them'.[82] The 'Crisis of *versus*' appears only as something undesirable, threatening, fatal; absolute difference must be reaffirmed if there is to be a happy ending.

As in the invasion narratives of the 1950s, as well as in *Signs*, this is achieved by showing how the arrival of the alien brings the human characters together into a unified whole. Towards the end of the film, for instance, Steven and Jasmine are united in a makeshift wedding ceremony. 'I should have done this a long time ago', he says, implying that the proposal of marriage has been prompted by the invasion. Meanwhile, Constance and David – who begin the film as divorcees – find that their separation is forgotten in the shadow of the alien other. As they act as witnesses to the marriage of Steven and Jasmine, the two characters are initially framed in five separate shots (unlike the bride and bridegroom, who are always pictured together). On the sixth shot, however, Constance reaches into frame to take David's hand, gently touching the wedding ring that he has never removed. Cutting has been cast aside. As in the 'last supper' sequence of *Signs*, separation has been overcome both at the level of the diegesis and in the organization of the film itself. When the other invades, humans come together.

Echoing the narratives of the 1950s, this union of a small number of central human characters in *Independence Day* functions metonymically, for the wedding scene is immediately followed by one of the most (in)famous moments in the film, when the President addresses the resistance fighters in unmistakably humanist terms:

> Mankind – that word should have new meaning for all of us today. We can't be consumed by our petty differences any more. We will be united in our common interest. Perhaps it's fate that today is the fourth of July, and you will once again be fighting for our freedom. Not from tyranny, oppression, or persecution, but from annihilation. We're fighting for our right to live, to exist. And should we win the day, the fourth of July will no longer be known as an American holiday, but as the day when the world declared in one voice: 'We will not go quietly into the night. We will not vanish without a fight. We're going to live on, we're going to survive. Today, we celebrate our independence day.'

This independence, of course, is an independence from the other. 'Mankind' finds its 'new meaning' when 'petty differences' between humans are set aside in the finding of 'one voice'. The 'Family of Man' is reborn.

Its triumphant voice speaks, in fact, at this very moment in the film, for, as William V. Spanos has pointed out, the naturalized, transparent 'we' is one of the hallmarks of humanism.[83] To say 'we' is to assume that more than one subject can be represented by a single utterance.

'We' – together with the related terms 'our' and 'us' – privileges identity over difference. 'We' unites. In this respect, these 128 words spoken by the President contain fifteen separate affirmations of humanism: the head of the republic says 'we' on nine occasions, 'our' five times, and 'us' once. And, as Jean-François Lyotard has pointed out:

> In a republic, the pronoun of the first-person plural is in effect the linchpin for the discourse of authorization. Substitutable for a proper name, *We, the French people* . . ., it is supposedly able to link prescriptions (such as articles in codes, court rulings, laws, decrees, ordinances, circulars, and commands) onto their legitimation 'in a suitable way'. Take an obligatory prescription: *It is an obligation for x to carry out act* α. The legitimation of this obligation can be written thus: *It is a norm for y that 'it is obligatory for x to carry out act* α*'.* The republican regimen's principle of legitimacy is that the addressor of the norm, *y*, and the addressee of the obligation, *x*, are the same. The legislator ought not to be exempt from the obligation he or she norms. And the obligated one is able to promulgate the law that obligates him or her. In speaking the law, the former decrees that he or she must respect it. In respecting the law, the latter decrees it anew. Their names, *x* and *y*, are in principle perfectly commutable between at least the two instances of normative addressor and prescriptive addressee. They are thus united in a single we, the one designating itself by the collective name 'French citizens'. The authorization is then formulated thus: *We decree as a norm that it is an obligation for us to carry out act* α. This is the principle of autonomy.[84]

Autonomy and independence hang over the whole of the President's speech: the human does not in any way depend upon the alien for meaning or its future. 'Man' is autonomous, independent, intact, in control, a law (*nomos*) unto 'himself' (*autos*).

Earlier in the film, Captain Hiller asks a question to which he expects no answer, but to which *Independence Day*, in fact, repeatedly responds. As he approaches the crashed spacecraft that houses the alien whom he will soon 'welcome' with a punch, Steven shouts abuse at his opponent. 'Who's the man?', he taunts. 'Who's the man?' In one sense, of course, this is not a question at all; it is merely a rhetorical gesture, a verbal confirmation of the supremacy that he has just materially demonstrated. And yet, taking the question at face value, I think that there is a sense in which the film consistently seeks to make a clear distinction between who is and who is not a man (women are very much relegated to the margins of this particular war of the worlds), between who is and who is not on the side of 'Man'. While *Mission to Mars* blurs the line between the human and the alien by appealing to a common point of origin, *Independence Day* continually retreats to the simple humanism of the 1950s, preferring instead to call up the ghost of *The War of the Worlds* and tell a tale of unequivocally evil extraterrestrials.

I lost my heart to a starship trooper

One year after the global success of *Independence Day*, *Starship Troopers* (dir. Paul Verhoeven, 1997) took humanism and spectacular militarism to something of an extreme. If Roland Emmerich's film revisited routes marked out by the invasion narratives of the 1950s, Verhoeven's movie had its very roots in Eisenhower's America, for it was based upon a novel first published by Robert A. Heinlein in 1959. The film recounts the war waged by the human Federal Forces against a monstrous race of 'bugs' from the planet Klendathu. As in Heinlein's book, the Federation is thoroughly undemocratic:[85] a clear distinction exists between citizens – those who 'accep[t] personal responsibility for the safety of the body politic'[86] by enrolling for military service – and non-citizens, who are deprived of the right to vote.

Near the beginning of the film, the four central characters – Rico, Carl, Dizzy and Carmen – are informed by Mr Rasczak, a teacher of one of their classes,[87] that violence is 'the supreme authority from which all other authorities derive'. Inspired by Rasczak's words, and perhaps also by the Federation's relentless propaganda, Rico decides to sign up for Federal Service. His parents, however, are unhappy with his choice, and his father – who dreams only of having a son at Harvard – ridicules the teachings of Rasczak, who repeatedly offers extremely reactionary opinions (in Heinlein's novel, he even goes on to denounce Karl Marx as a 'disheveled old mystic . . . turgid, tortured, confused, and neurotic, unscientific, illogical . . . [a] pompous fraud'[88]). Verhoeven's film, in fact, frequently aligns the politics of the Federation with Nazism: the official state propaganda, for instance, recalls, in both tone and composition, the scenes of the Nuremberg congress captured in Leni Riefenstahl's *Triumph of the Will* (1935), while the uniform of the military's intelligence wing is unmistakably fashioned after that of the Nazis. In *Starship Troopers*, the political has been thoroughly aestheticized, a move that Walter Benjamin famously identified as one of the hallmarks of fascism.[89]

However, strictly according to the textual economy, the Federation would seem to have adopted the correct approach to politics and, moreover, to extraterrestrials. The liberal, democratic beliefs of Rico's parents lead only to death, for, at the very moment when they forgive their son and implore him to 'come on home', the skies turn black and the video transmission is terminated. The alien 'bugs' have attacked Earth, killing over 8 million people in an instant. War is declared, and Rico, who had been considering leaving the military, commits himself to the conflict with a renewed passion. As in *Independence Day*, the ensuing war of the worlds is presented as what one of the Federation's broadcasts names a 'crisis for humankind'. At an emergency meeting of the Federal Council in Geneva, Sky Marshal Dienes announces: 'We must meet the threat with our valour, our blood, indeed with our very lives, to ensure that human civilization, not insect, dominates this galaxy now and always.' Recalling the President's speech in *Independence Day*, the language of Marshal Dienes is gathering, inclusive, hailing. It is precisely, in fact, an example of what Althusser would call ideology at work.[90] The use of the first-person pronoun, together with its possessives, interpellates all those who are listening. There is a human 'we', and if a listener responds to the speaking of this 'we', he or she must be human. And if there is a 'we', there must be a 'not-we', a 'Them', an altogether alien other. If ideology, as Althusser puts it, interpellates individuals as subjects, then it might be said that Dienes's speech is fashioned to recruit subjects of and for the Federation, subjects who are unquestionably human.

Human or alien. 'Us' or 'Them'. The options, the oppositions, are clear. But, although *Starship Troopers* concludes with an affirmation of absolute difference, it first hints, like *Independence Day*, that the human and the extraterrestrial might not automatically be wholly distinct. In fact, it seems to me that the film's principal project is to establish and enforce the difference between the two categories, to hold them absolutely apart in the face of fear.

In Heinlein's original novel, humanism is called into question by the very technology and technique of modern warfare. The starship troopers that give the book its name are, as the text recounts in some detail, hypnotised,[91] injected with special drugs,[92] and, above all, sent into combat encased within powered, cybernetic suits.[93] The latter, in particular, render the traditional, pure and autonomous subject of humanism distinctly problematic: 'If the suit hadn't already been told to jump,' recounts the narrator, near the beginning of the book, 'I guess I wouldn't have got out of there.'[94] One year before the concept of the cyborg was first proposed in the pages of *Astronautics*,[95] Heinlein's narrator had realized that '[t]he secret lies in negative feedback and amplification'.[96] 'Maybe,' he muses, 'they'll be able to do without us someday.'[97]

Although Paul Verhoeven had memorably explored some of the consequences of cyborg citizenship[98] in *Robocop* (1987), the cybernetic suits, the drugs, and the hypnosis are all excluded from his adaptation of *Starship Troopers.* In their absence, however, the possibility of an unstable opposition between the human and the inhuman nonetheless remains an issue. When Carl, Rico and Carmen arrive at the military's enrolment centre, they are greeted by an officer who remarks, on learning of Rico's destination, 'Mobile Infantry made me the man I am today.' The suggestion that certain stereotypical activities 'make the man' is nothing new, but as the administrator speaks, the camera cuts to a close-up of his prosthetic hand, before pulling back to reveal a distinct lack of legs. Meanwhile, at the beginning of the film, Rasczak is also missing a limb, but when he reappears much later in the narrative, he wears a prosthetic arm. Humans, it transpires, rely upon a whole series of prosthetic devices to win the war against the aliens: spaceships, bullets, missiles, and helmets all have a key role to play (and when the latter are removed, as the fatal accident during training proves, the unprotected 'authentic' head is all-too-human). Behind these additions, it becomes increasingly difficult to detect a 'pure' human being, and less still one that might be capable of defeating the aliens.

These, however, are marginal moments, and they are soon overshadowed by the central story of how the humans come to triumph over the extraterrestrial 'bugs'. The conflict itself reveals, as the deranged General puts it, echoing *Independence Day*'s Doctor Okun, 'They're just like us – they want to know what makes us tick so that they can kill us.' In the second half of this sentence lies, I think, the textual justification for the sheer force with which the film reaffirms the principles of humanism. The benign interaction between the human and the alien witnessed in *Mission to Mars* has once again been replaced by a situation in which there can be only one survivor. 'We're in this for the species, boys and girls', says Carl, and the Federation's eventual success marks the elevation of the human species over its terrible other.

The extreme violence with which humanism is restored is not accidental. Whereas *Independence Day* enlisted state-of-the-art special effects to create a sense of the spectacular (the film is a fine example of what have come to be known as 'event movies'), *Starship Troopers* inclines more towards the visceral. Bodies – both human and alien – are repeatedly dismembered. Limbs, heads, brains and blood – both red and green – bounce and drip across the screen with remarkable regularity.[99] Heinlein's novel provides the beginnings of an explanation for this violence. In the final meeting of the History and Moral Philosophy class, one of the students questions the validity of Mr Dubois's brutal beliefs.[100] He is quick to respond:

> Anyone who clings to the historically untrue – and thoroughly immoral – doctrine that 'violence never settles anything' I would advise to conjure up the ghosts of Napoleon Bonaparte and of the Duke of Wellington and let them debate it. The ghost of Hitler could referee, and the jury might well be the Dodo, the Great Auk, and the Passenger Pigeon. Violence, naked force, has settled more issues in history than has any other factor, and the contrary opinion is wishful thinking at its worst. Breeds that forget this basic truth have always paid for it with their lives and freedoms.[101]

Not only must Verhoeven's film bring the meaning of the alien back into line with the narratives of the 1950s, but this restoration must be done (and be *seen* to be done) with maximum force. The bugs are not merely destroyed; they are destroyed in a manner that is as vivid as it is vicious. 'The only good bug is a dead bug', says one of the survivors of the razing of Buenos Aires, rewriting and – more importantly – rehumanizing an infamous line from *Beneath the Planet of the Apes* (dir. Ted Post, 1970),[102] and it seems to me that this brief remark neatly captures the film's overall approach to the alien. There can, in *Starship Troopers*, be no peaceful co-existence, no sharing of space and sense. There is, rather, just one solution, phrased with chilling precision by Rico: 'Kill 'em, kill 'em all!' Extraterrestrials must be made extinct if humans are not to disappear like Dubois's Dodo. As in the invasion narratives of the 1950s, aliens bring only death and destruction to the human race. Once again, it is a question of 'Us' or 'Them', 'Us' versus 'Them'. The binary opposition between the human and the alien seems to have been restored. The 'Crisis of *versus*' with which *Mars Attacks!*, *Red Planet* and *Mission to Mars* concern themselves appears to have been negated.

Loving/loathing the alien

'Alien love', then, somehow manages to exist alongside a more traditional 'alien hatred'. *Independence Day* and *Mars Attacks!* share a summer and a soundstage, but little else; *Signs* arrives later than *Mission to Mars* and *Red Planet*, but looks far further back into the past for inspiration. The ghost of the 1950s haunts at the very moment of its rewriting and ridicule. And the films discussed in this chapter are merely a small selection from texts produced since 1982 – the year of *E.T.* – that continue to rely upon an understanding of the extraterrestrial as absolutely other and unequivocally evil. In the realm of cinema alone, I might just as readily have invoked examples such as *Aliens*, *Predator* (dir. John McTiernan, 1987), *The Hidden* (dir. Jack Sholder, 1988), *They Live* (dir. John Carpenter, 1988), *Alien 3*,[103] *The Faculty* (dir. Robert Rodriguez, 1998), and *Pitch Black* (dir. David Twohy, 2000). The 'versus' is still very much with 'us'.

To equate the recent rise of 'alien love' with the perfect disappearance of the past and the absolute erasure of humanism would, therefore, be to ignore the irreducible plurality of the present. But how can this plurality be explained? It is tempting to invoke Raymond Williams's assertion that any given historical moment consists of dominant, residual, and emergent meanings,[104] but this would not, I feel, allow me to do much more than acknowledge the simple fact that the present is plural in its dealings with extraterrestrials. I want, rather, to *account* for that plurality, to understand why 'alien love' and 'alien hatred' can court simultaneous credibility. The answer might, in fact, be relatively straightforward. Perhaps 'alien love' is not actually that different from 'alien hatred'. Perhaps *Independence Day* and *Mission to Mars* are not, in one particular sense, all that alien to each other. Perhaps, as in Tom Wolfe's analysis of Radical Chic, little has really changed. Perhaps 'alien love', for this very reason, might be better understood as Alien Chic.

3

I want to be leaving; or, tracking alien abduction

Let the ship slide open, and we'll go inside of it,
Where we are not human.

PATTI SMITH, 'Birdland'[1]

'I want to believe'

What if aliens were real?

So far, my focus has fallen upon fictional extraterrestrials. Sometimes, however, aliens are not held at the comfortable distance that imagination ultimately affords. Some encounters with creatures from galaxies far, far away are far, far closer. I am referring to alien abduction, and I want in this chapter to ask what the contemporary popularity of the phenomenon might reveal about the strange similarity between 'alien love' and 'alien hatred'. Why should 'alien love', as I suggested at the end of the previous chapter, be understood as Alien Chic?

'Real-life' cases of alien abduction are rarely taken seriously.[2] They are often seen as something of a joke, or perhaps the property of the 'lunatic fringe'. To believe that aliens really exist and are taking members of the human race on a daily basis is to risk being mocked as eccentric, or simply as a consumer of too much conspiracy theory.[3] And actually to claim to have been abducted is to risk ridicule and charges of insanity.[4] 'I do not know of a single witness who has gone public in the United States', notes Whitley Strieber, 'and not suffered economic and social hardship as a result.'[5] Even Strieber, who has published several books about his own experiences with aliens, began by assuming that he had gone mad. 'At first, I thought I was losing my mind', he recalls on the opening page of his well-known memoir, *Communion*, before going on to detail bouts of depression, anxiety and thoughts of suicide.[6]

But cultural criticism frequently involves taking the apparently unimportant or incredible entirely seriously. Culture, as I noted in the introduction, is simply what signifies. And alien abduction has come to signify with remarkable force: one survey has suggested that 'from several hundred thousand to several million Americans may have had abduction or abduction-related experiences'.[7] A poll conducted in 1997 by *Time* magazine and the CNN television channel revealed that 17 per cent of Americans believe that abduction is a genuine phenomenon.[8] Even Elaine Showalter, who sceptically dismisses such figures as 'pseudostatistics and projections',[9] eventually concedes, in a book published towards the end of the 1990s, that 'maybe we're witnessing the birth of a folk religion, with aliens functioning much like the angels who have sprouted all over the country as the millennium approaches'.[10] At the beginning of the twenty-first century, abduction is a widely-recognized phenomenon, part of the fabric of everyday life. People believe.

This, however, was not always the case. As the historian David M. Jacobs has made clear, alien abduction was once considered to be merely 'the fringy "stepchild" of the UFO phenomenon'.[11] In fact, most of the research conducted into reports of flying saucers in the 1940s and 1950s tended to concern itself with relatively straightforward aerial sightings. Aliens, at this time, tended to remain at a distance, and abduction was very rarely an issue. So much so, in fact, that when a small group of 'contactees' took the bold step of announcing that 'the benevolent beings they called Space Brothers had given them a mission to perform on Earth', they were quickly denounced by the 'new UFO organizations . . . [which] spent large amounts of time and energy trying to dissociate themselves from them'.[12]

It was not until 1965 that the first prominent publication of a case of abduction took place:

> The event had occurred in 1957 in Brazil. Antônio Villas-Boas was the son of a rancher. He was working on his father's farm at night when he saw a UFO land near him. Four large-headed, small Beings quickly came out of the object and forced Villas-Boas inside. They took off his clothes and spread a clear, odorless liquid over his body. They then cut his chin and collected some blood into a cup. Villas-Boas claimed that a small, naked female Being then entered the room. She had thin blond hair, large slanted eyes, high cheekbones, an ordinary nose, a small, thin-lipped mouth, and a sharply pointed chin. Her body looked human, her feet were small, and her hands were long and pointed. She was about four and a half feet tall. She began to hug and caress him. He became uncontrollably sexually excited. They had intercourse twice. Then the female Being abruptly broke off their intimacy and left Villas-Boas with the feeling that he was being treated like 'a good stallion to improve their . . . stock'. He was then let off the object.[13]

While the account of this incident attracted a certain amount of interest, David M. Jacobs notes:

> To UFO researchers at the time, this report seemed ridiculous and lurid; it reeked of pulp science fiction. Having spent the better part of the 1950s battling the contactees, they did not need another outlandish case to complicate their job of winning scientific legitimacy for the phenomenon.[14]

A year after the publication of the Villas-Boas case, however, one of the most famous instances of alien abduction came to light.

On 19 September 1961, Betty and Barney Hill were driving from Montreal to their home in Portsmouth, New Hampshire, when they noticed a strange object in the night sky. Stopping the car near Indian Head to investigate, the Hills were met by the crew of a 'pancake-like disc'.[15] 'Near hysteria',[16] the couple tried to drive to safety, but a strange beeping sound was suddenly heard, and the Hills 'began to feel an odd tingling drowsiness . . . From that moment, a sort of haze came over them.'[17] When they returned to consciousness, Barney was still driving the car, but they were now near Ashland, 35 miles south of Indian Head. Two hours had elapsed.

Although they could remember nothing further, the Hills remained unsettled about the period of 'missing time', and, in January 1964, they began a process of hypnosis and regression with Dr Benjamin Simon. This would eventually reveal that the couple had been abducted and taken into the flying saucer, where they were subjected to various physiological tests, including the insertion of a pregnancy-testing needle into Betty's abdomen.[18] The mystery had been solved. 'I felt so overwhelmed and relieved', recalled Barney. 'Now parts of my life that had been missing were added to it again. Parts of my life were being put back together.'[19] Two years later, the Hills received widespread publicity when a journalist named John G. Fuller wrote an article about their experiences for the popular publication, *Look*. When the issue in question broke the magazine's circulation record, Fuller's account was quickly expanded and published as *The Interrupted Journey: Two Lost Hours Aboard a Flying Saucer*. A television movie, *The UFO Incident* (dir. Richard A. Colla), followed in 1975.

It is generally accepted that the modern history of alien abduction begins with the case of Betty and Barney Hill.[20] Many of the now-familiar themes – an encounter at the roadside, a period of 'missing time', physiological probings (particularly of a sexual nature), a fascination with the human reproductive process, and telepathic communication, for instance – were discussed in great detail for the first time in Fuller's book. But, for David M. Jacobs, although the number of accounts of alien abductions steadily increased after the publication in 1966 of the Hills' story, it was not until the appearance in 1981 of Budd Hopkins's *Missing Time: A Documented Study of UFO Abductions*[21] that the subject was recognizable as a discrete entity:

> Unlike most UFO researchers, who treated abduction cases as simply another 'sighting' category, Hopkins investigated seven abduction cases for patterns, similarities, and convergences. He found that the question of inexplicable one- to two-hour gaps of time was more pervasive than had been realized in the past. Among other things, he discovered the significance of an unaccountable bodily scar that often accompanied abduction reports. He demonstrated that a person could be an abductee without having a UFO sighting and that abduction accounts could be hidden beneath the surface of strange 'screen memories'. Hopkins's research confirmed the prevalence of the examination that seemed to take place with nearly every abductee.[22]

In short, *Missing Time* made a decisive contribution to what Jodi Dean has called '[t]he turn to abduction',[23] and it is no coincidence that many contemporary studies of abduction – whatever their perspective – continue to invoke Hopkins as some kind of pioneer.[24]

Since 1981, the profile of alien abduction has continued to rise, and the phenomenon is now recognizable beyond the specialized fields of UFOlogy and abduction studies. Thirty years after the publication of *The Interrupted Journey*, a film like *Independence Day* could, as Jodi Dean acutely observes,

> presume an audience familiar with the fact that thousands of Americans say they have been abducted and sexually traumatized by aliens.
>
> This presumption makes sense. *Abduction*, Harvard professor John Mack's account of his work with abductees,

> received extensive media attention when it was released in 1994. Books by Whitley Strieber and Budd Hopkins have been best-sellers, with Strieber's *Communion* reaching number one on the *New York Times* best-seller list in May 1987.[25]

Meanwhile, by 1998, the motifs of abduction had become so familiar in western culture that Michael Marshall Smith could both casually allude to and subvert them in his strange novel, *One of Us*.[26] In short, I think that there is a sense in which abduction can now be taken for granted. Its procedures, its patterns and properties, are generally recognized. If people believe, they at once believe that they know what a typical abduction might involve.

In *Aliens in America*, Jodi Dean asks what aliens might reveal about contemporary American attitudes towards truth, judgement, legitimation and reality. As a political theorist, her approach and conclusions inevitably differ somewhat from mine, but I want nonetheless to cling to her belief that 'the discourse on UFOs and alien abduction . . . says something about *us*'.[27] More specifically, I want to stress that it reveals how the relationship between 'Us' and 'Them' is subject to change. What my rather brief history of abduction means to mark is a gradual but important shift in what happens when encounters between the human and the alien occur in western culture. In the 1940s, when the term 'flying saucer' was first popularized,[28] aliens tended to keep their distance, to remain a presence only in the skies. But, with time, that distance has dwindled. Encounters have become ever closer, and researchers have repeatedly found themselves having to revise their models, rethink their positions. Extraterrestrials have not stood still. What once seemed an adequate account no longer quite does justice to the current closeness of aliens.

The well-known distinction between different types of 'close encounters' first proposed in 1972 by J. Allen Hynek now seems a little limited, in fact. Hynek's categories – which were popularized five years later by Spielberg's *Close Encounters of the Third Kind* – were as follows:

A close encounter of the first kind is one in which 'no interaction of the UFO with the environment or the observers is reported'.[29] The craft, that is to say, is merely observed.

A close encounter of the second kind can be said to have occurred '[w]hen the reported UFO . . . leaves a visible record of its visit or encounter with human observers'.[30] Examples might include marks left upon the ground, or interference with electrical or mechanical equipment.

A close encounter of the third kind is one in which 'the presence of animated creatures is reported . . . (I say "animated" rather than "animate" to keep open the possibility of robots or something other than "flesh and blood")'.[31]

For Hynek, who spent many years advising the Unites States Air Force about UFOs, the latter category is 'the most bizarre and seemingly incredible aspect of the entire UFO phenomenon'. He would, he adds, 'gladly omit this part if [he] could without offense to scientific integrity'.[32] In 1972, that is to say, a close encounter of the third kind was somewhat unsettling, distinctly strange, even for an expert. This, for Hynek, was the closest that aliens came. Since then, however, researchers have supplemented Hynek's categories, adding close encounters of the fourth and fifth kinds.[33] Things have changed.

Close Encounters of the Fourth Kind was, in fact, the name that C. D. B. Bryan chose for his exhaustive account of the landmark conference on abduction that took place at the Massachusetts Institute of Technology twenty years after the publication of Hynek's book. Many of those who attended the event – Budd Hopkins, Thomas E. Bullard, David M. Jacobs, and John E. Mack, for instance – had worked closely with people who claimed to have been abducted by aliens. Some, such as Carol Dedham and Alice Bartlett, were there actually to relate their intimate experiences with extraterrestrial beings.[34] My own position is somewhat different. To the best of my knowledge, I have never been abducted, and have never even met anyone who claims to have been taken. I have no interest in passing judgement, in seeking to determine the veracity of testimonies, or in undertaking my own empirical enquiries. As I stressed at the beginning of chapter 1, I am interested in meanings, and I want to examine in detail how alien abduction signifies in the work of one particular researcher.

Close encounters of the Harvard kind

If Budd Hopkins is the 'father' of modern abduction, John E. Mack is probably the *enfant terrible.* His notoriety can be traced, in part, back to a well-publicized dispute with the Harvard Medical School, where he is Professor of Psychiatry and Director of the Center for Psychology and Social Change. After the publication in 1994 of his book, *Abduction: Human Encounters with Aliens*, Mack was called to account by an official committee of his colleagues, which claimed to have, as one of the Deans put it, concerns about the nature of Mack's work with abductees. Eventually, in August 1995, after a legal battle over the question of academic freedom, the university retreated.[35] 'John Mack is just as he started out,' reported one of the members of the Special Faculty Committee, 'a perfectly full-fledged member of the Harvard faculty with no adverse action taken.'[36]

What was it in Mack's book that provoked such a response? What did he say about abduction that caused his colleagues such concern? It was not, it seemed, the fact that a Pulitzer-Prize-winning[37] professor had been spending considerable amounts of time listening to people who claimed to have been abducted by aliens (and whose case histories are reproduced at length in *Abduction* and its subsequent companion volume, *Passport to the Cosmos*). For, when Mack received a letter from the Harvard Medical School, it was implied in it that no one would have been too worried if the book had merely identified a previously-unknown psychiatric syndrome. The scandal, rather, stemmed from Mack's *interpretation* of the abduction narratives, particularly his belief that his 'findings might require a change in our view of reality'.[38]

Abduction and *Passport to the Cosmos* are very much exercises in interpretation. At the beginning of the latter text, Mack summarizes his project:

> I wish to stress at the outset that I am not . . . seeking to establish the material reality of the alien abduction phenomenon . . . Rather, I am more concerned with the meaning of these experiences for the so-called abductees and for humankind more generally. In that sense this book is not simply about abductions but has to do with what such anomalous experiences and related phenomena can tell us about ourselves and our evolving knowledge of the nature of reality.[39]

At stake, in other words, is not truth but meaning. What, Mack repeatedly asks, does abduction mean? Having spent almost a decade analyzing dozens of abductees – or, to use the term that he often prefers, 'experiencer participants' – he comes to a somewhat startling conclusion. Close encounters of the fourth kind are, he declares, overwhelmingly benign, and should, as such, be welcomed. Humans should learn to love aliens.

'The story', he writes, 'would go something like this' (I quote at length simply because this is a key passage):

> It all starts with the ultimate creative principle, which abductees call variously God, Source, Home or the One . . . From some primal beginning . . . everything we now know of as this universe came almost instantaneously into being . . .
>
> Human beings, having been formed originally by the God force, retained some experience of a relationship to it. But then something else happened. We developed a consciousness, a self-awareness, different from other species in that we came to know our own mortality, that our time on this Earth was limited, and that this body at least would die . . .
>
> Until perhaps the middle of the eighteenth century, people in the West – as well as the indigenous peoples of the

> Earth, who have never lost their connection with the Creator – experienced their advanced understanding of the material world in the context of a cosmos that was ensouled, in which God continued to inhere. But sometime in that century . . . many people in Western society became in large part 'secular'. They lost their sense of connection with the . . . ultimate creative principle. The universe came to consist largely of dead matter, energy, and space, and our pleasures, for the most part, became restricted to earthly emotional connections and material satisfactions.
>
> This approach . . . has led to some big problems . . . [W]e have created increasingly efficient methods for taking precious, non renewable materials from the Earth. As a result we have begun to exceed our energy resources, and by expelling into the air, land, and water the poisonous by-products of our consumption that we have not found a way to get rid of safely, we are killing off many of the planet's life-forms.[40]

There is hope for the fallen and doomed human race, however. According to Mack, aliens offer salvation, 'balance',[41] a timely reminder that everything (every thing) in the universe is connected and that there is, as one of the abductees puts it, 'no difference in the essence of any being'.[42] And this reminder acts at once as an important 'intervention',[43] for many of the abductees report being given a warning that, unless humans learn to understand their cosmic connection, the present ecological crisis will end in their apocalyptic demise. 'From this perspective', as Mack puts it in the closing paragraphs of *Passport to the Cosmos*, 'the alien abduction phenomenon is largely an opportunity or a gift.'[44]

Aliens, in other words, are to be celebrated, loved, embraced. They are here to help, and humans face extinction without them. In this respect, Mack takes a decisive step that David M. Jacobs is unwilling to take. For the latter, extraterrestrials

> appear to be neither malevolent nor benevolent. They do not seem to be here to help us or to harm us. They are here for themselves. They are doing what they want to do, without consideration for our wishes. They appear to have no concern with the central issues and problems of human survival.[45]

For this very reason, I think that Mack's books are particularly fine examples of 'alien love', and their difference from earlier approaches to abduction is radical. All you need is love. But this 'alien love', I want to suggest, soon turns into Alien Chic.

Terror is by no means absent from the case histories presented by Mack, of course, and his admirable commitment to detail means that he is never unaware of such feelings in his patients. The fear, however, is fleeting, and trauma quickly gives way to love:

> As I will document in detail in several case examples, the traumatic, rapelike nature of the abduction memories, or even of the process itself, may become altered as the abductees reach new levels of understanding of what is occurring, and as their relationship to the beings themselves changes in the course of our work.[46]

A young woman named Eva experiences precisely such a transformation. 'Like most abductees,' writes Mack,

> Eva has had disturbing, even terrifying, encounters with alien beings. But her determination to give herself to the process, to surrender the need to control and resist its intensity and meaning, has enabled Eva to move beyond fear and trauma to a place of greater inner balance and personal power. It is characteristic of her to write in her journal following an abduction experience that left her feeling very tired that she *hoped* she had been taken 'on a journey'.[47]

As is so often the case, love leads to sex. Isabel, another of Mack's patients, fondly recalls her erotic encounter with an extraterrestrial being:

> It was different than sex with a human being, physical sex. It was more – I know this is going to sound dumb – but it's like having spiritual sex. It wasn't just on the outside. It was more internal. I remember feeling that whoever did this cared enough about me that they felt the state I was in, that I felt distressed, and that they came and helped me. It didn't feel like, 'Oh my God, who did this without my permission!' I just felt, 'Thank you'.[48]

Sex with an alien is better than sex with another human. The whole cosmos, and not merely the Earth, moves. For another particularly enthusiastic abductee, the encounter is 'better than the best sex or the best anything you could have, better than fly-fishing for a week'.[49] What was a source of embarrassment and unease for Betty and Barney Hill is now celebrated in explicit detail. In fact, as Elaine Showalter has pointed out, some contemporary accounts of alien abduction 'closely resemble women's pornography, from the soft-core rape fantasies of bodice busters to the masturbation fantasies recounted by writers like Shere Hite or Nancy Friday'.[50] The alien love doll has come to life.

'Ontological shock'; or, reality isn't what it used to be

The work of John E. Mack does far more than merely rewrite earlier understandings of abduction, however. More radically, it calls for a rethinking of reality itself:

> Quite a few abductees have spoken to me of their sense that at least some of their experiences are not occurring within

> the physical space/time dimensions of the universe as we comprehend it. They speak of aliens breaking through from another dimension, through a 'slit' or 'crack' in some sort of barrier, entering our world from 'beyond the veil' . . . They experience the aliens, indeed their abductions themselves, as happening in another reality, although one that is as powerfully actual to them as – or more so than – the familiar physical world.[51]

In short, a new 'ontological paradigm' is required to make sense of abduction. 'I do not expect', warns Mack, 'that the material presented in this book will have much impact on the minds of those who believe that the laws of physics as encompassed by the Newtonian/Einsteinian system are the full definition of reality.'[52] Tradition trembles.

As a psychiatrist, Mack might well be familiar with a certain well-known passage from Freud's *Introductory Lectures on Psychoanalysis*:

> In the course of centuries, the *naïve* self-love of men [*sic*] has had to submit to two major blows at the hands of science. The first was when they learnt that our earth was not the centre of the universe but only a tiny fragment of a cosmic system of scarcely imaginable vastness. This is associated in our minds with the name of Copernicus, though something similar had already been asserted by Alexandrian science. The second blow fell when biological research destroyed man's supposedly privileged place in creation and proved his descent from the animal kingdom and his ineradicable animal nature. This revaluation has been accomplished in our own days by Darwin, Wallace and their predecessors, though not without the most violent contemporary opposition. But human megalomania will have suffered its third and most wounding blow from the psychological research of the present time which seeks to prove to the ego that it is not even master in its own house, but must content itself

> with scanty information of what is going on unconsciously in its mind.[53]

Scandal hovers over each name mentioned here. In 1633, Galileo was sentenced to life imprisonment for discussing Copernican theory in his *Dialogue on the Two Chief World Systems*, and Rome ordered the burning of the treatise. Several centuries later, the theories of evolution and natural selection were widely denounced (Darwin once playfully referred to T. H. Huxley, a prominent supporter, as his 'good and admirable agent for the promulgation of damnable heresies!'[54]), and still prove unacceptable to some American school authorities. And Freud himself, of course, encountered what Ernest Jones called 'a storm of opposition'[55] to his findings. Years before the Nazis publicly burned them, his books were being attacked by respected professionals:

> At a congress of German Neurologists and Psychiatrists that took place in Hamburg in 1910 Professor Wilhelm Weygrandt, a *Geheimer Medizinalrat*, gave forcible expression to the state of alarm, when Freud's theories were being mentioned, by banging his fist on the table and shouting: 'This is not a topic for discussion at a scientific meeting; it is a matter for the police'. Similarly, when Ferenczi read a paper before the Medical Society of Budapest, he was informed that Freud's work was nothing but pornography and that the proper place for psycho-analysts was prison.[56]

Freud makes few direct appearances in Mack's two books, but, in the closing pages of *Abduction*, not long after he has alluded to Freud's development of a 'new wa[y] of knowing',[57] Mack effectively returns to the scandalous scene conjured up by the father of psychoanalysis:

> As I come to the end of this story I cannot help wondering what it might take to bring about the shift in consciousness, the change of paradigm that is implicit in what the abductees

> have undergone. It would appear that what is required is a kind of cultural ego death, more profoundly shattering (a word that many abductees use when they acknowledge the actuality of their experiences) than the Copernican revolution which demonstrated that the earth, and therefore humankind, did not reside at the center of the cosmos.[58]

Once again, nothing less than the figure of 'Man' is at stake. For Mack, alien abduction – like the findings of Copernicus, Darwin, Wallace and Freud – poses a profound challenge to humanism. 'The UFO abduction phenomenon', as he puts it in *Passport to the Cosmos*,

> seems especially well suited to challenge the anthropocentric humanistic worldview. It suggests that we are but one of the higher forms of intelligence that have evolved in the cosmos, and not the brightest one at that. It reveals technologically superior beings whom we do not understand, who confront us with the fact of our lack of autonomy, power, and control, and who may even be mating with us without our permission.[59]

'We' are not alone, but 'we' are not quite who 'we' thought 'we' were, either. Encounters with extraterrestrials 'seem to be created, as if by design, to shatter . . . the previously held idea of reality . . . and topple the experiencer from the sense of being a member of a uniquely intelligent life-form at the peak of the Great Chain of Being'.[60] Things are beginning to change; there is a 'spiritual rebirth taking place in Western culture'.[61] The figure of Man, to recall once again Michel Foucault's famous image, is in the process of being erased from the sand by an incoming tide. Humanism is coming to an end, and can finally be terminated with the help of 'alien love'.

I have already identified some of the problems that arise when the absolute end of 'Man' is announced, and I think that Mack's work, while fearlessly and fascinatingly pioneering, runs into similar difficulties when it tries to read 'alien love' as the epitaph of anthropocentric discourse. Rather than take Mack at his word, I want to suggest that his words, and those of the abductees, unwittingly perpetuate the humanism that is allegedly overturned. Humanism, that is to say, abducts abduction from a pure beyond, and manages, against all odds, to live on. The new 'now' secretes the old 'then'. The human remains.

Abduction abducted; or, when is a step not a step?

While the beyond, in all its senses, fascinates Mack, neither *Abduction* nor *Passport to the Cosmos* makes reference to *Beyond the Pleasure Principle*, one of the strangest texts in the corpus of psychoanalysis (Freud even told Ferenczi, 'Much of what I am saying in it is pretty obscure, and the reader must make what he [*sic*] can of it'[62]). First published in 1920, the essay promises to step beyond that which had dominated psychoanalysis for so long.[63] Beyond, that is to say, the pleasure principle. But Freud never quite makes or takes that step. *Beyond the Pleasure Principle*, as Derrida has pointed out, takes Freud nowhere new. It takes him nowhere at all, in fact, for the text is '*a-thetic*',[64] without thesis. Instead, it

> advances without advancing, without advancing itself, without ever advancing anything that it does not immediately take back . . . [D]espite several marching orders and steps forward, not an inch of ground is gained; not one decision, not the slightest advance in the question which occupies the speculator, the question of the PP as absolute master.[65]

For all his attempts, Freud finds himself in a state of paralysis,[66] unable to hold himself to his word. The promised 'step beyond the PP will have remained interdicted'.[67] The mastery of the pleasure principle is, against all odds, reinforced.

When is a step not a step? When it is a step beyond. That joke works far better in French, where the signifier '*pas*' can mean either 'step' or 'not'. Every *pas* is a step . . . and is not (a step). Three of Derrida's footnotes, in fact, lead the reader to 'Pas', his remarkable essay on the work of Maurice Blanchot.[68] And, on closer inspection, 'To speculate' often follows in the footsteps of Blanchot, who once published a work entitled *Le Pas au-delà*,[69] a phrase that Derrida uses on several occasions in his essay,[70] even if the English translation does not always preserve the pun and never explicitly acknowledges this particular debt.[71]

Like the later *Writing of the Disaster*,[72] *Le Pas au-delà* is a book 'for which there is no generic term'.[73] Philosophy, fiction, fragment, confession: no combination of these categories can come close to naming or taming the sheer strangeness of Blanchot's text. Paul de Man once noted that '[r]eading Maurice Blanchot differs from all other reading experiences',[74] and while the pages of *Le Pas au-delà* have held me captive for many hours, I have to confess that I am still not sure what the book is 'about'. It may even be, like *Beyond the Pleasure Principle*, a-thetic. As in Freud's text, death would seem to be the problem – it makes an appearance on the opening page, after which it never really gives up the ghost – but *Le Pas au-delà* repeatedly side-steps certainty and decidability, preferring instead to privilege signifier over signified.

Blanchot suffered from what could be called a passion for the '*pas*'. Indeed, as Derrida points out, it can be heard in the titles of several of his works: *Faux <u>pas</u>*, *La <u>Pa</u>rt de feu*, and *L'Es<u>pa</u>ce littéraire*.[75] On one occasion, there is even a double-stepping over the sound: *Celui qui ne m'accom<u>pa</u>gnait <u>pas</u>*.[76] This doubling, Derrida continues, even extends to the 'two', the '*deux*', that might be heard in '*au-delà*' (or, as 'Pas' puts it, '*o-2-la*').[77] It seems to me that Derrida inherits something of Blanchot's fascination with the '*pas*', the step that is not (a step), and I think that it is possible to read his long-standing resistance to the 'apocalyptic tone' in philosophy as a meditation upon the impossibility of taking once and for all a step beyond. At the risk both of over-stepping the mark and anticipating an argument that I will develop in the following chapter, I might even venture to suggest that deconstruction, as a measured working-within, has at its heart the *pas au-delà*. With this in mind, I want to read the *pas au-delà*, the step not beyond, that troubles John E. Mack's project, turning 'alien love' into Alien Chic.

In *Passport to the Cosmos* (a title that contains its own '*pas*'), Mack notes that, since the publication of Budd Hopkins's *Intruders*[78] in 1987, 'some investigators have come to see the creation of a race of human/alien hybrid offspring as an important, if not *the* central purpose or meaning of the abduction phenomenon'.[79] This is something that will be familiar to readers of Octavia E. Butler's *Xenogenesis* trilogy,[80] the first volume of which appeared in the same year as *Intruders.* While Mack goes on to differentiate his understanding of the hybrid project from that of Hopkins and David M. Jacobs, it nonetheless remains a central aspect of his work. Meanwhile, recent cultural theory has often turned to hybridity as a way of thinking beyond essentialism and humanism. But, whereas theorists such as Donna J. Haraway, Gloria Anzaldúa and Paul Gilroy have, when invoking the radical potential of hybridity, always been sure to offer examples,[81] Mack concedes that he finds himself faced with 'the absence of solid evidence of actual pregnancy, genetic changes, or the physical existence of the hybrids themselves'.[82] It soon becomes clear, in fact, that it is not the abductees who are becoming hybrid beings. Rather, samples are being taken from their bodies to be used elsewhere in the creation of the new species. As Jacobs acutely observes, the hybrid project 'is not a program of reproduction, but one of *production*'.[83] Two different species are making a third.

This fundamental elsewhere, this absence, is one of the moments at which humanism reaffirms itself in a space that is declared by Mack to be beyond anthropocentric thinking. It seems to me that *Abduction* and *Passport to the Cosmos* describe a heightened presence or *self*-presence of the human being abducted. In its involvement in the hybrid project, which happens elsewhere and involves others, the human subject finds itself reassured, marked out as authentic and absolutely different from the inhuman. There is, in other words, a close encounter with humanism. An individual who has been chosen to participate in the hybrid project cannot already be a hybrid being; he or she must, on the contrary, be a fine specimen of the purely human. And if that person is subjected to a host of probing medical procedures (an occurrence repeatedly described in Mack's two books), he or she must, I think, be different from the aliens engaged in the examinations. Why else would they need to know about human physiology? Why else would they bother abducting such an individual? It seems to me, moreover, that the entire logic of abduction (etymologically, a drawing-away-from) affirms the predetermined and proper space from which the human being is taken. You have to be abducted from somewhere, after all. And what is abducted, I think, is the purely human.

These may sound like somewhat abstract theoretical objections. But the narratives presented by Mack do support such a reading. In the chapter of *Passport to the Cosmos* devoted to the hybrid project, Mack returns to the story of Eva, whose experiences were recounted at some length in *Abduction*. After the publication of the earlier book, in fact, Eva wrote an entire thesis about her encounters, from which Mack quotes the following passage:

> I have also had several sexually oriented encounters with the Beings. During the process of writing this thesis, I came to understand that the sexual connotation of the experiences was only a metaphor used to enable me to understand certain intrinsic and subtle personal metamorphoses. In reality, the encounters were a collection of diverse communions, Godly and sacred encounters allowing me to touch, experience, and remember additional aspects of my-Self. In one encounter I learned that the impregnation process I experienced . . . served as a process for the elevation of my conscious awareness into an individuated Being who is on a path of Self-discovery back to God, learning and experiencing along the way wholeness, completion, non attachment, and most of all, humility.[84]

This sense of wholeness is reinforced when Eva tells Mack that the encounter with aliens is all about 'becoming aware . . . about seeing, perceiving, feeling, experiencing more of who I truly am'.[85] Not who *we* truly are, in the cosmic sense upon which Mack insists, but 'who I truly am'. The encounter with alien alterity brings the human self-same into focus. Descartes is reformulated, reanimated: I am abducted, therefore I am.

In this respect, Mack's account of abduction is closer than it might initially appear to the interpretation offered in Whitley Strieber's *Communion*. While Mack regularly acknowledges Strieber's work, he seeks to take matters several steps further, particularly with respect to anthropocentrism. In short, Strieber is less willing than Mack to articulate a break from humanist discourse. He explicitly acknowledges, in fact, that his close encounters with aliens bring about a heightened, deepened, expanded sense of being human. '[T]he most important thing about [the experience]', he notes at one point, 'was its essentially *human* effect. I was a human being, and my part of things involved having a human experience.'[86] And while it is true that Strieber's most basic ontological assumptions are apparently called into question by the encounters, a clear reinforcement of (the) human being is repeated towards the end of *Communion*:

> I do not wish to imply by this anything beyond a human context. It is possible for man [*sic*] to become more whole, for each of us to make our private journey back to the place of emergence, and find there the simplest and most real of truths: that we are all at heart the same, that every body contains every soul and has room for every act without reference to its quality. There is a deep, objective awareness of self and universe that is available to all of us.[87]

While the original (pre-encounter, pre-abduction) self is changed, even 'giv[en] up',[88] a more whole, authentic human being comes to take its place.

Mack, on the other hand, declares an undoing of anthropocentric discourse, an overcoming of humanism. It seems to me, however, that Eva's words actually describe the occupation of a position similar to that of Whitley Strieber. She, too, achieves 'wholeness, completion, [and] non-attachment', and it comes as no surprise that her thesis shares its title with Strieber's book: *Communion*.[89] Abduction is abducted from beyond the limits of the human, and firmly returned to the space of anthropocentrism. The human remains. The step beyond is not (a step).

Eva is not the only one of Mack's patients to have been drawn into the hybrid project. Peter, to whom chapter 13 of *Abduction* is devoted, has also found himself involved, and his experiences have led him to discover that he has what Mack calls 'a dual human/alien identity'.[90] During one meeting, Peter even changes voices and begins to speak as an extraterrestrial. This shift is explicitly marked out in Mack's account: not only does Peter's voice become 'a kind of monotonous droning',[91] but the signifiers themselves undergo a telling change. Suddenly, the 'they' which Peter has been using to refer to the alien beings becomes a 'we'. This linguistic alteration, I think, attests to an absolute distinction between the human and the inhuman that Mack's text unconsciously supports. In fact, although Peter has more than one identity, and is taking part in the hybrid project, his dual identity is precisely that: a *dual* identity. There are two distinct components – one human, one alien – and each is identical to itself. By his own admission, he is 'split in two', and '[the] human part is just resisting the alien part, the part that knows, the part that has so much information to bring here'.[92] As in the case of Eva, the encounter with otherness reinforces the otherness of the other and the self-sameness of the self-same. Peter, like Eva, participates in the hybrid project, but remains distinctly non-hybrid (for each half is separate). And if there is, on Mack's part, a need to consider 'the difficult task of reconciling [Peter's] human and alien identities',[93] those identities cannot already be combined, convoked, in council with each other.

Derrida has taught his readers that even an apparently innocent punctuation mark can signify with remarkable force. In *Of Spirit*,[94] for instance, Heidegger's inconsistent use of quotation marks is shown to make his relationship to Nazism somewhat undecidable. It seems to me that John E. Mack's punctuation demands similar attention. When he writes of Peter's 'human/alien identity' (and this is always the formulation), it seems to me that the oblique marks a distinction, a cut, a distance. It is a line uncrossed. The 'human' and the 'alien' are condemned to face each other across a divide. Hyphenation (human-alien), of course, would have conveyed – as the etymology implies – togetherness, joining, hybridity. Elsewhere, in fact, Mack does employ the hyphen to close the gap between the human and the alien: the index to *Abduction*, for instance, points readers in the direction of 59 separate references to 'human–alien communication'. But, when discussing the dual identities of Peter and five other abductees, Mack always writes 'human/alien'.

I think that this distinction, which is entirely consistent, further punctures Mack's project. To resurrect for a moment an obsolete formulation,[95] it might be said that the oblique, at a stroke, obliques his belief that abduction 'seems especially well suited to challenge the anthropocentric humanistic worldview'. Humanism's sacred binary opposition between the human and the inhuman returns precisely when an extreme form of 'alien love' is being invoked as the ultimate step beyond. While some things have certainly changed – the brief history of abduction with which I began this chapter has change at its very heart – humanism remains, returns. There is still an 'Us', and this is absolutely distinct from 'Them'.

'Alien love', that is to say, is abducted by the logic of 'alien hatred'. The binary opposition between 'Us' and 'Them', human and inhuman, resurfaces. What might, at first glance, appear to be a radically different approach to the extraterrestrial – aliens are welcomed; close encounters are benevolent and beneficial – turns out to be merely a different way of shoring up the traditional distinction between human and alien. It is for this very reason that I prefer to describe the present moment not as one of 'alien love', but rather of 'Alien Chic'. As in Tom Wolfe's sense of Radical Chic, the movement from rejection to embrace of the other is decidedly superficial. The underlying, informing principles of 'Us' and 'Them' are untouched by the gesture. And, as Wolfe is quick to note, there is also a sense in which a celebration of the other is a celebration of the other *as other*, as entirely distinct from the self, the same, the not-other. 'Radical Chic, after all', he concludes, 'is only radical in style; in its heart it is part of Society and its traditions.'[96]

As I briefly noted in the introduction, I think that the same is true of what I am calling 'Alien Chic'. Even though recent years have seen a dramatic shift in the way that aliens are inscribed in western culture, the rise of 'alien love' does not mark a disappearance of humanism. On the contrary, it seems to me that the distinction between 'Us' and 'Them' is preserved, strengthened, underlined by the widespread welcoming of aliens. This means that the traditional subject of humanism finds hope and confirmation in Alien Chic, and it is precisely this effect – this continued reign of a human subject over its inhuman objects – that I will explore in the following chapter.

Before I turn to alien-themed objects, however, I want briefly to revisit Tom Wolfe's essay on Radical Chic. About one third of the way into the text, Wolfe notes that the phenomenon emerged at a moment of great social change in New York City:

> By the 1960s . . . the erstwhile 'minorities' of the first quarter of the century had begun to come into their own. Jews, especially, but also many Catholics, were eminent in the media and in Culture. So, by 1965 . . . New York had two Societies, 'Old New York' and 'New Society'. In every era, 'Old New York' has taken a horrified look at 'New Society' and expressed the devout conviction that a genuine aristocracy, good blood, good bone – themselves – was being defiled by a horde of rank climbers. . . . In the 1960s this quaint belief was magnified by the fact that many members of 'New Society', for the first time, were not Protestant.[97]

It is in the subsequent struggle between New and Old that Radical Chic finds its purpose. What better way for the 'New Society' to establish its credentials, to display its wealth and power, than to support – in the most spectacular way possible – 'worthy causes'?

> New arrivals have always had two ways of certifying their superiority over the hated 'middle class'. They can take on the trappings of aristocracy, such as grand architecture, servants, parterre boxes, and high protocol; and they can indulge in the gauche thrill of taking on certain styles of the lower orders. The two are by no means mutually exclusive; in fact, they are always used in combination.[98]

The 'gauche thrill', of course, comes from knowing that nothing is really threatened by *nostalgie de la boue*. 'Such affectations', Wolfe concludes, 'were meant to convey the arrogant self-confidence of the aristocrat as opposed to the middle-class striver's obsession with propriety and keeping up appearances.'[99] 'Risks' can be taken, 'love' for something forbidden can be professed, only because the traditional distinction between 'Them' and 'Us' is actually confirmed and preserved in the gestures of Radical Chic. The potential social crisis, the result of significant change, is thus neatly avoided. *Plus ça change* . . .

I am suggesting that Alien Chic emerges in response to a recent and far more wide-ranging crisis in humanist discourse. While there is nothing new about the concept of posthumanism – H. P. Blavatsky wrote of the '*post-Human*' in the late nineteenth century, for instance[100] – it was not until the 1990s that the term made a genuinely noticeable impact upon western culture. There were occasional sightings at earlier moments – Ihab Hassan's essay, 'Prometheus as performer',[101] appeared in the late 1970s, for example – but as the millennium approached, a whole series of critics explicitly raised the question of posthumanism.[102] While their approaches frequently differed, these thinkers shared a suspicion that humanism was in a state of crisis.

By 2002, the Modern Language Association of America had taken an interest, announcing in one of its newsletters that 'the future may hold more interest in an environment entirely without human beings: the subject term "the posthuman" is currently under evaluation [for inclusion in the *MLA International Bibliography*] after appearing six times since 2000'.[103] Meanwhile, at approximately the same moment (and, moreover, beyond the walls of the university), the audience of BBC Radio 4's popular *Start the Week* programme was being invited by Francis Fukuyama to consider the possibility that the future would be inhabited by posthuman beings.[104] Such creatures, but perhaps not Radio 4 listeners, would probably be happy dancing to the latest release from *Posthuman Records*, the label set up at the turn of the millennium by Marilyn Manson.

Many of the critics who have taken up the question of posthumanism (notably Donna J. Haraway, N. Katherine Hayles, R. L. Rutsky and Elaine L. Graham) have focused upon the way that recent developments in techno-science have unsettled many of the assumptions of humanist discourse. As Haraway argued in her wonderful, hugely influential 'Cyborg manifesto', the binary oppositions that were once so sacred to humanism – organism/machine, reality/fiction, human/animal, physical/non-physical, and self/other, for example – have now been deconstructed: 'By the late twentieth century, our time, a mythic time, we are all chimeras, theorized and fabricated hybrids of machine and organism; in short, we are cyborgs. The cyborg is our ontology; it gives us our politics.'[105] This means that the humanist subject finds its foundations disturbed, and Haraway concludes that '[p]erhaps, ironically, we can learn from our fusions with animals and machines how not to be Man, the embodiment of Western logos'.[106]

By the turn of the millennium, however, Haraway felt that 'cyborgs could no longer do the work of a proper herding dog to gather up the threads needed for critical inquiry',[107] and her more recent book, *The Companion Species Manifesto*, 'tr[ies] to convince readers that dogs might be better guides through the thickets of technobiopolitics in the Third Millennium of the Current Era'.[108] Cyborgs, she suggests, are merely 'junior siblings in the much bigger, queer family of companion species'[109] that poses a radical challenge to the 'Family of Man'. And it is precisely here, in the understanding of relationships between humans and animals, that a further challenge to humanism has begun to emerge. As Cary Wolfe points out, in his fascinating book, *Animal Rites*, a cursory glance at recent American popular culture – but perhaps not the discipline of cultural studies – reveals that humanism's tradition of 'taking it for granted that the subject is always already human'[110] is no longer convincing:

> Over the past several years *Time*, *Newsweek* and *U.S. News and World Report* have all run multiple cover stories on new developments in cognitive ethology that seem to demonstrate more or less conclusively that the humanist habit of making even the *possibility* of subjectivity coterminous with the species barrier is deeply problematic, if not clearly untenable. And PBS and cable television – most recently in the big-budget PBS series on 'the animal mind' hosted by *Nature* executive producer George Page – have made standard fare out of one study after another convincingly demonstrating that the traditionally distinctive marks of the human (first it was possession of a soul, then 'reason', then tool use, then tool *making*, then altruism, then language, then the production of linguistic *novelty*, and so on) flourish quite reliably beyond the species barrier.[111]

In short, 'the "human", we now know, is not now, and never was, itself'.[112]

This, I want to suggest, is precisely the context within which Alien Chic emerges. More specifically, it seems to me that Alien Chic is a reaction to the contemporary crisis in humanist discourse. Just as the binary oppositions that structured humanism find themselves unsettled, Alien Chic – like Radical Chic – offers a subtle reinforcement of the older way of the world, in which 'Us' and 'Them', human and alien, self and other, are absolutely distinct. And while that distinction does not rely upon the hatred of the 1950s, the love of the present for all things alien nonetheless goes hand in hand with anthropocentric assumptions.

But why love? Why reinscribe the border between the human and the extraterrestrial by declaring a *fondness* for the latter? Why not simply turn back the clock to the hatred of the past? This, I must admit, puzzled me for a while. And then I remembered the moment in *A Lover's Discourse* at which Roland Barthes, under the subheading 'declaration', writes of '[t]he amorous subject's propensity to talk copiously, with repressed feeling, to the loved being'.[113] Love, quite simply, affords more opportunities than hatred for excessive public display. It is far easier, I think, to signal love with a positive exhibition of aliens – especially if they take the form of commodities – than it is to show hatred with negativity. This particularly applies in the case of the wide range of alien-themed objects currently available, a selection of which I will consider in the following chapter. If consumption involves desire, love is already implicated in the acquisition of alien objects. And love, in turn, requires display.

Alien Chic, then, is a defence mechanism, a trend with which 'we' reassure 'ourselves' about who 'we' are at a moment of immense uncertainty. When 'our' difference from machines and animals is no longer obvious, 'we' turn to the alien for its instant difference ('I may be a cyborg, but at least I'm not one of *those*'). 'We' love 'Them', and loving 'Them' as a 'Them' confirms 'Us' as 'ourselves'. As Tom Wolfe puts it, in the very first paragraph of 'Radical Chic', '*Amo ergo sum*'.[114] 'Alien love', in the end, is structurally similar to 'alien hatred' in its carving up of the world into binary oppositions. Both tendencies rely upon what Philip Roth calls, in a rather different context, '[t]he fantasy of purity'.[115] Alien Chic is a humanism. To give Descartes yet another twist: I love E.T., therefore I am.

4

Alien objects, human subjects

You play with my world like it's your little toy.

BOB DYLAN, 'Masters of war'[1]

An alien is for life, not just for Christmas

If my enquiry into the phenomenon of Alien Chic began with laughter, it has ended with several large boxes of alien objects, for the writing of this book has been a process punctuated by moments at which friends, colleagues and students have generously donated alien-themed toys and gadgets to my ever-expanding collection. Without wishing to sound ungrateful, I am sure that finding these gifts did not involve having to look too hard, for, as I noted in the introduction to this book, such items are readily available in contemporary western culture. Aliens, it would seem, make good gifts.

As my collection has grown, I have increasingly come to wonder about the relationship between objects and the human subjects to whom they belong. Why do people desire objects in their lives? Why, to put it in vaguely Leibnizian terms, are there some things, rather than no things?[2] Why collect? What, more specifically, does it mean to own an alien object, to display it, play with it, live with it? What effect does the ownership of these items have upon the possessing subject? Why on earth (off Earth?) would anyone wish to change his or her voice into that of an alien, take drugs with the help of an extraterrestrial, or save money in an 'Alien Encounter Fund' collection tin? While I do not intend to produce a psychology, phenomenology or sociology of toys,

I do want to build upon the conclusions of the previous chapter by reading a selection of alien-themed objects, treating them as texts, instances of culture, signifiers.

It might be tempting – particularly for an unreconstructed Marxist, or an Arnoldian defender of 'sweetness and light' – to dismiss the contemporary parade of alien-themed objects as duplicitous or unimportant. For the 'sad militant',[3] to borrow a concept from Michel Foucault, there would be little to say, and little need to engage with these disposable commodities in detail. But constrictive value judgements of this kind have no place in what I understand to be cultural criticism. Quite simply, if something signifies, it is the business of the cultural critic.

In this respect, I have always taken strength from Marshall Berman's assessment of Walter Benjamin's writings on Paris and Baudelaire. Benjamin, he notes, was not very good at being a traditional Marxist:

> His heart and his sensibility draw him irresistibly toward the city's bright lights, beautiful women, fashion, luxury, its play of dazzling surfaces and radiant scenes; meanwhile his Marxist conscience wrenches him insistently away from these temptations, instructs him that this whole glittering world is decadent, hollow, vicious, spiritually empty, oppressive to the proletariat, condemned by history. He makes repeated ideological resolutions to forsake the Parisian temptation – and to forbear leading his readers into temptation – but he cannot resist one last look down the boulevard or under the arcade; he wants to be saved, but not yet.[4]

Berman does not mean this as a criticism. On the contrary, he is wise enough to see how '[t]hese inner contradictions, acted out on page after page, give Benjamin's work a luminous energy and poignant character'.[5] The pious, pure, ascetic, and the orthodox rarely make for exciting reading.

It is not even the case, I think, that Benjamin was attempting to be on such intimate terms with capitalism that its secret workings, its weakest link, lay at his fingertips, for what emerges from the *Arcades Project*, the heartbreaking *Moscow Diary*,[6] and many of his shorter pieces, is something very close to a genuine love of commodities. On the one hand, Benjamin knows that the beckoning arcades of Paris are the 'temples of commodity capital',[7] but he cannot deny, on the other hand, the pleasure that comes from their contemplation. As a good cultural critic, he simply acknowledges that the arcades are, for better or worse, part of the culture upon which his gaze has fallen. They must, as such, be considered. As one of his early drafts has it: 'In *The Arcades Project*, contemplation must be put on trial. But it should defend itself brilliantly and justify itself.'[8]

With Benjamin in mind, I want to allow myself to be seduced a little by the objects that lie on the desk before me. This, I think, is the only real way to find out what they mean, and what, moreover, they mean for the human subject to whom they belong. As a cultural critic, what kinds of stories can I tell about them, and what do they tell me about the culture from which they have emerged? What is at stake in alien objects?

My own private alien: Theorizing the object

Walter Benjamin was a prolific collector,[9] and there is a sense in which *The Arcades Project* stands as an immense, chaotic, intoxicating, convoluted collection of observations and quotations. Perhaps unsurprisingly, a short section of the work is actually devoted to the practice of collecting.[10] 'What is decisive in collecting', Benjamin suggests, 'is that the object is detached from its original functions in order to enter into the closest conceivable relation to things of the same kind. This relation is the diametric opposite of any utility.'[11]

Several decades later, Jean Baudrillard came to a similar conclusion in *The System of Objects*. The book – which, incidentally, was Baudrillard's first – opens by acknowledging the 'ever-accelerating procession of generations of products, appliances and gadgets'[12] that had begun to flood the cultures of late capitalism by the end of the 1960s. The sheer number of such items, he notes, has a tendency to overwhelm the human subject, making the Enlightenment fantasy of producing an encyclopaedia of objects impossible:

> [E]veryday objects (we are not concerned here with machines) proliferate, needs multiply, production speeds up the life and death of such objects – yet we lack the vocabulary to name them. How can we hope to classify a world of objects that changes before our eyes and arrive at an adequate system of description?[13]

The System of Objects, accordingly, is neither encyclopaedia nor 'exhaustive catalogue'.[14] It is, however, concerned with the place of objects in culture and 'the processes whereby people relate to them and with the systems of human behaviour and relationships that result therefrom'.[15]

One of Baudrillard's principal projects is to unsettle the commonplace understanding of the 'consumption' of everyday items such as furniture, cars, watches, cigarette lighters, and stockings (in this respect, it is very much haunted by *Mythologies*, even if Roland Barthes's text is never actually acknowledged[16]). For Baudrillard, consumption 'is surely not that passive mode of absorption and appropriation which is contrasted to the active mode of production, thus counterposing two oversimplified [*naïfs*] patterns of behaviour [*comportement*] (and alienation)'.[17] It is, rather, 'an active form of relationship (not only to objects, but also to the community [*la collectivité*] and to the world), a mode of systematic activity and global response on which our entire cultural system is founded'.[18] In this active relationship, something crucial happens to the human subject, and Baudrillard makes this particularly clear in the section of the book devoted to the practice of collecting. While I would hesitate to call myself a true collector of alien-themed objects – I have amassed a modest collection purely in the name of research, and I have no plans to expand it further now that *Alien Chic* is finished – I do think that Baudrillard's analysis offers the beginning of an explanation of the contemporary popularity of such items.

He begins by making a distinction between 'practical' and 'pure' objects. The former are, quite simply, 'put to use',[19] employed in the functional manner for which they were intended (a refrigerator, for instance, is merely used to preserve perishable goods). As such, the 'practical object' is of no interest to the collector. A pure object, however,

> devoid of function or abstracted from its use, takes on a strictly subjective status: it becomes an object in a collection. It ceases to be a carpet, a table, a compass or knick-knack in order to become an 'object'. A collector will say 'a beautiful object', and not 'a beautiful statuette'.[20]

The ghost of Walter Benjamin watches over this passage, but it seems to me that Baudrillard takes the theory of collecting – and, by extension, the theory of objects – one step further, brings it up to date and into line with the findings of structuralism and poststructuralism, by enquiring into the effect that collecting has upon the acquiring subject.

Objects, he proposes, confer a certain sense of mastery:

> Between the world's irreversible evolution and ourselves, objects interpose a discontinuous, classifiable, reversible screen which can be reconstituted at will, a segment of the world which belongs to us, responding to our hands and minds and delivering us from anxiety. Objects do not merely help us to master the world by virtue of their integration into instrumental series, they also help us, *by virtue of their integration into mental series*, to master time, rendering it discontinuous and classifying it, after the fashion of habits, and subjecting it to the same associational constraints as those which govern the arrangement of things in space.[21]

And, if collecting marks an attempt to be in a position of security, it also involves, Baudrillard adds, a search for singularity and distinction:

> The particular value of the object, its exchange value, is a matter of the cultural and social domain. Its absolute singularity, on the other hand, arises from the fact of being possessed by me – and this allows me, in turn, to recognize myself in the object as an absolutely singular being.[22]

Objects, that is to say, confirm the human subject *as a subject*, as something that is not an object, not inanimate, not inhuman. By marking the object's difference, the subject collects itself into being. While the real is absolutely unmasterable, objects nonetheless grant the subject '*the possibility, from the present moment onwards, of continually experiencing the unfolding of his* [*sic*] *existence in a controlled, cyclical mode, symbolically transcending a real existence the irreversibility of whose progression he is powerless to affect*'.[23] This has a decidedly Lacanian inflection, particularly in its allusion to a symbolic mastery of an untameable real, and the sentence, in fact, is immediately followed by a reference to a famous psychoanalytic story of symbolic mastery: the *fort/da* game.

Near the beginning of *Beyond the Pleasure Principle*, Freud describes a 'game played by a little boy of one and half and invented by himself'.[24] The child – Freud's eldest grandson, Ernst, in fact[25] – was usually well-behaved, but

> had an occasional disturbing habit of taking any small objects he could get hold of and throwing them away from him into a corner, under the bed, and so on, so that hunting for his toys and picking them up was often quite a business. As he did this he gave vent to a loud, long-drawn-out 'o-o-o-o', accompanied by an expression of interest and satisfaction. His mother and the writer of the present account were agreed in thinking that this was not a mere interjection but represented the German word '*fort*' ['gone']. I eventually realized that it was a game and that the only use he made of any of his toys was to play 'gone' with them. One day I made an observation which confirmed my

> view. The child had a wooden reel with a piece of string tied round it. . . . What he did was to hold the reel by the string and very skilfully throw it over the edge of his curtained cot, so that it disappeared into it, at the same time uttering his expressive 'o-o-o-o'. He then pulled the reel out of the cot again by the string and hailed its reappearance with a joyful '*da*' ['there']. This, then, was the complete game – disappearance and return.[26]

It would have been easy for an observer to smile at this curious activity, and quickly dismiss it as meaningless child's play. But, as Freud once noted, the material upon which psychoanalysis bases its observations 'is usually provided by the inconsiderable events which have been put aside by the other sciences as being too unimportant – the dregs, one might say, of the world of phenomena'.[27] The apparently unimportant *fort/da* game, Freud proposes, has a meaning:

> It was related to the child's greatest cultural achievement – the instinctual renunciation (that is, the renunciation of instinctual satisfaction) which he had made in allowing his mother to go away without protesting. He compensated himself for this, as it were, by himself staging the disappearance and return of the objects within his reach.[28]

But why did little Ernst willingly restage what must have been a distressing experience in the form of a game? What motivates such a compulsion to repeat? Freud offers a tentative explanation: 'At the outset he was in a *passive* situation – he was overpowered by the experience; but, by repeating it, unpleasurable though it was, as a game, he took on an *active* part.'[29]

The object, in other words, finds itself reeled into a situation of mastery and comfort. It seems to me that the alien objects to which I wish to turn are compelled to repeat this general tendency, thus pulling their owners back to the safety of humanism. *Da*. When Baudrillard writes, therefore, that 'what you really collect is always yourself',[30] I think that the verb in question should be understood in all of the senses available in the English language. Collecting objects allows the subject to collect itself, to put itself together and into a position of apparent mastery, *and* at once to regain control of itself in the face of a terrifyingly unruly real.[31] As Baudrillard puts it, in a later text:

> We have always lived off the splendor of the subject and the poverty of the object. It is the subject that makes history, it's the subject that totalizes the world. Individual subject or collective subject, the subject of consciousness or of the unconscious, the ideal of all metaphysics is that of world subject; the object is only a detour on the royal road of subjectivity.[32]

This is the familiar dream of humanism. And if this is traditionally true of objects in general, I think that the anthropocentric impulse is even more apparent when the phenomenon of alien-themed objects is opened to analysis.

Don't Bogart that bug-eyed monster

We went looking for ice cream, and we found an alien bong. It was a quiet, sunny afternoon in the small market town of Frome, in the west of England. We were walking back to the car, enjoying a cone of the delicious local gooseberry and elderflower, when I spotted the head of an alien in the window of a tobacconist. Three multi-coloured hookah-style pipes led from the porcelain skull.

I have my suspicions that the object was not really intended for the smoking of tobacco. When I lived in northern California in the early 1990s, it was impossible to wander around cities like Berkeley without encountering what were still called, in a hangover from the 1960s, 'head shops' (there may well now be a newer term for such places), the windows of which displayed a remarkably diverse range of smoking devices, often advertised as being 'for use with tobacco'. I can even remember a café on Haight Street, just across the bay in San Francisco, where a variety of giant hookahs – 'for tobacco only' – could be hired for a hour's communal use. Tobacco is probably less socially acceptable than cocaine in modern California, of course, but the fact that this establishment was within sight of the junction of Haight and Ashbury made the insistence upon tobacco all the more incongruous. The famous crossroads is not what it once was (a Gap clothing store now stands on one corner), but I am happy to report that the spirit of the 1960s was still just about alive in the early 1990s, for I am fairly sure that I caught the occasional whiff of other substances being smoked from the hired hookahs.

To the best of my knowledge, Charles Baudelaire never wrote about extraterrestrials. Given his interest in hashish, however, I think that he might have been intrigued by the alien bong. Although he was clearly fascinated by the strange green jelly-like substance that had become fashionable among 'a certain class of dilettante',[33] Baudelaire much preferred the pleasures offered by wine, and devoted a whole section of *The Flowers of Evil* to the drink, the soul of which sings a 'melody of light and brotherhood'[34] to the poet at one point. That wonderful image reappears in 'On wine and hashish compared as means of augmenting the individuality',[35] a text in which Baudelaire seeks to establish a firm binary opposition between the two intoxicants:

> On the one hand we have a drink that stimulates the digestion, fortifies the muscles, and enriches the blood. Even taken in great quantities, it will cause only slight disturbances. On the other hand we have a substance [hashish] that troubles the digestion, weakens the physical constitution, and may produce an intoxication that lasts up to twenty-four hours. Wine exalts the will, hashish destroys it. Wine is physically beneficial, hashish is a suicidal weapon. Wine encourages benevolence and sociability. Hashish isolates. One is industrious, in a manner of speaking, the other

> essentially indolent. . . . Finally wine is for those people engaged in honest labor, those who are worthy of drinking it. Hashish is among the solitary pleasures, and is favored by miserable idlers. Wine is useful and produces fruitful results; hashish is useless and dangerous.[36]

In spite of his suspicion, however, Baudelaire readily tried hashish, and recalled his experiences in texts such as 'On wine and hashish' and the related 'Poem of hashish'.[37] Although he never explicitly identifies it as such, it seems to me that what Baudelaire records in these pieces is the suspension of the knowing subject of humanism.[38] 'The individual's conscious nature', he notes,

> disappears from time to time. Objectivity, which has produced a number of pantheistic poets and all of the great actors, assumes such force that your confused perceptions cannot distinguish your own being from that of others. You are the tree that sighs in the wind singing to nature vegetal melodies.[39]

The hashish, 'dissolved in a cup of very hot black coffee',[40] in turn dissolves the humanist subject, renders it an inhuman object:

> Imagine that you are seated, smoking a pipe [of tobacco]. Your attention lingers a moment too long on the spirals of bluish clouds that drift slowly upward from the pipe's bowl. The idea of a evaporation – slow, uninterrupted, and obsessive – grips your mind and soon you will apply this idea to your own thoughts, to your own thinking process. Through some odd misunderstanding, through a type of transposition or intellectual quip, you feel yourself vanishing into thin air, and you attribute to your pipe (in which you fancy yourself crouched like packed tobacco) the strange ability to *smoke you*.[41]

The self is a cloud, dispersed, displaced, exhaled and lost in air. And even when the intoxication has faded, an unmistakable uncertainty remains:

> When the first rays of daylight enter your room, your first sensation is one of profound astonishment. Time stands fixed. A moment ago it was night, now it is day. 'Have I slept? Have I spent all night in an intoxicated slumber that suppressed the notion of time, so that the entire night seemed to have passed in the space of a second? Or rather was I caught in the veil of a sleep crowded with visions?' This is a matter which cannot be determined.[42]

This is a matter which cannot be determined. The knowing subject of humanism is still in disarray, fragmented: 'Your personality, which you have cast to the four winds, can only be regained by the greatest efforts of will.'[43]

Baudelaire might not have found hashish quite so 'troubling', quite such a 'chaotic demon',[44] if he had smoked it through the alien bong, for the item in question, by placing an absolutely alien object at the centre of the scene of consumption, tempers the suspension of the smoking and knowing subject a little. However potent the substance inhaled, the evaporation of subject into object described by Baudelaire will always be checked somewhat by the irrevocable presence of the extraterrestrial, the utterly inhuman. However hard the hit, the drug's temporary home stands out as an anchoring device. What could be more inhuman, less of a human subject, than an alien object? The extra-terrestrial head recapitulates to the smoking subject that he or she – however high – can never be as inhuman as the alien object that is providing the intoxication.

In this respect, it seems to me that the alien bong is the perfect recreational object for a historical moment at which the subject of humanism finds itself in a state of crisis. It allows its owner, its user, to smoke himself or herself à la Baudelaire, but simultaneously to be marked out as distinct, grounded, human. The subject can be suspended and supported in one blow; he or she may, like Baudelaire, see the infinite, but at once remain resolutely finite. The actual design of the object, moreover, suggests the collective humanist 'we' to which I referred in chapter 2, for the alien bong – with its three pipes – is intended for use by a group. And – as in the invasion narratives of the 1950s, *Independence Day*, *Signs* and *Starship Troopers* – this group comes together when it faces the absolutely other. What Baudrillard calls '[t]he immemorial privilege of the subject'[45] is never truly challenged by this most object-like object. For humanism, that is to say, the alien bong confers a safe and happy high. Inhale but remain hale. Just say 'know'.

The face that launched a thousand spaceships

Becoming an alien has never been easier, thanks to the Alien Mask Voice Changer. This grey, plastic, full-facial mask is fitted with an internal microphone which connects to a small speaker that can be clipped to the owner's belt. When the mask is worn and the switch flicked, the wearer's voice is instantly transformed into that of an alien.

Claude Lévi-Strauss would probably have liked this object. He did, after all, devote an entire book to masks (not of the alien variety, admittedly, but rather those belonging to Pacific Northwestern Native American cultures). One of the projects of *The Way of the Masks* was to call into question the decidedly atomistic account that a functionalist anthropologist might offer:

> It would be misleading to imagine . . . as so many ethnologists and art historians still do today, that a mask and, more generally, a sculpture or a painting may be interpreted each for itself, according to what it represents or to the aesthetic or ritual use for which it is destined. We have seen that, on the contrary, a mask does not exist in isolation; it supposes

> other real or potential masks always by its side, masks that might have been chosen in its stead and substituted for it. In discussing a particular problem, I hope to have shown that a mask is not primarily what it represents but what it transforms, that is to say, what it chooses *not* to represent. Like a myth, a mask denies as much as it affirms. It is not made solely of what it says or thinks it is saying, but of what it excludes.[46]

Lévi-Strauss's commitment to the primacy of culture is convincing, seductive, and alluring. But I think that there is a sense in which his desire to see patterns and to make connections – to 'gathe[r] scattered threads',[47] as the book's closing sentence has it – leads him away from investigating the finer points of the relationship between a mask and its wearer. Although he acknowledges that 'a mask is not primarily what it represents but what it transforms', and although he amasses a vast array of empirical information, there is no real theory of the mask. To be fair, of course, this may simply not be the business of anthropology. Near the beginning of the book, in fact, Lévi-Strauss reveals what ultimately motivated his enquiry:

> Looking at these masks, I was ceaselessly asking myself the same questions. Why this unusual shape, so ill-adapted to their function? Of course, I was seeing them incomplete because in the old days they were topped by a crown of swan or golden eagle feathers . . . intermingled with some thin reeds adorned with 'snowballs' of down that quivered with every movement of the wearer . . . But these trimmings, which may be seen in old photographs, rather accentuate the strangeness of the mask without shedding any light on its mysterious aspects: why the gaping mouth, the flabby lower jaw exhibiting an enormous tongue? Why the bird heads, which have no obvious connection with the rest and are most incongruously placed? Why the protruding eyes, which

> are the unvarying trait of all the types? Finally, why the quasi-demonic style resembling nothing else in the neighboring cultures, or even in the culture that gave it birth?[48]

Five questions, but no real consideration of the relationship between mask and masked. Or, to be more precise, no real consideration of the relationship between object and subject. It is this very aspect of the Alien Mask Voice Changer that accounts, I think, for its contemporary appeal.

A mask conceals, brings about a certain transformation of something that already exists. It dissimulates, suspends. To wear a mask is to become someone or something different, other, or perhaps merely to hide an original identity. And it seems to me that it is precisely this original identity that is emphasized for the owner of the Alien Mask Voice Changer. While there is a sense in which the possessing and wearing of this object suggests a willingness to welcome and celebrate the alien, I think that – as with all cases of Alien Chic – there is also a distinct humanism, a confirmation of the human itself, at work.

The entire logic of the Alien Mask Voice Changer, in fact, rests upon the assumption that the wearer is not already alien, that he or she is – like John E. Mack's abductees – a fine specimen of the purely human. Why else would the subject require this special device to alter his or her original appearance? If the subject already looked and sounded like an extraterrestrial (whatever that might mean), the mask would be wholly superfluous.[49] In other words, the mask assumes – and, moreover, confirms – that its owner is not already alien, but is, rather, something entirely different, which can be temporarily transformed into an extraterrestrial. The mask, that is to say, is an object *for* a subject, a human subject. It disguises something, transforms something that must necessarily precede its acquisition. It is, moreover, an impermanent barrier that holds its spectators at a distance from the secret, the truth that lies beyond pretence. And, in both cases, this point of origin is nothing less than the human face.

A mask normally requires the prior presence of a face, which will be transformed, hidden, dissimulated. But more precisely, an *alien* mask requires the original presence of a *non*-alien face. By wearing the object, that is to say, the subject confirms prior ownership of a human face, and the human face traditionally carries with it the privilege of presence, the assurance of authenticity in western culture. The Alien Mask Voice Changer reproduces, moreover, what is presently the conventional image of the extraterrestrial. While the aliens of the invasion narratives of the 1950s were uniformly evil, there did not seem to be any consensus concerning their appearance. Although working with primitive technology and, more often than not, tiny special-effects budgets, the filmmakers nonetheless managed to produce a remarkably diverse range of aliens. The invader of *The Thing from Another World*, for instance, bears no resemblance to the eponymous extraterrestrial from *The Blob* (dir. Irwin S. Yeaworth Jr., 1958) or the creatures that populate *This Island Earth* (dir. Joseph Newman, 1955). In recent years, however, popular culture has tended to homogenize its aliens, frequently depending upon what are usually known as 'greys'. These aliens – with their small and spindly bodies, large heads, and almond-shaped eyes – are now instantly recognizable *as aliens*, and have appeared in numerous films and television series, in Microsoft's 'Webdings' symbols, as well as upon many of the alien-themed objects mentioned in the introduction to this book.

The Alien Mask Voice Changer – like the alien bong and the Alien Encounter Fund collection box, to which I will turn in a moment – relies entirely upon this look, this shorthand. There is no question that the plastic face should be read as extraterrestrial. It is a stereotype, a cliché, a given. The object, that is to say, is excessively obvious in its simulation of the face of the alien. This, in turn, dissimulates what already exists, and what already exists is neatly confirmed as human. I mask, therefore I am.

Do masks have voices? Lévi-Strauss at least alluded to the possibility in the original French title of his book, *La Voie des masques*, in which '*la voix*' of masks also makes itself heard. The Alien Mask Voice Changer certainly has a voice, for one of its main features is its ability to transform human speech into what it claims to be extraterrestrial sound. And, like the face, the voice has been habitually associated with authenticity and presence in western culture. Jacques Derrida has done much to expose the pervasiveness of this tendency, particularly in early texts such as *Of Grammatology*, *Speech and Phenomena*,[50] *Writing and Difference*, and *Dissemination*. From the Pre-socratic philosophers, and on through figures such as Plato, Hegel, Leibniz, Rousseau, Saussure, Lévi-Strauss, Heidegger, and Searle, western thinking has, Derrida observes, been characterized by 'the debasement of writing, and its repression outside "full" speech'.[51] In nowhere but the latter, according to this long metaphysical tradition, can truth, presence, *logos* reside. By the same token, the written word is seen as dangerous, secondary, exterior, fatal. Only the voice is true.

It seems to me that the Alien Mask Voice Changer finds itself – perhaps unconsciously – speaking up for phonocentrism. As with the facial component of the object, I think that the transformation brought about by the microphone and the amplifier at once confirms the source, the primary material, *as* source, *as* primary material. What the device amplifies and distorts is the authentic human voice, and the temporary absence for which the object is responsible in turn underlines the precession of that voice. If, that is to say, the wearer's words are changed into alien sounds (and the very name of the object emphasizes change), it follows that he or she does not already speak in or with an alien tongue. The mask's effect – its gimmick, as it were – relies upon a firm distinction that it inscribes between the human and the extraterrestrial. However much I mask my real voice, I nonetheless – in masking – speak of its prior presence. The microphone amplifies the authentic.

By temporarily suspending the face and the voice – two features commonly associated with genuine human presence – the Alien Mask Voice Changer effectively affirms the pre-existence of the unquestionably human subject (if I must call upon an external object to make myself look and sound like an alien, I cannot already resemble or even be an extraterrestrial; I must, rather, possess a face and a voice which are non-alien, and which can be manipulated by the device in question). When the object is removed, when the amplifier is silenced, the original features return to the scene. The alien object has been cast aside, and the abducted human subject is restated, reinstated, welcomed back to Earth. *Fort/da*.

Saving my-self

In his charming essay on book collecting, Walter Benjamin recalls a moment at an auction when, driven by 'the ardent desire to hold on to [an edition of Balzac's *Peau de chagrin*] forever',[52] he found himself successfully bidding more than he could really afford for the volume. The following morning, he coyly adds, involved a trip to a local pawnshop.

Building a collection of alien-themed objects can be a similarly expensive business. If I had bought every such item that I have stumbled across while researching and writing this book, I, too, would probably have been driven to the verge of financial ruin. Fortunately, help is at hand, in the form of the Alien Encounter Fund collection box. This small tin – a modern variation on the familiar 'piggy bank' – has a slot at the top for the insertion of money. A silver and black label is wrapped around the cylinder, and printed at the top of each side are the words 'Alien Encounter Fund'. In each case, the signifier 'Alien' is printed in a shade of green that perfectly matches the skin of the little extraterrestrial that is pictured beneath. On one side, additional text reads: 'SAVE HERE FOR A TRIP TO ANOTHER PLANET OR BEYOND', while the other side carries the following message:

> Please give generously so that I can afford:
> - An English/Alien phrase book
> - My own tailored spacesuit
> - A seat on the Shuttle
> - The first trip to Mars

The Alien Encounter Fund collection tin seems to be another straightforward instance of 'alien love'. Once again, a close encounter with extraterrestrials is to be welcomed. It is, moreover, something worth saving for. On closer inspection, however, this example of 'alien love' turns into a classic case of Alien Chic.

The most noticeable word on the label is 'ALIEN'. Not only is it printed in capital letters and in a larger size than all the other signifiers, but it is also the only term to be written in green. The difference is clear, and it seems to me that the tin, like all other instances of Alien Chic, celebrates the alien only ***as alien***. If, moreover, the owner of the money box needs to start amassing an Alien Encounter Fund, it follows that he or she cannot already be among aliens. He or she, rather, must currently be among humans (the object offers no alternative to these two categories). This is implied in several ways.

First, one of the items which will apparently be purchased with the contents of the tin is an 'English/Alien phrase book'. As the entire label is written in the former language, the subject for whom this object is designed – the 'I' of the phrase 'so that I can afford . . .' – is presumed both not to be already fluent in 'Alien'[53] ***and*** to be able to understand English (the label would, if this were not true, be meaningless). The object proceeds, that is to say, within the space of English, which is distinguished from 'Alien'. Whoever understands the message written upon the label, therefore, is confirmed as a human being.

Second, the object assumes familiarity with certain terrestrial phenomena: phrase books, tailoring, the Space Shuttle and, above all, capital. Would an alien understand the significance of a phrase book or a tailored space suit? Do aliens even need spacesuits? The seats on the Space Shuttle, meanwhile, are presumably designed for the human frame. But would an extraterrestrial require or even fit into a seat? The gelatinous mass of *The Blob* would certainly pose problems in this respect, as would the mischievous beach ball that causes so much trouble in *Dark Star* (dir. John Carpenter, 1974). And, finally, what guarantee is there that an alien would understand the concept of capital, or even the basic circulation of money? Texts such as *E.T.*, *Brother from Another Planet* (dir. John Sayles, 1984), and the *K-PAX* trilogy[54] have, in fact, have playfully examined what happens when visitors from other worlds encounter everyday human practices, and it seems to me that, in a similar manner, the Alien Encounter Fund tin implicitly naturalizes the prior existence of various human conventions.

Above all, Baudrillard's suggestion that the collector of objects really collects him- or herself finds further resonance in this particular example of Alien Chic, for the item both forms part of my collection *and* is designed for the collection of money (a human phenomenon). I collect and save myself several times over. The alien is celebrated, but humanism is saved from disappearance by the very gesture of celebration. 'Man' remains in mint condition. My reward for loving the alien is myself. *Quid pro status quo.*

Three alien-themed objects, three confirmations of the human subject. In collecting these items, it would seem that I have – to return to Baudrillard's proposition – collected myself. The alien – and I have no desire to forget this – is enjoyed and willingly exhibited, but this 'alien love' is, I think, simultaneously a love of the principles of humanism, in which the human is understood to be absolutely distinct from its array of others. The alien objects are, in other words, examples of the wider culture of Alien Chic, in which, perhaps against all odds, humanist discourse is repeated. Once again, aliens are loved *as aliens*, and their status here as collectable objects ensures, to return to the words of Baudrillard, 'the splendor of the subject'. Playing with aliens does not necessarily involve toying with the security of the subject. The human remains, finds plenitude and shelter in the embrace of Alien Chic. 'Man' lives.

Is this the end of the story? Is there only one way to imagine the relationship between the human and the alien? Is anthropocentric discourse insurmountable, inevitable, eternal? Absolutely not. There is, I want to propose, a different way to intervene, to think, to object.

What is to be done; or, theorizing posthumanism

As I noted towards the end of the previous chapter, the term 'posthumanism' is anything but alien to contemporary western culture. This invasion has come at a price, however, for there is often a remarkable reluctance actually to theorize posthumanism, to think carefully about what the prefix 'post-' might mean in this context. In some accounts, posthumanism is simply apparent: it needs no theorizing, and only the most foolish or self-absorbed of cultural critics would actually spend time speculating about something that was staring him or her in the face. '"Man"', as Steve Beard confidently puts it, 'does not have to be theorized away; the intersection of consumerism and techno-culture has already done the job.'[55] All that was solid has melted into air. A posthumanism that is truly 'post-' has arrived, and theory, like 'Man' 'himself', no longer has a place.

I am not quite ready to be seduced by such an approach. It is, I think, too easy, too complacent, too premature. It cannot, moreover, possibly account for the fact that Alien Chic – which might at first glance seem to mark the end of humanism – actually relies upon the humanist concept of 'Man', even when – as in the work of John E. Mack, for instance – that very figure is pronounced dead. Posthumanism, I want to suggest, needs to be imagined otherwise, and needs above all to reconsider the untimely celebration of the absolute end of 'Man'. What Derrida calls the 'apocalyptic tone'[56] should be toned down a little, for, as Nietzsche once pointed out, it is remarkably difficult to cut off the human(ist) head through which we (continue to) 'behold all things'.[57]

While I am not for one moment interested in preserving humanism, in keeping its head firmly upon its shoulders, I do think that it is worth remembering the tale of a certain mythical beast that effortlessly re-membered itself. 'The hydra throve on its wounds', recalls Ovid, 'and none of its hundred heads could be cut off with impunity, without being replaced by two new ones which made its neck stronger than ever.'[58] Apocalyptic accounts of the end of 'Man', it seems to me, ignore humanism's hydra-like capacity for regeneration and, quite literally, recapitulation. In the approach to posthumanism upon which I want to insist, the glorious moment of Herculean victory cannot yet come, for humanism continues to raise its head(s).

N. Katherine Hayles has done much to reveal the dangers of what might be called apocalyptic or complacent posthumanism.[59] This, in fact, is precisely how her fine book, *How We Became Posthuman*, opens:

> This book began with a roboticist's dream that struck me as a nightmare. I was reading Hans Moravec's *Mind Children: The Future of Robot and Human Intelligence*, enjoying the ingenious variety of his robots, when I happened upon the passage where he argues it will soon be possible to download human consciousness into a computer. To illustrate, he invents a fantasy scenario in which a robot surgeon purees the human brain in a kind of cranial liposuction, reading the information in each molecular layer as it is stripped away and transferring the information into a computer. At the end of the operation, the cranial cavity is empty, and the patient, now inhabiting the metallic body of the computer, wakens to find his consciousness exactly the same as it was before.
>
> How, I asked myself, was it possible for someone of Moravec's obvious intelligence to believe that mind could be separated from body? Even assuming such a separation was possible, how could anyone think that consciousness in an entirely different medium would remain unchanged, as if it had no connection with embodiment? Shocked into awareness, I began to notice he was far from alone.[60]

Moravec, Hayles concludes, 'is not abandoning the autonomous liberal subject but is expanding its prerogatives into the realm of the posthuman',[61] for the seemingly posthumanist desire to download consciousness into a gleaming digital environment is itself downloaded from the distinctly humanist matrix of Cartesian dualism. Humanism survives the apparent apocalypse and, more worryingly, fools many into thinking that it has perished.

Moravec's fatally seductive narrative does not 'exhaust the meanings of the posthuman',[62] and *How We Became Posthuman* offers an admirably nuanced approach that seeks to avoid the 'lethal . . . grafting of the posthuman onto a liberal humanist view of the self'.[63] What remains to haunt the book, however, is the possibility that humanism will haunt or taint posthumanism, and it is precisely this problem – a problem of what remains, a problem of remains – that is raised by the phenomenon of Alien Chic.[64] If Hayles's project is to imagine a posthumanism that does not fall into the kind of trap that ensnares Moravec, mine is slightly different (though not unrelated), involving instead an attention to what of humanism itself persists, insists, and ultimately *desists.*[65] I want, in short, to ask an apparently straightforward question, with deliberately Leninist overtones: if traces of humanism find their way into even the most apocalyptic accounts of the posthumanist condition, *what is to be done*?

I chose to begin the introduction to my earlier book on posthumanism with a reference to an image from the cover of *Time* magazine that I have since realized raises the problem of human(ist) remains.[66] The issue in question dates from the first week of January in 1983, a moment at which, according to the *Time*-honoured tradition, the magazine was expected to announce the winner of its 'Man of the Year' award. There was, however, something strange about this particular victor. 'Several human candidates might have represented 1982', the magazine's publisher explained to his readers, 'but none symbolized the past year more richly, or will be viewed by history as more significant, than a machine: the computer.'[67] There had been previous years in which the honour was not, strictly speaking, bestowed upon a 'real' person (GI Joe towered over 1950, while Middle Americans dutifully represented 1969, for instance), but this time something far more dramatic had occurred. Humans had failed to leave their mark.[68] 'Man of the Year' had given way to 'Machine of the Year', and what looked like humanism's epitaph loomed over the cover's striking scene: 'The computer moves in.'

The event did not go unnoticed. Three weeks later, *Time*'s letters page carried over thirty responses to the award. Only a handful of the readers who chose to write in were happy with the magazine's decision.

Irving Kullback of New Jersey was one of these: 'I never dreamed', he gushed, 'that *Time*'s Man of the Year would be living in my house, my TRS-80. You made a great choice.' Perhaps predictably, however, most responses were hostile. 'An abomination', fumed Andrew Rubin of Los Angeles. 'You blew it', sighed Joseph A. Lacey of Redding, California. 'The Man of the Year has no soul', declared the more metaphysically-inclined Shakti Saran of Allston, Massachusetts, while Ohio's Joseph Hoelscher finally understood the real meaning of the box office success of the year: 'Your cover relegates man to a papier-maché dummy and glorifies a machine. No wonder ET wanted to go home.'[69]

These irate readers need not have worried too much about 'Man'. 'He' was still alive, still in the picture. Quite literally, in fact, as I realized several months after submitting the manuscript of *Posthumanism* to the publisher. In my haste to draw attention to the obvious headline and the presence of the computer at the centre of the picture, I had overlooked the significance of the somewhat pathetic anthropomorphic figure that sat to the left, looking on.[70] Here, in the margins of the image, another side of the story began to emerge. Why, if the computer has 'moved in' should there be a human witness? What might such an onlooker reveal about the apparent apocalypse? If 'we' have truly been abducted from the space of humanism, why is 'Man' still pictured? If 'Man' is present at 'his' own funeral, how can 'he' possibly be dead? What looks on lives on. The end of 'Man' was suddenly in doubt. Long before I had begun to think about Alien Chic, I had come up against the problem of knowing what to do with human remains.

Margins. Remains. The inside and the outside. Death. The work of Jacques Derrida once again announces itself. As I briefly suggested in chapter 2, although Derrida distanced himself from the apocalyptic tendencies of anti-humanist thinkers such as Louis Althusser and Michel Foucault, he did not for one moment advocate a return to humanism. If 'Man' could not be forgotten in an instant, he argued, it did not follow that 'Man' was inevitable. On the contrary, there was a different way to intervene, and this alternative approach was proposed in some detail in 'The ends of Man', an essay first published in 1968.

Derrida begins by turning his attention to the manner in which some of his contemporaries were conducting their 'questioning of humanism'[71] by 'affirming an absolute break and absolute difference'[72] from established anthropocentric thought. Such 'transgressions', Derrida points out, can all too easily become 'false exits', as the 'force and the efficiency' of tradition effect a stricter and more naïve reinstatement of 'the new terrain on the oldest ground'.[73] The outside carries the inside beyond the apparent apocalypse. The new secretes the old; the human remains.

Unease with what he would later term the 'apocalyptic tone' does not, however, mark the end of Derrida's critique. Neither, moreover, does it lead to a call for a simple surrender to the humanism that had dominated French philosophy in the post-war years. Refusing to give up, Derrida suggests that there is a second way to challenge the hegemony and heredity of humanism. 'I don't destroy the subject; I situate it',[74] he told the audience of the famous Baltimore 'Languages of Criticism and the Sciences of Man' conference in 1966. And, two years later in 'The ends of Man', he proposes

> attempting the exit and the deconstruction without changing terrain, by repeating what is implicit in the founding concepts and the original problematic, by using against the edifice the instruments or stones available in the house, that is, equally, in language. The risk here is one of ceaselessly confirming, consolidating, *relifting* (*relever*), at an always more certain depth, that which one claims to be deconstructing. The continuous process of making explicit, moving towards the opening, risks sinking [*risque de s'enfoncer*] into the autism of the closure.[75]

Alone, however, this would still not be enough, and Derrida goes on to suggest that there is no 'simple and unique'[76] choice to be made between the two methods of challenging anthropocentrism. A 'new writing' is needed, he concludes, and this 'must weave and interlace the two motifs'.[77] This, in short, 'amounts to saying that it is necessary to speak several languages and produce several texts at once'.[78] The ease of speed and the speed of ease had found themselves called into question.

I think that Derrida's reluctance to be seduced by the 'apocalyptic tone' bears repeating today, as posthumanism begins to find its feet within the university[79] (and, of course, as Alien Chic continues its invasion of western culture). There is a sense in which it might be tempting to affirm an absolute break with humanism, and to shy away from attending to what remains of humanism in the posthumanist landscape. From one perspective, this would be perfectly understandable: posthumans are far more exciting, far sexier than humans. To misquote Donna Haraway, I, for one, would rather go to bed with a cyborg than a 'Man' of reason.[80] And it would be extremely comforting to believe that overcoming humanism can be accomplished by simply celebrating all things alien, by rushing to love what was once loathed. But things are not that straightforward, for the human haunts. It follows that someone has to do the dirty work: humanism requires attention. The familiar, easy announcements of a complete change of terrain, a pure outside, need to be complemented by work that speaks to humanism's ghost, to the reappearance of the inside within the outside. Both halves of the signifier in question demand attention: posthumanism is as much *post*humanist as it is post*humanist*.[81]

This should not be read as a regressive or reactionary gesture. To engage with humanism, to acknowledge its persistence, is not necessarily to support humanism. Derrida's call for critics to repeat 'what is implicit in the founding concepts and the original problematic' is by no means a demand for a simple, straightforward, compulsive repetition of those concepts. Deconstruction, rather, as he has insisted on various occasions, consists in repeating things '*in a certain way*',[82] in order to expose the overwhelming uncertainty of even the most apparently certain discourses. As *Mémoires for Paul de Man* puts it:

> [T]he very condition of a deconstruction may be at work, in the work, *within* the system to be deconstructed; it may *already* be located there, already at work, not at the center

> but in an excentric center, in a corner whose eccentricity assures the solid concentration of the system, participating in the construction of what it at the same time threatens to deconstruct. One might then be inclined to reach this conclusion: deconstruction is not an operation that supervenes *afterwards*, from the outside, one fine day; it is always already at work in the work; one must just know how to identify the right or wrong element, the right or wrong stone – the right one, of course, always proves to be, precisely, the wrong one.[83]

The troublesome element is always already there, often in the margins, where it seems unimportant. But Derrida's gaze is repeatedly drawn to the fringes, to the apparently minor detail that actually unsettles the certainty of the entire system. For him, to take a line from Don DeLillo's *Valparaiso*, 'major things are implied in minor moments'.[84] In *Dissemination*, for instance, the Greek term *pharmakon* – used by Plato to describe the status of the written word – is singled out for attention. Because *pharmakon* can signify (among other things) either 'poison' or 'remedy', Derrida declares the meaning of Plato's pronouncements upon writing to be undecidable. Any attempt to write matters in stone – whether by the philosopher himself or by his various translators and commentators – would be 'as violent as it is impotent',[85] as narrow as it is unjust. 'Only a blind or grossly insensitive reading', Derrida concludes, attacking a powerful critical heritage, 'could indeed have spread the rumor that Plato was *simply* condemning the writer's activity.'[86] An entire philosophical tradition is unsettled by a single word, a single word that was there all along.

I want to argue for a posthumanism that is not afraid to repeat humanism *in a certain way*, and with a view to the deconstruction of anthropocentric thought. If the pure outside is a myth, it is, I think, nonetheless possible to 'lodg[e] oneself within traditional conceptuality in order to destroy it',[87] to reveal the internal instabilities, the fatal contradictions, that expose how humanism is forever rewriting itself as posthumanism. Repetition, that is to say, can be a form of questioning: to restate is not always to reinstate. There is a frighteningly fine line between insurrection and resurrection, and contemporary western culture consistently encourages its subjects to avoid taking risks.[88] But this particular risk, I think, must be measured against the alternative, for, as N. Katherine Hayles shows so well, there is nothing more terrifying than a posthumanism that claims to be terminating 'Man' while actually extending 'his' term in office.

How might this somewhat abstract theory work? How might deconstruction invite a reconsideration of the apparent certainties of humanist discourse? A good place to begin, it seems, is at the beginning. As I noted in the introduction to *Alien Chic*, the human being described by René Descartes is a figure of certainty and authority, entirely known and knowable to itself. I want, however, to revisit *in a certain way* the moment in the *Discourse on the Method* at which Descartes tells his fantastic tale of simians, humans, and automata.[89] What if his wonderfully confident anthropocentrism actually pulled itself apart? What if the 'ontological hygiene'[90] that Elaine L. Graham locates at the heart of humanism were always already in crisis, always already distinctly unhealthy? What if a certain 'ontological choreography'[91] were secretly at work in the text? What if humanism were alien to itself?

Descartes asserts his anthropocentrism on the grounds that it would be impossible for a machine that looked like a human to possess enough different organs to enable it to respond to the infinite unpredictability of everyday life. Sooner or later, as countless subsequent science fiction narratives conveniently testify, the truth will out. Absolute and natural difference will eventually *tell itself*. There is, however, something of a blind spot, an aporia, in Descartes's account, for if a machine – quite in keeping with the spirit of his fantastic scenario – were constructed in such a way that it had what might be called 'an organ for every occasion',[92] it would, *according to the letter of Descartes's own argument*, no longer be possible to maintain a clear distinction between the human and the inhuman. Given enough organs, a machine would, after all, be capable of responding, and responding in a manner utterly indistinguishable from that of a human being. Reason, no longer that which 'distinguishes us from the beasts', would meet its match, its fatal and flawless double.

On closer inspection, in other words, there lies within Cartesian 'ontological hygiene' a real sense in which, to take a line from one of Philip K. Dick's novels, '[*l*]*iving and unliving things are exchanging properties*'.[93] In the margins of the text, the sacred lines of humanism cross themselves (out), and the moment at which humanism insists becomes the moment at which it nonetheless desists. Quite against his will, quite against all odds, Descartes has begun to resemble Deckard,[94] the troubled protagonist of *Do Androids Dream of Electric Sheep?*[95] and *Blade Runner* (dir. Ridley Scott, 1982) who utterly fails to police the boundary between the real and the fake, the human and the inhuman. The philosopher's monkey gets the better of him; it monkeys around with humanism. Refusing merely to ape the human, it becomes a simian simulacrum (a 'simulacrian', if you will), a copy for which there is no longer an original. Humanism has slipped away from itself, and the *Discourse on the Method* has begun to tell a story not unlike that of Donna J. Haraway's *Simians, Cyborgs, and Women.*

The very structure of humanism, to use Derrida's words, 'bears within itself the necessity of its own critique';[96] its inside turns itself inside out. I think that the trick – and this would certainly not be what Haraway calls a 'god-trick'[97] – is to learn something that the characters who encounter the strange building in Mark Z. Danielewski's *House of Leaves*[98] know all too well: the straightforward distinction between inside and outside is not always that straightforward. The boundaries that ought to fall into line with common sense, the laws of science and the land, turn out to be far more uncertain. Things are not what they seem. As I see it, the task of posthumanism is to uncover those uncanny moments at which things start to drift, of rereading humanism *in a certain way*, against itself and the grain. This, of course, involves a careful rethinking of the meaning of the 'post-', and while Derrida's philosophy implicitly demands a cautious approach to the prefix in question, it seems to me that Jean-François Lyotard's writings on the postmodern might be more immediately relevant to the work of theorizing posthumanism along these lines.

After the publication in 1979 of *The Postmodern Condition*,[99] Lyotard spent much of the rest of his life urging his readers to resist easy, complacent understandings of the postmodern. Essays such as 'Answer to the question: What is the postmodern?' and 'Note on the meaning of "post-"'[100] repeatedly confounded popular opinion by insisting, among other things, that the postmodern should not be seen as a historical period, and even that postmodernity precedes modernity. It is, however, to a text first published in 1987 that I want to turn here.

'Rewriting modernity' opens with the suggestion that its title 'seems far preferable to the usual headings, like "postmodernity", "postmodernism", "postmodern", under which this sort of reflection is usually placed'.[101] Developing his earlier insistence that the signifier 'postmodern' 'simply indicates a mood, or better, a state of mind',[102] Lyotard goes on to declare that,

> Postmodernity is not a new age, but the rewriting of some of the features claimed by modernity, and first of all modernity's claim to ground its legitimacy on the project of liberating humanity as a whole through science and technology. But as I have said, that rewriting has been at work, for a long time now, in modernity itself.[103]

Modernity and postmodernity, that is to say, should not be thought of as entirely distinct entities: postmodernity is the rewriting of modernity, which is itself 'constitutionally and ceaselessly pregnant with its postmodernity'.[104] The 'post-' is forever tied up with what it is 'post-ing'. This is no cause for despair, and should not for one moment be confused with Habermas's claim that modernity is a project that still calls for (and, moreover, is capable of) completion.[105] Lyotard's postmodern, on the contrary, attends to the modern in the name of questioning. The 're-' of the rewriting, as he puts it, 'in no way signifies a return to the beginning but rather what Freud called a "working through" . . .'.[106]

The brief paper to which Lyotard is alluding at this point was composed in 1914, shortly after Freud had completed his analysis of the Wolf Man, and makes an important theoretical distinction between remembering (*Erinnern*), repeating (*Wiederholen*) and working-through (*Durcharbeitung*). The latter term refers to the delicate situation that arises when a patient initially resists the procedure of analysis. 'One must', Freud stresses,

> allow the patient time to become more conversant with this resistance with which he has now become acquainted, to *work through* it, to overcome it, by continuing, in defiance of it, the analytic work according to the fundamental rule of analysis. Only when the resistance is at its height can the analyst, working in common with his patient, discover the repressed instinctual impulses which are feeding the resistance; and it is this kind of experience which convinces the patient of the existence and power of such impulses. The doctor has nothing else to do than to wait, and let things take their course, a course which cannot be avoided nor always hastened.[107]

The traumatic event, that is to say, cannot be remembered as such, cannot be simply and surely brought back to consciousness. But neither can it be forgotten, for if the patient could turn his or her back on the past, he or she would not require the help of the analyst. This strange condition, this twilight zone, is the predicament of anamnesis. Faced with such a situation, analysis must move slowly, and Freud concludes that this 'working-through of the resistance may in practice turn out to be an arduous task for the subject of the analysis and a trial of patience for the analyst'.[108] There can be no simple settling of scores, no sudden breaks with the troublesome past.

Lyotard is quick to heed Freud's warning. Cultural analysis, he proposes, can learn from psychoanalysis. Modernity, that monstrous 'Thing' with which postmodernity is trying to come to terms, must be worked through, patiently rewritten: 'Rewriting, as I mean it here, obviously concerns the anamnesis of the Thing. Not only that Thing that starts off a supposedly "individual" singularity, but of the Thing that haunts the "language", the tradition and the material with, against and in which one writes.'[109] And it is precisely this elaborate, laborious, labyrinthine rewriting that Lyotard labels postmodernity.

I want to borrow Lyotard's borrowing, to carry it – along with the work of Derrida – to the space of posthumanism.[110] Both thinkers, it seems to me, invite a careful (re)consideration of the signifier in question. From a perspective informed by their thought, the 'post-' of posthumanism does not – and, moreover, cannot – mark or make an absolute break from the legacy of humanism. 'Post-'s speak (to) ghosts, and cultural criticism must not forget that it cannot simply forget the past. The writing of the posthumanist condition should not seek to fashion 'scriptural tombs'[111] for humanism, to write tradition into silence; it must, rather, take the form of a critical practice that occurs *inside* humanism, and should consist not of the wake but the working-through of anthropocentric discourse. Humanism has happened and continues to happen (it is the very 'Thing' that makes 'us' 'us', in fact), and the experience – however traumatic, however unpleasant – cannot be erased without trace in an instant. The present moment may well be one in which the hegemony and heredity of humanism feel a little less certain, a little less inevitable, but there is a real sense in which the crisis, as Gramsci once put it, 'consists precisely in the fact that the old is dying and the new cannot be born'.[112] The scene is changing, but the guard is not. Not yet, not now. A working-through remains underway, and this coming-to-terms is a gradual and difficult process that lacks sudden breaks. An uneasy patience is called for.

Ted Mooney's haunting novel, *Easy Travel to Other Planets*, knows and writes this very demand. In its strange near-future world, humans – called upon in countless ways to rethink established assumptions about their relationship to the inhuman – are beginning to experience 'a new emotion, one that no one had ever felt before'.[113] But these are early days, for the characters and the text cannot yet name this feeling. 'It's like . . . I don't know,' someone remarks, 'it's like being in a big crowd of people without the people. And you're all traveling somewhere at this incredible speed. But without the speed.'[114] Travel to a wholly other space, where no trace of the human remains, is not easy; tradition is still working, being worked-through, worked-over, worked out. Or, more precisely (and this is probably the most difficult point to grasp), it is working through *itself*.[115] 'We' ignore this at 'our' peril, for speed no longer signifies success or succession.[116] And if this gentle, gradual working-through is at once an engagement with humanism, it does not follow that things stand still, that the deliberate reckoning with the weight of tradition means a blindness towards things to come. If, to invoke Paul Celan, there are still songs to be sung beyond the human,[117] posthumanism marks the recognition that humanism, always already in disharmony with itself, forever sounds of other airs, other heirs. 'Questioning', as Heidegger once insisted, 'builds a way',[118] and I think that questioning humanism – posthumanism itself – begins to build ways for being different in the future. 'We' have nothing to lose but 'our' selves.

This rather laborious working-through of seventeenth-century philosophy and poststructuralist theory has, I realize, temporarily abducted me from the arms of the alien. In the following chapter, therefore, I want to pursue the implications of my understanding of posthumanism for the culture of Alien Chic. How might cultural criticism adequately reckon with this curious and contradictory phenomenon? How is humanism's working-through of itself, its self-undoing, actually manifested in texts that deal with alien beings? If, that is to say, humanism continues to haunt the present moment, how is it nonetheless possible to trace the ways in which Alien Chic is at once haunted by an uncanny alternative called posthumanism?

5

A Crisis of *versus*: Rereading the alien

There were shades to him which dimmed what I kept expecting to find.

DON DELILLO, *Americana*[1]

'Who are all these beautiful people?': Watching *Roswell*

Roswell knows its moment.[2] It knows, moreover, that it knows its moment, for as it narrates the adventures of a group of teenage aliens doing their best to fit into a small community in New Mexico, it at once narrates the contemporary culture of Alien Chic. Roswell, of course, is the holy city of UFOlogy, the alleged site of an infamous flying saucer crash to which all true 'X-philes' must make a pilgrimage. There is, in fact, a sense in which the signifier itself has become, as Richard Vine put it in his timely review of the series, 'an established brand name in what passes for the global counter-culture'.[3] And this is precisely where *Roswell* begins, setting its pilot episode during a week in which the city is due to celebrate the legendary close encounter of 1947. The opening scene takes place in the CrashDown Café – a diner, situated opposite the UFO Center, where staff wearing extraterrestrial badges, aprons and headgear serve 'alien-themed greasy food' – and sees one of the waitresses asking her customers if they 'are here for the crash festival' (a spectacular event, complete with plummeting UFO, which forms the backdrop to the episode's climax). From the outset, that is to say, Alien Chic makes its presence felt, and the series goes on repeatedly and playfully to invoke the cultural phenomenon to which it owes its existence.

But as it knowingly acknowledges Alien Chic, *Roswell* also exemplifies the trend. While the extraterrestrials of the 1950s were almost always vile monsters, here they are immaculately groomed teenage sex symbols. And this is not merely a diegetic question, for the characters have been repeatedly presented – in popular magazines or the fan-produced *Roswell 2004 Calendar*,[4] for instance – as objects of desire. Perhaps unsurprisingly, a brief search of the internet reveals dozens of websites devoted to deciding whether or not Max is more handsome than Michael, or Isabel more alluring than Tess. 'Who are all these beautiful people?', asks a BBC webpage devoted to the series.[5] They are, it would seem, aliens with whom to fall in love.

But if *Roswell* is a particularly glossy example of Alien Chic, if it thrives upon a conventional opposition between the human and the extraterrestrial (aliens are loved, once again, *as aliens*), I want to suggest that this is by no means the end of the story. Things are not what they seem, for familiarity turns out to be somewhat deceptive. The series, in fact, ceaselessly starves the humanism upon which it seems to feed, both calling forth and calling into question the belief in an absolute difference between the human and the inhuman. If such an opposition undoubtedly drives the narrative (and without it there would be no Alien Chic), it simultaneously leads to a drift away from the orbit of humanism. The familiar turns uncanny as humanism reveals itself to have been always already housing the alien of posthumanism.

I was a teenage teenager; or, why aliens need (V)isas

What could be more predictable, more formulaic, than a teenage drama set in and around a high school?[6] If the archetypal (American) teenager is not to be found at the drive-in or the diner, he or she will surely be sulking at the back of the classroom, dodging the Hall Monitor, or, at the very least, inhaling illegal substances somewhere on the premises. For obvious reasons, most teenage drama has something to say about the institution of education, and teenage identity, more often than not, is articulated in a struggle against the values posed and imposed by such a system. Within teenage fictions, education is, quite simply, familiar to the point of invisibility, 'blanched with the anemic pallor of the obvious', to use Heidegger's wonderful phrase.[7] I want to suggest, however, that in *Roswell*, its very obviousness actually has the strange effect of destabilizing the metaphysical opposition between the human and the inhuman. Education, it transpires, educes the possibility of posthumanism.

Although one of his books has made an appearance in *Melrose Place*,[8] I do not know if the makers of *Roswell* have ever read the work of Jean-François Lyotard. And Lyotard, if he were still alive, would probably not be a fan of the series. Commercial television, he once concluded, was not really tuned in to the needs of philosophy:

> Yet, can he [the philosopher] make something known by speaking for a quarter of an hour one evening in front of a camera . . . maybe his face, take a good look . . . maybe also his name, but that's less likely . . . and what is least likely is that he will make known what he believes he has to say, since that has already taken him one or two thousand written pages and several years (he is not young), so that it should be impossible for him to say all that in fifteen minutes.[9]

In the opening pages of *The Inhuman*, however, Lyotard contemplates the relationship between education, the human, and the inhuman, in a way that raises an intriguing question about *Roswell*:

> If humans are born humans, as cats are born cats (within a few hours), it would not be . . . I don't even say desirable, which is another question, but simply possible, to educate them. That children have to be educated is a circumstance

> which only proceeds from the fact that they are not completely led by nature, not programmed. The institutions which constitute culture supplement this native lack.[10]

Humans, that is to say, *become* human with time and a little encouragement. Left entirely to their own devices, they would probably never make the leap, never take up their places within the symbolic order. Culture may well be ordinary, as Raymond Williams insisted,[11] but it is also what makes 'us' ordinary human beings. In the absence of cultural institutions such as schools, 'we' would not be human. 'We' (if, that is, 'we' could still be called 'we') would remain inhuman, non-human, a-human, posthuman. 'Our' apparently natural state of being, of being *human*, is, it follows, anything but natural. It is, rather, a question of culture and the lead of education. 'Our' source lies not, as humanism proposes, in nature, but in culture. 'Our' origins are, in other words, profoundly non-original. Once upon a time, 'we' were aliens. The other is all that 'we' once were. 'We' are made; the 'we' is made.

If Lyotard's somewhat disarming argument is considered alongside Althusser's insistence that the cultural institutions that function as Ideological State Apparatuses – and school, of course, is singled out as the dominant ISA[12] – must continually *re*state and *re*work their claims upon their subjects, the line that humanism confidently inscribes between the human and the inhuman becomes even less certain. 'We' need to be kept in check, kept human. The inhuman is never too far away. Through its institutions, its apparatuses – education, law, religion, morality, ethics, common sense – culture ceaselessly (re)makes humans (why else would 'we' need such entities in our adult lives?). And the very presence of such institutions in *Roswell* testifies to the work that humanism must perform in order to maintain its hegemony. If school exists – and, moreover, exists as *a legal requirement* – 'we' cannot originally, naturally, eternally be the 'we' of humanism. There is, as Lyotard suggests, a 'native lack' with which to reckon and wrestle.

From this perspective, there is a sense in which teenage rebellion is a rebellion against humanism. When *Roswell*'s human characters refuse to take the edicts of education as a given, or engage in a delicate game of trickery against figures of authority like Sheriff Valenti and Miss Topolsky, they are effectively alien-ating themselves, turning away from the human. To challenge both school and law is to challenge the culture of humanism and the humanism of culture.[13] Max, Michael and Isabel might actually be aliens, but the actions of human characters like Liz and Maria also go some way towards the earning of such a label. The familiar theme of teenage alienation is, in other words, taken somewhat literally in *Roswell*: human teenagers are almost as alien(ated) as the aliens they befriend and desire.

Meanwhile, the aliens' longing to fit in, to lie low and play the game, is profoundly humanist in intent, for, unlike their human allies, the extraterrestrials *want* culture to pass for nature, in order that they can be viewed and treated as ordinary, authentic human beings. 'Everything has to be normal', says Max at one point, even if 'normal' has suddenly begun to look like a look, a host of conventional gestures. The alien simulates the human; the human makes itself alien. The borders of humanism have been crossed. In a further twist, Michael's tendency to miss many of his classes is understood by his art teacher to be a symptom of ordinary teenage rebellion: his absence is neither unusual nor suspicious. The school has seen it all before, and even expects a certain percentage of its pupils to behave in such a manner (why else would records of attendance be kept?). One of the most fundamental institutions of humanism, that is to say, actually predicts the possibility of posthumanism, caters for it, structures its rituals in accordance. Teenagers, it seems, would not be teenagers if they did not act a little inhuman, a little alien-ated, from time to time. The inhuman (alien) passes for human (teenager) by appearing inhuman (alien-ated truant), and the traditional opposition between the real and the simulated suddenly finds itself even deeper in crisis. Youthful rebellion, so often dismissed as nothing more than an unfortunate and unpleasant side-effect of growing up, turns out to pose a curious challenge to the hegemony and heredity of humanist discourse. For humanism, teenagers are nothing but trouble, and trouble, as Judith Butler has mischievously pointed out, need not always be seen in negative terms.[14]

(Posthu)manly sports and jobs for life (but not as we know it)

If no teenage drama is complete without high school, no American high school is complete without sport. While sport certainly plays a compulsory part in British state schooling – I have both physical and mental scars to prove it – a higher value appears to be placed upon such activities in the United States, where it often appears that there can be no education without physical education.[15] And, in keeping with tradition, the narrative of *Roswell* sports an interest in games. From the brief glimpse of the gymnasium provided in the opening episode, to Kyle's distinctive jacket and status as all-round 'jock' (he is identified as 'Student Athlete of the Month' at one point), sport is always part of the fabric of life at West Roswell High, part of the *mise en scène*. While this is perfectly predictable, obvious to the point of transparency, the ordinary actually has extraordinary implications. In sport, humanism meets its match.

As the first scene of the pilot episode makes clear, the aliens have powers and abilities that are noticeably different from those of their human classmates: with bare hands, Max miraculously heals Liz's life-threatening gunshot wound. It might appear that this is the true mark of the alien, the locus of absolute difference, but it seems to me that the familiar institution of sport implies the inescapable presence of people with differing powers and abilities *within the human race itself.* Without such variation, in fact, sport would not be possible, for if everyone possessed entirely equal talents, there could be no such thing as competition. While there are, of course, established rules to which all players must conform – a referee or umpire is always on hand to ensure that this is the case, and to punish any transgressors – there is, as Don DeLillo's *End Zone* shows so memorably, a differend[16] that divides, that *must* divide, team from team, competitor from competitor. In the breathless second section of the novel, for instance, the narrator briefly outlines the metaphysics of (American) football: 'Each play must have a name. The naming of plays is important. All teams run the same plays. But each team uses *an entirely different system of naming*.'[17] In competition, at the very heart of sport, lies the untying of humanism's insistence upon an underlying likeness. Events such as the Olympic Games might be held aloft as a global celebration of human achievement and spirit, but, from this perspective, they are at once the murmur of the irreconcilable differences that mark posthumanism. The medals and the trophies, the cheques and the champagne, all point to the fact that sport relies upon a fundamental *difference* between its players. Once again, in its entirely familiar *mise en scène*, *Roswell* reveals that humanism's sacred sameness fails to qualify.

But sport is not the only ordinary feature of school life to imply that humans differ quite radically from each other in ability. An early episode entitled 'Monsters' is framed around the events of 'Futureweek', during which pupils are subjected to a series of personality tests and eventually informed by Miss Topolsky where their futures ideally lie: 'I want', she announces, 'to help you discover exactly what's right for you.' It seems to me, however, that the seemingly banal ritual of careers guidance further undermines humanism's faith in identity, simply because it acknowledges that human beings do quite different things with their lives. People, as Topolsky goes on to suggest, have different 'strengths'. This, in fact, makes the whole practice of careers guidance a possibility, for if everyone were exactly the same, there would be no need for such a system of advice. And *Roswell* even shows, in precise detail, the wide variety of futures eventually offered to the pupils: writing, law enforcement, psychology, professional football, and retail. No two people, however, have the same 'strengths'. If 'Futureweek' is intended to 'discover exactly what's right' for each student, it follows that certain professions would be unsuitable, 'wrong'. Difference is at work everywhere, both in the present and the future. The aliens' absolute alterity might appear to lie in their extraordinary abilities, but 'Futureweek', like the equally familiar institution of sport, implies that there is no such thing as an ordinary, standard, essential, human ability. Aliens differ from humans, but humans differ from themselves.

I do not even think that the series ultimately permits the strange powers of the extraterrestrials to stand as a sign of absolute otherness. While the aliens are certainly immune to the established laws of physics – Michael bends the bars that cover the window of the Sheriff's office; Isabel reheats food with a casual wave of her hand; Max dissolves the bullet and heals the wound in Liz's stomach[18] – their powers are not, it transpires, without limits. In the episode entitled 'Leaving normal', for instance, Liz's grandmother suffers a stroke shortly after arriving to visit her family. As her favourite relative lies on the verge of death in a hospital bed, Liz asks Max to use his curative powers. But Max, it is now revealed, cannot always defer death: 'Liz, when I saved you,' he explains, 'it was because you were shot. There was a bullet in you. Something was happening to you that wasn't supposed to happen. It was before your time. But I can't just heal people – I'm not God.' In this instance, there is little that he can do.[19] The grandmother's time, quite simply, has come, and after a final few moments together with her granddaughter, she passes away. The aliens' powers are no match for the oldest problem of them all. While life can sometimes be preserved – as Liz's first encounter with Max would prove – on other occasions, it cannot. Death is undying.

Meanwhile, 'Leaving normal' also quietly reveals that the extraterrestrials' seemingly miraculous abilities are shared by certain humans, for, upon her arrival at the hospital, Liz's grandmother is revived by electric shocks that are administered by a team of doctors. With the right training and equipment, that is to say, humans can sometimes be brought back from the dead *by other humans.* Death does not always have to win. At times it can be tamed, overcome, deferred by human hands. What appears to be a trait exclusive to the aliens is actually a quality shared by certain members of the human race. And if those qualities are mutual, the boundaries marked out with such confidence and clarity by anthropocentrism have been breached. Medicine doctors humanism.

I've got UFO under my skin

As Liz lies close to death on the floor of the CrashDown Café, Max's intervention brings about a strange insight into her innermost thoughts and childhood memories. Her life, it might be said, flashes before his eyes. 'We can connect with people', he later explains, apparently identifying yet another mark of the truly alien. But once again, it seems to me that *Roswell* fails, in the tales that it actually tells, to make this characteristic into a sign of absolute difference.

Frank Sinatra once assured his listeners that 'you have a head start' in life and love 'if you are among the very young at heart'.[20] There is, it would seem, no love like young love; the two words go together, as another of Sinatra's songs has it, 'like a horse and carriage'.[21] Like education, romance is a familiar feature in teenage fiction, and at the heart of *Roswell* lies a touching love story. At the very beginning of the first series, Liz develops strong feelings for Max, her saviour, but is already romantically involved with Kyle, the son of Sheriff Valenti. To make matters worse, she cannot be sure that Max is really interested in her: does he share her passion, or has he revealed his alien secret and bared his soul out of mere compassion?[22] In the meantime, Kyle has grown increasingly suspicious about the amount of time that Liz has been spending in Max's company, and it is at this point that other members of the football squad, in a delicate gesture of solidarity with their teammate, assault Max in a darkened alley.

Liz discusses the dilemma with her grandmother, who suggests that 'if it isn't complicated, he probably isn't a soulmate'. 'Complicated', I think, is the perfect word to describe the intricate series of connections that *Roswell* traces between its human characters. Love and friendship are seen to lie at the heart of everyday teenage life, influencing how people connect, disconnect, and reconnect with others. And these connections are as strange as they are complicated. Love, in particular, moves in mysterious ways. It cannot, as Liz comes to realize, be mastered or rationalized. 'The tough thing about following your heart', she says, shortly after leaving Kyle,

> is what people forget to mention, that sometimes your heart takes you places you shouldn't be, places that are as scary as they are exciting, and as dangerous as they are alluring. And sometimes your heart takes you places that can never lead to a happy ending. And that's not even the difficult part. The difficult part is when you follow your heart, you leave normal, you go into the unknown, and once you do, you can never go back.

Love is shrouded in mystery. In its distance and difference from what is 'normal', it is 'unknown'. Romance, however thrilling, however 'alluring', is never simple, predictable, measurable. 'It's complicated', is all that Liz will, or can, say to Kyle when bringing their relationship to an end.

Platonic friendship, meanwhile, is no less complex, no less alien to reason and common sense. Although the affair between Liz and Kyle is broken off early in the first series, there remains another man, besides Max, in her life. Alex Whitman has been a close friend to Liz for many years, but the episode entitled 'Blood brother' sees this friendship thrown into crisis. When Max is injured in a car crash and taken to hospital, a routine blood test threatens to reveal his extraterrestrial origins. Realizing that the sample must be intercepted and replaced with a test tube of human blood, Liz asks Alex to be a donor. Although this conveniently saves the day, Max urges Liz not to tell Alex the truth, and a tale about drug abuse is quickly concocted. But Alex is no fool, and realizes that something else it at stake. He decides to confront Liz, arguing that a friend ought to be able to confide in another friend. Liz, however, insists that a *true* friend would respect silence and secrecy:[23]

Liz: I need you to believe in me, even though I can't . . . I can't tell you what you want to know.
Alex: Because of Max.
Liz: No. Forget Max, Alex. This is between us. Look, I told you before that this was complicated. Well, maybe it's not. There is a right side and there is a wrong side, and if you choose the wrong side right now, Alex, something really terrible is going to happen to all of us. I am begging you, Alex, if five years of friendship have meant anything to you, please trust me. I swear to you, I am on the right side.

Although Alex is quite clearly upset by Liz's concealment, he remains faithful, respects her silence, and takes her side (without, of course, knowing what that side might be).[24]

How can this strange and powerful bond possibly be explained, rationalized, figured? Common sense, logic and reason would all surely compel Alex to refuse to help Liz without knowing why he is placing himself in a position of danger ('What I just did, I could get arrested for', he says, shortly after donating his blood), and yet he continues to stand by and support his friend. How, moreover, can Liz hope to honour her acquaintance with Alex when her friendship and romantic involvement with Max pull her in an entirely different direction? How can a friend lie to a friend at the request of another friend (and, adding insult to injury, actually admit to the deception)?

Things are evidently, as Liz might put it, 'complicated', and *Roswell*, tellingly, does not try to resolve matters. It has no answers. It shows the existence of connections between people, but it does not (or cannot) explain the phenomenon. Such an approach marks, I think, yet another way in which the series troubles the opposition between the human and the alien upon which, as an example of Alien Chic, it nonetheless relies. While the aliens clearly have the ability to connect with people in mysterious ways, everyday human life involves the making of similarly mystifying connections with others.[25] Love and friendship are just as bizarre, just as inexplicable. However 'normal', they are utterly strange.

On the third hand; or, from Alien Chic to 'A Crisis of versus*'*

The dark secret at the heart of *Roswell* is thus revealed: '[t]he other is in the same'.[26] What seems, at first glance, to be little more than a glossy example of Alien Chic turns out to be far more complicated, far more undecidable.[27] There is, in other words, a third stage beyond the two that I have already outlined at length in earlier chapters. On the one hand, aliens are widely celebrated in contemporary western culture, and this rise of 'alien love' might suggest that there has been a clean break from the past. On the other hand, however, 'alien love' relies upon precisely the same binary opposition as 'alien hatred', permitting the patterns of the past to endure. But, to borrow a delightful flourish from Nabokov,[28] on the *third* hand, a close reading reveals that Alien Chic's central binary opposition is always already unstable. Alien Chic is certainly at work, but it is at once reworked, worked over, worked-through by its own assumptions. The human is never quite at home with itself, and never without the alien. In the most familiar themes of everyday teenage life – alienation, rebellion, love and friendship, uncertainty about the future – *Roswell* unearths resources for a rethinking of the relationship between the human and the inhuman, between 'Us' and 'Them'. Within its stories, the signifiers 'human' and 'alien' are rearticulated until the relationship between them is no longer one of absolute difference. Neither the human nor the alien is ever entirely revealed in the plenitude of opposition; there is a repeated deferral, an endless retreat from humanism.

It would be possible, I think, to continue this line of enquiry by rereading *in a certain way* any of the recent examples of Alien Chic considered in previous chapters, showing how the reconstruction of anthropocentric discourse is at once its deconstruction. I want instead, however, to end this book by travelling back to my point of departure, to the text to which I owe the journey that has ended with *Alien Chic*. Might the 'third hand' also touch the 'alien hatred' of the 1950s? Was the opposition between the human and the extraterrestrial uncertain even then?

Pod Almighty; or, the strange case of *Invasion of the Body Snatchers*

Things are not what they seem. When he returns to Santa Mira after a brief absence, the protagonist of *Invasion of the Body Snatchers* – Miles Bennell – discovers that a strange condition has suddenly begun to affect many of the town's residents, leading them to believe that relatives, friends, and colleagues are impostors. Although a local psychiatrist named Danny Kaufman casually dismisses the affair as 'an epidemic mass hysteria', Miles soon discovers that Santa Mira is actually being invaded by an alien force, which is quietly spreading doubles of the human inhabitants. These fakes are particularly difficult to spot because they look, sound and remember exactly like the individuals they have supplanted.

This immediately sets *Invasion of the Body Snatchers* apart from many of the other alien invasion films of the period, in which the other is visibly, obviously other. In *The War of the Worlds* and *It! The Terror from Beyond Space*, for instance, the difference between humans and non-humans *tells itself*, and no one could ever mistake the latter for the former. Siegel's film, however, 'has no visible monster',[29] no obvious enemy. There is, nonetheless, a difference between the human and the inhuman, and the telling of this difference comes to occupy a central position within the narrative. As Vivian Sobchack has pointed out, the aliens in *Invasion of the Body Snatchers* give themselves away by '*not* doing something',[30] by failing to behave in a certain way. The precise nature of this defining lack becomes apparent when, near the beginning of the film, Miles discusses recent events in Santa Mira with Wilma:

> *Wilma*: Let's have it. You talked to him – what do you think?
> *Miles*: It's him. He's your Uncle Ira all right.
> *Wilma*: He is *not.*
> *Miles*: How is he different?

Wilma: That's just it – there is no difference you can actually see. He . . . He looks, sounds, acts, and remembers just like Uncle Ira.

Miles: Then he *is* your Uncle Ira. Can't you see that? No matter how you feel, he is.

Wilma: But he isn't. There's something missing. He's been a father to me since I was a baby. Always when he talked to me there was a special look in his eye. That look's gone.

Miles: What about memories? There must be certain things that only you and he would know about.

Wilma: Oh God . . . I've talked to him about them. He remembers them all down to the last small detail, just like Uncle Ira would. But, Miles, there's no emotion. None. Just the pretence of it. The words, gestures, the tone of voice – everything else is the same, but not the *feeling*. Memories or not, he *isn't* my Uncle Ira.

Wilma's suspicions are confirmed at a later stage in the narrative by the alien double of Danny Kaufman:

'Danny': Miles, you and I are scientific men, you can understand the wonder of what's happened. Now just think: less than a month ago, Santa Mira was like any other town – people with nothing but problems. Then, out of the sky, came a solution: seeds, drifting through space for years, took root in a farmer's field. From the seeds came pods which have the power to reproduce themselves in the exact likeness of any form of life.

Miles: So that's how it began – out of the sky.

'Danny': Your new bodies are growing in there. They're taking you over cell for cell, atom for atom. There's no pain: suddenly, while you're asleep, they'll absorb your minds, your memories, and you're reborn into an untroubled world.

> *Miles*: Where everyone's the same?
> *'Danny'*: Exactly.
> *Miles*: What a world. We're not the last humans left – *they'll* destroy you.
> *'Danny'*: Tomorrow you won't want them to. Tomorrow you'll be one of us.
> *Miles*: I love Becky. Tomorrow, will I feel the same?
> *'Danny'*: There's no need for love.
> *Miles*: No emotion? Then you have no feelings, only the instinct to survive. You can't love or be loved, am I right?
> *'Danny'*: You say it as if it were terrible. Believe me, it isn't. You've been in love before – it didn't last, it never does. Love, desire, ambition, faith – without them life's so simple, believe me.

The difference cannot be seen. In the complete absence of 'bug-eyed monsters', the essential distinction between the human and the inhuman moves from the physical to the metaphysical: humans have feelings, but aliens do not.[31] This binary opposition supports the film's humanism in four principle ways. First, there is a belief in an absolute difference between the human and the inhuman. Second, this difference is hierarchical. Third, there is an appeal to a uniquely human essence that cannot be replicated. Fourth, there are clearly identifiable rules according to which a simple versus – humans versus aliens – may be maintained.

But what if things are not what they seem? What if there is, within the text's margins, a posthumanist alternative? What if there is, in fact, a 'Crisis of *versus*'? I want in what follows to inhabit the explicit humanism of Siegel's film *in a certain way*. My initial point of dwelling will be a brief, apparently minor moment in the text. Here, I suggest, humanism begins to falter, begins to announce an impossibility that will have been the possibility of posthumanism.

'I did not have sexual relations with that woman'; or, what's a nice legume like you doing in a place like this?

Approximately half way through the film, Miles returns home to find Becky, Teddy, and Jack relaxing on the patio. When the latter indicates that he is having trouble igniting the barbecue, Miles makes his way to the greenhouse for a can of lighter fluid. The long shot that captures his entrance is notably canted, immediately implying that something is awry. Sure enough, an alien pod lies in the lower left-hand corner of the frame.[32] Miles suddenly catches sight of the pod bursting open, and calls out to Jack, who, together with the women, rushes in to discover four pods discharging vaguely human shapes. Jack takes up a pitchfork, only to be restrained by Miles, who insists that the invaders pose no danger 'until they're completely formed'. A little later, Miles finds himself alone with the alien objects, which now resemble himself, Jack, Teddy, and Becky. Armed with the pitchfork, he approaches Becky's double, a medium close-up capturing the familiar face of his lover beneath the strange foam. In a canted reverse shot, Miles stands with the weapon raised. A subsequent close-up provides a clearer view of 'Becky's' face. The film cuts back to a close-up of Miles: the pitchfork is still raised but an anguished expression now troubles his features. He begins to wilt, to lean to his right. He lowers the weapon, unable to destroy the body (Carmen Dragon's ominous score, which had been frantically building to a climax, falls at this point, implying failure).[33] Eventually, he moves forward to his own replica and, with scant hesitation, stakes the body.

It seems to me that what the greenhouse scene effectively describes – quite contrary to what the film declares[34] – is an uncertainty regarding the meaning of the alien, an uncertainty that marks the invasion of posthumanism into the heart of humanism. Miles knows that the object before him is an inhuman fake that must be destroyed at all costs (this is doubly apparent because the real Becky is standing outside the greenhouse), and yet he responds as if it/she were human. It would appear that, as in *Roswell*, love is the problem. Because the alien reminds him of Becky, Miles cannot avoid acting as if it/she were the true object of his desire.[35] His uniquely human feelings, that is to say, lead him to place his lover in a position which threatens her very existence, her very future as a human being. Although '[s]exuality and sexual difference', as Cyndy Hendershot has pointed out, 'are *the* measures of humanity in the film',[36] it would seem that they are at once the measures of posthumanism. To be human is to desire, to possess emotions, but to desire is to trouble the sacred distinction between the human and the inhuman. Miles loves Becky, but Miles also acts as if he loves an alien legume. Things are most certainly not what they seem.

Lacan among the legumes

The filming of *Invasion of the Body Snatchers* began in Hollywood on 23 March 1955.[37] On the same day, thousands of miles away in Paris, Jacques Lacan was speaking to the audience of his seminar about the need to remember that the human subject is the subject of the unconscious and, as such, lies 'beyond the *ego*'.[38] In one respect, of course, these simultaneous moments could not be more dissimilar: while Don Siegel's film sets out to raise humanism, Lacan spent much of his life trying to raze it. His approach, he once agreed, was 'a-human',[39] something particularly apparent from the opening paragraph of his most famous essay, where it is stressed that the theory of the mirror stage 'leads us to oppose all philosophy directly issuing from the *Cogito*'.[40] Psychoanalysis, for Lacan, was no friend of humanism:

> To be a psychoanalyst is simply to open your eyes to the evident fact that nothing malfunctions more than human reality. If you believe that you have a well-adapted, reasonable ego, which knows its way around, how to recognize what is to be done and not to be done, and how to take reality into account, then there is nothing left to do but send you packing.[41]

Without knowing whether or not Lacan ever saw *L'Invasion des profanateurs de sépulture,* as it was known in France,[42] and without forgetting for one moment the differences between Lacanian psychoanalysis and B-movies, I want to stage a certain invasion, to allow Lacan's account of desire to seep into the gap opened up within *Invasion of the Body Snatchers* by Miles's hesitation before the inhuman.

Love, for Lacan, is far from simple. Desire and romance bring no true connection, for what any subject really wants from a partner is something impossible:

> Aristophanes' myth ties up [*noue*] the pursuit of the complement in a moving, and deceptive, way [*de façon pathétique, et leurrant*], by articulating that it is the other, its sexual other half [*sa moitié sexuelle*], that the living being seeks in love. To this mythical representation of the mystery of love, analytic experience substitutes the search by the subject, not for the sexual complement, but for the part of him- or herself, lost forever, that is constituted by the fact that he or she is only a sexed living being, and that he or she is no longer immortal.[43]

Neither half of the loving couple can truly satisfy the other, for neither person has what the other really wants. Each is bound to desire, bound to lack, bound to the Other. At the end of the day (and, moreover, all through even the most passionate of nights), two hearts never quite beat as one. There is, as the notorious *Encore* seminar repeatedly insists, *no such thing as a sexual relationship.*[44]

Following this lead, Catherine Belsey concludes that True Love – the arrest of desire in the triumphant discovery of another who can fill the gap in being – is an impossibility. 'Desire', she writes, '. . . cannot be contained by the stable, institutional, public *legality* which is marriage. On the contrary, desire, which is absolute, *knows no law.*'[45] Desire is unruly, troubling, ongoing. It never falls under the control of the subject of humanism. It mocks mastery. It is precisely, as Lacan once put it, 'the *desire for something else*',[46] a point articulated with discreet charm in Luis Buñuel's *That Obscure Object of Desire* (1977), where the woman with whom the male protagonist is obsessed is played by two completely different actresses who regularly switch places. He appears not to notice. Neither does desire.[47]

I think that the greenhouse scene marks a point at which *Invasion of the Body Snatchers*, quite contrary to its intention, admits something of Lacan's account. As an authentic human being, Miles ought – within the textual economy – to be able to destroy Becky's double, but something spoils the beautiful simplicity of humanism. When he falters, unable to distinguish between the two figures, Miles quite simply does not know what he is doing. His failure is a failure of humanism, of the faith in an absolute difference between the human and the inhuman. If, as Derrida once remarked, deconstruction 'never proceeds without love',[48] the converse would seem also to be true: love cannot proceed without a certain deconstruction taking place in its wake. Because he desires Becky, the film declares Miles to be undoubtedly human. And yet, the scene in the greenhouse proceeds to describe how Miles's desire renders him incapable of distinguishing between his human lover and an inhuman double. Desire leads him astray (his name, after all, suggests distance as much as love[49]). That which defines at once defiles. The sacred position set aside for the heterosexual couple is rendered untenable. True Love – the true mark of the human – turns out to have been truly unattainable, for desire escapes its vows and the aisle of every ceremony. As the late Antony Easthope put it:

> A traditional humanism had tried to separate what people do into an inside and an outside, to mark off civilisation from barbarism, human and inhuman, Theseus and the centaur. Against this view psychoanalysis demands humility, which means that we have to take human and inhuman together, as equal possibilities.[50]

And 'equal possibilities' equal the impossibility of humanism. *Invasion of the Body Snatchers* ends up walking arm in arm with Lacan.

On closer inspection, however, the marginal greenhouse sequence is not the only moment in *Invasion of the Body Snatchers* at which humanism trembles. At first glance it would appear that a straightforward binary opposition informs the entire narrative: humans love and bond into families; aliens do not, repeatedly invading the space of romance and domesticity. The Belicecs' discovery of the strange body in their house, for instance, triggers a chain of events that disrupts the relationship between Miles and Becky. First, as Nancy Steffen-Fluhr points out, Jack's phone call to the restaurant 'interrupts an intimate dinner which Miles had arranged as part of his plan for seducing Becky, the focus of his teenage lusts',[51] and although the strange events actually drive Becky to Miles's house for the night, they also bring Teddy and Jack, further disturbing Miles's seduction plan.

The following morning (bound by the Hays Code, the film can only allude to the possibility that the unmarried couple shared the same bed), Miles enters the kitchen to find Becky already at the stove, preparing his breakfast. The score suggests harmony and tranquillity, and each character occupies his/her correct position according to the discourse of patriarchal domesticity – she cooks, he sits and waits – until a noise from the basement startles them. Although they are relieved to discover that it is merely an engineer attending to the gas meter, it is later implied that this apparently friendly character (played, incidentally, by Sam Peckinpah) was working not for the gas company but for the alien invaders (might he have been responsible for placing the pods in the greenhouse?).

To make things worse, as soon as this crisis is resolved and harmony restored (the score changing accordingly), Jack enters the kitchen just as Miles and Becky are embracing and declaring their love for each other. Teddy, he reports, is still shaken from the uncanny events of the previous night, and he feels that it would be unwise for them to return home. 'Would you mind taking in a couple of boarders for a while, or do you, uh, have something else in mind?' he asks, suppressing a knowing smile. 'Well, I was toying with an idea,' replies Miles, glancing towards Becky and then grinning lasciviously at Jack, before concluding, 'but you can stay.' Love and sex are further deferred, further disturbed by the aliens. As Nancy Steffen-Fluhr neatly concludes, the invasion 'prevent[s] Miles and Becky both from sleeping and from sleeping with each other'.[52] While they are fighting for a future in which it will be possible 'to love and be loved', as Becky puts it, the lovers have no time to be lovers, to do any of the things lovers are supposed to do. 'I want your children', sighs Becky to Miles, but as long as there is an alien presence in Santa Mira, there is little chance of this happening.

As the official site of love, the nuclear family is also targeted, and begins to flounder beneath the alien regime. Miles's very first close encounter with the effects of the invasion comes near the beginning of the film, when his car narrowly avoids striking a small boy, Jimmy Grimaldi, fleeing from home. The boy's mother explains that her son does not want to attend school, but Jimmy's grandmother later offers a different explanation: her grandson believes that his mother is an impostor. 'She's not my mother! Don't tell her where I am!', cries the boy, terrified of his own family.

With Miles when he first meets Jimmy Grimaldi is Sally, his assistant. Throughout the film, she remains a somewhat marginal figure, about whom the viewer learns very little, but the conversation that takes place as she and Miles drive back to his surgery makes it clear that she belongs to a happy family. This changes when she is converted by the aliens, however, for when Miles spies upon a meeting of the invaders at Sally's house, he sees her (or, to be more precise, her double) volunteer to place a pod in her baby's playpen. 'There'll be no more tears', she says coldly, no longer a mother, but an other.

As the narrative unfolds, a pattern emerges: Jimmy's mother is not his mother; Wilma's uncle is not her uncle; Becky's father is not her father; Sally, the good mother, now murders her child. In short, as Sumiko Higashi puts it, the 'nightmare of having loved ones replaced by pod creatures . . . occurs within the family unit'.[53] When love is killed by the invaders, the nuclear family becomes redundant, refuted, and replaced.

But things not quite what they seem, for the viewer learns at a very early stage in the narrative that both Miles and Becky have recently undergone divorces.[54] Although this conveniently sets up a future romance between childhood sweethearts, it simultaneously calls the institution of marriage and the ideal of True Love into question by revealing that desire has already failed to honour and obey the will of the lovers. Families were falling apart long before the aliens arrived. Love, elsewhere the mark of humanity, is once again revealed to be no guarantee that the human subject will be able to distinguish between appropriate and inappropriate partners. Miles and Becky might appear to be the perfect couple, but there is no textual evidence to differentiate this relationship, this choice of partners, from their previous failures. No reason is given for the dissolution of Becky's marriage, and the only information provided about Miles's divorce lays the blame upon the demands of his profession, upon the fact that he 'was never there when dinner was on the table'.[55] And precisely because there is no suggestion that he will give up his work as a doctor in order to spend more time with Becky, it is not certain that the future will be one in which all shall be well. True Love is not, in other words, entirely true, for the permanence of the relationship remains in doubt. It is hardly surprising, therefore, that Miles should actually admit that love lies beyond his understanding:

> *Miles*: I found out that a doctor's wife needs the understanding of Einstein and the patience of a saint.
> *Becky*: And love?
> *Miles*: I wouldn't know about that – I'm just a *general* practitioner. Love is handled by the specialists.

Yes and no: Humanism, posthumanism, Alien Chic

Things are not what they seem. Appearances can be deceptive. While this is the message of *Invasion of the Body Snatchers*, it also turns out to be true of the film itself. As in *Roswell*, a seemingly straightforward humanism secretes its own alternative. The text, to return to Jacques Derrida's distinction, *declares* that it is possible to maintain a firm opposition between the human and the inhuman, but at once *describes* an entirely different state of affairs. Anthropocentrism is stalled as it is installed, rewritten as it is written, deposed as it is imposed. The subject of humanism is an impostor.

Both sides of the picture matter. In my attention to this drift away from anthropocentrism, I do not mean to say that *Invasion of the Body Snatchers* and *Roswell* are not humanist texts. What I do insist upon, however, is the fact that they are not *simply* humanist texts. I am not proposing an approach that 'will finish by answering *yes* or *no*',[56] neatly tying all of the signifying strands into a satisfying knot. As Derrida put it, in response to a question about his reading of Greek philosophy:

> As my colleagues know, each time I study Plato I try to find some heterogeneity in his own corpus, and to see how, for instance, within the *Timaeus* the theme of the *khôra* is incompatible with this supposed system of Plato. So, to be true to Plato, and this is a sign of love and respect for Plato, I have to analyze the functioning and disfunctioning of his work.[57]

Following Derrida, my point is that it is not possible to arrive at a moment of certainty, mastery, satisfaction. Meaning keeps on moving, and cultural criticism must learn to hear the 'yes' with the 'no', to read the disfunctioning alongside the functioning, to announce how every 'supposed system' is at once a deposed system. Humanism is there and not quite there. It comes and goes, it flickers, it drifts, and it is precisely this wandering that I want to call the possibility of posthumanism.

I should like to stress once again that I am not using the term in question to signify the obsolescence of humanism. The 'post-' does not mark an end, a break, or novelty; it identifies, rather, a patient reckoning with – a working-through of – what follows the prefix. This is not undertaken with a view to refining or refinding anthropocentrism; the engagement with tradition is avowedly critical in its commitment to an undermining. I want, in other words, to propose a posthumanism that is not afraid to tackle the traces of humanism that haunt contemporary western culture.

Those traces prove that stepping simply and suddenly beyond anthropocentric assumptions is not possible, for the past repeatedly informs and infiltrates the present. But, in the absence of a pure and ready beyond, the alternative does not have to be settling for the 'beyondless', to borrow a term from Beckett.[58] Humanism does not have to be the end, the whole, or the author of the story. The task, as I see it, is a matter of reading against the grain in order to unearth the ruins that anthropocentrism has hidden in and from itself. Humanism, in fact, is eternally and unwarily becoming alien to itself, becoming posthumanism.

The present participle towards the end of the previous sentence is respectfully addressed to N. Katherine Hayles. Although she begins her wonderful book with the recognition that discussing posthumanism in the past tense – *How We Became Posthuman* – is always going to be problematic,[59] I am still slightly troubled by her title. In my account, posthumanism is always ***becoming***, coming and yet going, and the difference of tense marks a tension, an ongoing questioning. As I suggested in the previous chapter, posthumanism is as much ***post***humanist as it is post***humanist***. From this perspective, it is not something straightforward, present, instantly graspable. Certainty and mastery – cornerstones, after all, of humanism – must be surrendered as cultural criticism comes to recognize that it is not possible to attach labels once and for all to moments, movements, discourses, texts.

It! The terror that looked a little familiar; or, invasion of Invasion of the Body Snatchers *(episodes II and III)*

There is another way to challenge the humanism of *Invasion of the Body Snatchers*, and this can be seen in the two avowedly anti-humanist remakes of Don Siegel's film. The movie, that is to say, has invaded more than once, and the compulsion to repeat and revisit the tale, to tell it anew, appears to be motivated in part by a desire to 'get it right', to settle an old score. Indeed, it has become almost conventional when writing about *Invasion of the Body Snatchers* to note that the film released in 1956 is not the film that Don Siegel originally made and intended for exhibition.[60]

When Siegel's first cut failed to please either Walter Wanger (the producer) or Allied Artists (the studio backing the project), the latter two parties began to re-fashion the product in various ways. Throughout the shooting period (March–April 1955), the film had carried the same title as the serial from which it derived: *The Body Snatchers.* Wanger, however, believed that this was too reminiscent of an earlier film, *The Body Snatcher* (dir. Robert Wise, 1945), and, in the summer of 1955, accepted the studio's suggestion of *They Came from Another World.* Don Siegel objected to the new title, however, and proposed *Sleep No More* (an alternative actually suggested by Kevin McCarthy, the actor who played Miles) and *Better Off Dead* in its place. Wanger forwarded these suggestions to the studio, along with two of his own – *Evil in the Night* and *World in Danger* – but Allied Artists finally settled upon *Invasion of the Body Snatchers* in late 1955. Don Siegel would later complain that this 'absurd title . . . cheapened the content of the story'.[61]

The struggle did not confine itself to the title. During post-production, the film itself was extensively re-edited. The most striking addition was a framing device, which Don Siegel was required to film almost five months after the completion of principal photography. As originally submitted to the studio, the film began *in medias res* with Miles's arrival at the railway station, and concluded with the scene where he runs wildly through the traffic, vainly attempting to warn passing motorists about the invasion. In an attempt to counter this bleak ending, which was viewed as uncommercially inconclusive, *Invasion of the Body Snatchers* was rearticulated as a long flashback that now concluded on a note of optimism (the psychiatrist believes Miles's bizarre story, realizes that immediate action is required, and notifies the FBI).

The imposition of this framing device has attracted a great deal of critical attention, much of it founded upon a tacit sense of conflict: Siegel versus the Studio; the Artist versus the System; the Maverick versus the Conservatives. Criticism, in other words, is invaded by its object;[62] it repeats the diegetic project of telling the difference between the fake and the real thing, and Siegel comes to resemble Miles, engaged in a desperate battle against a mindless enemy. Philip Kaufman certainly subscribed to such a view when publicizing his version of *Invasion of the Body Snatchers*, which was released in 1978:

> I started talking a lot to Don Siegel and I realised how he had been screwed over in the making of the original. They originally had a lot of comedy in the original, but after they previewed it in San Diego (Kevin McCarthy told me this, too), the studio made him take all the comedy out because they said a horror movie shouldn't have comedy. And they added a false beginning and ending because they wanted everybody to feel that everything was all right in the world, that the FBI could step in, and that there was something to be said for optimistic Hollywood endings.
>
> My feeling was to go back to Don Siegel's intention, or what he described to me as his intention at the time. Although our film goes over a lot of the same plot lines, it is more a sequel done twenty years later than a remake.[63]

Although it knowingly refers to Siegel's movie – Kevin McCarthy makes a brief appearance, still shouting at motorists, while Siegel himself has a cameo role as a taxi driver – Kaufman's film sets out to turn its back on the humanism of its predecessor, carefully cultivating a sense of obscurity through the use of low-key lighting, disorienting camera angles, a confusing soundtrack, and a meandering joke that lacks the closure of a punch line.[64] The most significant challenge, however, comes in the closing scene, where, to the wonderfully cynical sound of 'Amazing grace', a character who appears to be the protagonist is approached by an acquaintance named Nancy. She is evidently pleased to see him, evidently still human. When she calls his name and smiles, however, he turns, points directly at her (and into the camera), and utters the horrific scream used by the invaders to draw attention to the presence of a human being. The camera closes in on his gaping mouth until the screen is completely black. The human hero has failed, become inhuman. The ships will sail from the city's harbour, carrying pods to the rest of the world. There is no hope for the future.[65] As the director himself put it: 'In a way, it's apocalyptic, really . . . To put a rosy ending on [the film] just didn't seem in keeping with the nature of the nightmare we were trying to develop.'[66]

Writing in 1986, David Lavery predicted a third invasion of *Invasion of the Body Snatchers.*[67] This actually occurred in 1993, seven years earlier than Lavery expected. While Philip Kaufman widened the diegetic focus to the city of San Francisco, Abel Ferrara's *Body Snatchers* retreats far beyond the claustrophobia of Siegel's Santa Mira into an isolated military base, neatly described by one critic as 'at once an updated suburbia, a prison camp and a toxic waste dump'.[68] Presumably in an attempt to rethink the sexual politics of the story, *Body Snatchers* places a female character named Marti at the centre of things. Given Ferrara's reputation, it is perhaps surprising that, until the final reel, *Body Snatchers* is less consciously and consistently incoherent than Kaufman's remake. It appears, in fact, to be a relatively straightforward tale of the alliance formed between Marti and Tim against the alien invasion. The pair – who, like Miles and Becky, never quite find the time to turn their blossoming relationship into a true romance – escape in a helicopter, destroy the infested military base and several (if not all) of the vehicles carrying pods to the outside world, and head for safety.

But, as if suddenly remembering Kaufman's shocking *dénouement*, the film undermines its apparent humanism by concluding on a note of desperate ambiguity. As the helicopter lands in the city, a threatening low-angle shot frames the ground marshal. The score strikes a sustained minor chord, over which runs a non-diegetic repetition of a remark made by the double of Marti's stepmother at an earlier moment in the narrative. The words are distorted, excessively slowed: 'Where're you gonna go? Where're you gonna run? Where're you gonna hide? Nowhere, 'cause there's no one like you left.' The image of the marshal slowly fades and is replaced by the words 'THE END'. Have Marti and Tim 'escaped' into captivity? With whom is the marshal communicating via his headset? Have the aliens conquered the city, the country, the rest of the world? Is this 'THE END' of the human race? *Body Snatchers* offers no clear restoration of order, of humanism. As in Kaufman's film, there is no happy outcome.

The revisions proposed by Kaufman and Ferrara differ from Siegel's film in that they deliberately resist humanism. In seeking to tell a story about alien invasion without falling into the comforts and conventions of anthropocentrism, they go some way towards imagining a world in which, to return to the anti-humanist scene described by Althusser, 'Man' is reduced to ashes. Things appear to have changed. But things, of course, are never quite what they seem. Both films set out to challenge humanism by simply inverting the binary opposition between the human and the inhuman: the helpless humans finally become inhuman. While the emphasis quite clearly falls upon the half of the binary opposition habitually relegated by humanism, the certainty of the opposition itself is never called into question, never subject to invasion, never deconstructed. For this very reason, it seems to me that, although the world has been turned upside down, there is nothing to stop a further turn, a further revolution that would exactly restore the earlier order of things. Moreover, to allow a binary opposition (however inverted) between the human and the inhuman to remain *within* a challenge to humanism is at once to allow humanism (the belief, after all, in a binary opposition between the human and the inhuman) to remain within, to haunt, to invade. The repealed, once again, is repeated.

The strain of posthumanism that I am proposing would resist humanism not by turning its back, but by turning back *in a certain way*. If tradition cannot be simply overcome – if Alien Chic preserves something of the past – I think that the task must, to return to Derrida's words, become one of 'operating necessarily from the inside', folding tradition back upon itself until the implicit becomes explicit and brings impossibility to bloom. Posthumanist cultural criticism must, I think, learn to listen out for the deconstruction of the binary opposition between the human and the inhuman that is forever happening *within* humanism itself. Turning the world upside down will no longer do. The other is always already within. Humanism is merely pretending otherwise.

Conclusion: From difference to differance (with an 'a')

> Nothing lasts, and yet nothing passes, either. And nothing passes just because nothing lasts.
>
> PHILIP ROTH, *The Human Stain*[1]

It is the best of times, it is the worst of times for aliens. They have everything before them, they have nothing before them. It is their spring of hope, it is their winter of despair.

On the one hand, contemporary western culture, which once sought to repel extraterrestrials, now seems to have fallen in love with all things alien. The other is now welcomed, embraced, celebrated. If 'we' keep watching the skies, it is with love and longing in 'our' hearts. On the other hand, 'we' love them at a distance, and according to the familiar hierarchy of humanism. While aliens are allowed to invade 'our' lives on a daily basis, 'we' love 'them', quite simply, as a 'them'. They are desired only ever *as aliens*. Their otherness remains, not least at the level of the signifier, which continues to mean, and to mean something substantially different from 'human'. 'We' tell them that 'we' love them, but 'our' words reiterate the prejudices of the past. When 'we' fondly sigh, 'we' sigh as a 'we'. 'Alien love' preserves the absolute difference upon which 'alien hatred' was once constructed: an alien is still an alien. Little has changed. 'Alien love', accordingly, is Alien Chic.

But that, I want to insist, is not the end of the story. On the third hand, if the culture of Alien Chic is revisited with Derrida's way of reading in mind, it is possible to draw out the manner in which the binary opposition between the human and the inhuman is forever deconstructing itself. The extraterrestrial and the human can never be held absolutely apart, for there is always a contamination of the categories, a close encounter with crossings. In other words, humanism haunts, but is at once challenged in its revenance and reverie. What comes back does not have to be accepted on its own terms; it is, rather, possible to resist humanist discourse by listening to its narrative so carefully that the gaps in the tale, the unpredictable 'unsaids', signify as surely as the moments of intention. Anthropocentrism is imposed but deposed, written but rewritten, there but not quite there.

This is not to say that the human and the alien are exactly the same, that any sense of difference is abducted by a grand homogeneity. On the contrary, the approach to Alien Chic and humanism that I am proposing activates the differance (with an 'a') that has been quietly repressed by difference. I am, that is to say, interested in a more subtle illumination of what Stuart Hall has named a 'sense of difference which is not pure "otherness"'.[2]

Differance (with an 'a'), of course, is a neologism coined by Jacques Derrida in his brilliant rereading of Saussure. Saussure's radical move, proposed in the *Course in General Linguistics*, was to suggest that language is not 'a naming-process . . . a list of words, each corresponding to the thing that it names'.[3] If this were the case, words:

> would all have exact equivalents in meaning from one language to the next; but this is not true. French uses *louer* (*une maison*) 'let (a house)' indifferently to mean both 'pay for' and 'receive payment for,' whereas German uses two words, *mieten* and *vermieten*; there is obviously no exact correspondence of values.[4]

For Saussure, meanings are learned only with language, which, accordingly, determines and delimits what can be known. Language, furthermore, is a system that lies 'outside the individual who can never create nor modify it by himself [*sic*]'.[5] Meaning is the effect of the circulation of signs, each of which comprises a signifier (a sound or graphic mark) and a signified (the concept generated by the signifier). 'The bond between the signifier and the signified', Saussure stresses, 'is arbitrary'.[6] Pursuing this insight, the *Course in General Linguistics* concludes that language is a system of 'differences *without positive terms*'.[7] Meaning is the result of the difference between signs; meaning depends only upon difference.

And yet, although he insists that the sign is of an arbitrary character, Saussure nonetheless proposes that signifier and signified are 'intimately united',[8] appearing as one:

> Language can also be compared with a sheet of paper: thought is the front and the sound the back; one cannot cut the front without cutting the back at the same time; likewise in language, one can neither divide sound from thought nor thought from sound; the division could be accomplished only abstractedly, and the result would be either pure psychology or pure phonology.[9]

Meaning, that is to say, is fixed and fixable within a given linguistic community. Regardless of the arbitrary connection between signifier and signified, when one individual uses a certain signifier, others implicated in the linguistic 'contract' at that particular historical moment will understand precisely what the statement means.

In the late 1960s, Derrida suggested that Saussure had ultimately retreated from the full implications of his discovery into a more familiar metaphysics. This was perhaps most immediately evident in Saussure's insistence that, while *langue* exceeds human control, *parole* 'is always individual, and the individual is always its master'.[10] Intention, in other words, travels in the sign; humans control the meanings of their specific utterances, if not the larger linguistic system that makes meaning possible. Signs obey. For Derrida, however, the sign is more than merely arbitrary; it is at once radically unstable. The signifier does not lead purely and directly to its signified. Something gets in the way.

Derrida patiently returned to Saussure's insistence that the signifier signifies by being different from other signifiers, and not by simply referring to pre-existing concepts. This return was neither rejection nor simple resurrection of the *Course in General Linguistics*; it was, rather, a pursuing of Saussure's findings to their unsaid conclusion, an illumination of '[w]hat Saussure saw without seeing, knew without being *able* to take into account'.[11] If, Derrida noted, meaning depends upon difference, then meaning forever depends upon the *trace* of the other – the excluded, the different – within the same. 'Without a retention in the minimal unit of temporal experience,' he pointed out, 'without a trace retaining the other as other in the same, no difference would do its work and no meaning would appear.'[12] The signifier and signified, that is to say, are not held together in a unique bond, like two sides of a sheet of paper. The trace of the other within the same stalls such simplicity. And without the trace, meaning would be impossible: '*The trace is in fact the absolute origin of sense in general. Which amounts to saying once again that there is no absolute origin of sense in general. The trace is the differance* which opens appearance [*l'apparaître*] and signification.'[13]

The curious term 'differance' figures here, as elsewhere in *Of Grammatology*, but Derrida gives a more detailed account of his neologism in an essay simply entitled 'Differance', which was first delivered to a meeting of the French Philosophical Society in 1968. He begins by noting that the French term *différer* can mean both 'to differ' and 'to defer' (English, of course, uses two separate verbs):

> On the one hand, it indicates difference as distinction, inequality, or discernibility; on the other, it expresses the interposition of delay, the interval of a *spacing* and *temporalizing* that puts off until 'later' what is presently denied, the possible that is presently impossible. . . .
>
> In the one case 'to differ' signifies non-identity; in the other case it signifies the order of the *same*. Yet there must

> be a common, although entirely differant [*différante*], root within the sphere that relates the two movements of differing to one another. We provisionally give the name *differance* to this *sameness* which is not *identical*: by the silent writing of its *a*, it has the desired advantage of referring to differing, *both* as spacing/temporalizing and as the movement that structures every dissociation.[14]

Meaning depends upon difference, but also upon deferral. The signifier *defers* the full presence of the signified because the trace of other signifiers can never be wholly without:

> Differance is what makes the movement of signification possible only if each element that is said to be 'present', appearing on the stage of presence, is related to something other than itself but retains the mark of a past element and already lets itself be hollowed out by the mark of its relation to a future element.[15]

But if meaning depends upon the trace, upon differance (with an 'a'), it does not follow that differance (with an 'a') can truly be called the origin of meaning, for this would require it to be something that can be made present. Differance (with an 'a'), Derrida concludes, 'never presents itself as such. It is never given in the present or to anyone.'[16] It eludes the mastery of the signifying subject, even as it makes the signification of that subject possible. It is 'neither a *word* nor a *concept*',[17] neither a presence nor an absence: it exceeds, or deconstructs, such oppositions. Without differance (with an 'a'), there would be no meaning. But differance (with an 'a') shadows every moment of meaning with the trace of the other.

This, of course, makes a world of differance (with an 'a') to the relationship between the human and the extraterrestrial that lies at the heart of Alien Chic. Humanism would insist that the two categories are entirely and naturally distinct, but I propose that, rather than the human and the alien being absolutely different from each other, they actually inhabit a scene of differance (with an 'a'). The meaning of each term depends upon the trace of the other. The human forever differs from itself, finds its moment of plenitude and perfect presence deferred by the trace that nonetheless calls it into being.

In his fine book, *High Technē*, R. L. Rutsky suggests that '[a] posthuman subject position would . . . acknowledge the otherness that is part of us',[18] and I merely want to add that this otherness has *always* been part of 'us', parting 'us' from 'ourselves'. Posthumanism, as I see it, is the acknowledgement and activation of the trace of the inhuman within the human. In the end, absolute difference is abducted by differance (with an 'a'). In the end, 'Man' secretes the other within. In the end, close encounters are constitutive, and invasion is inescapable. In the end, humanism finds itself a little alien.

Notes

INTRODUCTION: THEY ALL LAUGHED

1 Ella Fitzgerald, 'They all laughed', *Ella Fitzgerald Sings the George and Ira Gershwin Songbook*, Verve Records, 1959.

2 Although its credits give a copyright date of 1955, the film was not actually released until early 1956. The larger history of the alien invasion films of the post-war years has been written about at length elsewhere, and I do not intend to repeat it here. See, for instance, Patrick Lucanio, *Them or Us: Archetypal Interpretations of Fifties Alien Invasion Films*, Bloomington and Indianapolis: Indiana University Press, 1987; Bill Warren, *Keep Watching the Skies! American Science Fiction Movies of the Fifties*, Jefferson, NC: McFarland, 1997; Brian Murphy, 'Monster movies: They came from beneath the fifties', *Journal of Popular Film*, 1972, vol. 1.1, pp. 31–44; Peter Biskind, *Seeing is Believing: How Hollywood Taught Us to Stop Worrying and Love the Fifties*, New York: Pantheon, 1983.

3 Nancy Steffen-Fluhr, 'Women and the inner game of Don Siegel's *Invasion of the Body Snatchers*', *Science-Fiction Studies*, 1984, vol. 11.2, p. 139.

4 For a fascinating collection of post-production documents, see Al LaValley (ed.) *Invasion of the Body Snatchers: Don Siegel, Director*, New Brunswick, NJ and London: Rutgers University Press, 1989, pp. 123–47.

5 Walter Benjamin, 'The author as producer', in *Understanding Brecht*, trans. Anna Bostock, London: New Left Books, 1973, p. 101.

6 Karl Marx, 'The Eighteenth Brumaire of Louis Bonaparte', in *Surveys from Exile: Political Writings, Volume 2*, ed. David Fernbach, Harmondsworth: Penguin, 1973, p. 146.

7 Neil Badmington (ed.) *Posthumanism*, Basingstoke and New York: Palgrave, 2000. I have recounted this coincidence on many occasions, and have often been asked if I have made up, or even 'sexed up', this curious chain of events. The narrative does, I readily admit, seem slightly fantastic,

a little too much of a convenient coincidence. It is, however, a true story, and this is precisely where my interest in Alien Chic began. Strange coincidences happen, and, like laughter, can often serve as the beginning of an unforeseen adventure. In fact, while putting the finishing touches to this introduction, I happened to reread one of Paul Auster's non-fiction books, in which the author – whose tales so often revolve around chance – tells his interviewers that he sees his job as being driven by an obligation 'to keep [himself] open to these collisions, to watch out for all these mysterious goings-on in the world' (Paul Auster, 'Interview with Larry McCaffery and Sinda Gregory', in *The Red Notebook and Other Writings*, London and Boston: Faber and Faber, 1996, p. 119). I feel much the same about cultural criticism, and *Alien Chic* will have a great deal more to say about 'mysterious goings-on in the world' and in the skies.

8 Jacques Derrida, *Dissemination*, trans. Barbara Johnson, London: Athlone, 1981, p. 25. Emphasis and capitalization in original. I shall return to Derrida's 'Crisis of *versus*' throughout this book, preserving the capital letter and the italics throughout. It should be noted, of course, that the 'Crisis of *versus*' is an allusion to Mallarmé's famous 'crisis of verse'.

9 As I was writing this introduction, the British press reported that alien contact lenses might, in fact, cause permanent damage to the wearer's eyes. See, for instance, Robin McKie, '"Alien" lenses put young eyes at risk', *Observer*, 9 November 2003, p. 11.

10 Raël, *Let's Welcome the Extra-Terrestrials: They Genetically Engineered All Life on Earth – Including Us!*, London and Los Angeles: Tagman Press, 2002. I am indebted to Jessica Mordsley for first bringing the Raëlians to my attention.

11 Erich von Däniken, *Chariots of the Gods? Unsolved Mysteries of the Past*, trans. Michael Heron, London: Corgi, 1971.

12 See, in particular, Raël, *The True Face of God*, Geneva: The Raëlian Foundation, 1998, pp. 19–78.

13 Ibid., p. 207. For artists' impressions of what the embassy will look like, see pp. 108–9.

14 Ibid., p. 184.

15 Jodi Dean, *Aliens in America: Conspiracy Cultures from Outerspace to Cyberspace*, Ithaca and London: Cornell University Press, 1998, p. 182. Emphasis in original.

16 Available: <http://www.sextoy.com> (accessed – not, I should add, from a Cardiff University computer – 12 December 2003).

17 Tom Wolfe, 'Radical Chic', in *Radical Chic and Mau-Mauing the Flak Catchers*, London: Cardinal, 1989, p. 86.

18 Ibid., p. 6.

19 Ibid., p. 11. Emphases in original.

20 Ibid., p. 40.
21 See, in particular, ibid., pp. 26–7.
22 Ibid., p. 37.
23 Ibid., pp. 6, 7.
24 Ibid., p. 31.
25 Ibid., p. 21.
26 Ibid., p. 91. Wolfe explains '*nostalgie de la boue*' in the following manner: '[It] is a nineteenth-century French term that means, literally, "nostalgia for the mud"' (p. 32).
27 Tony Davies, *Humanism*, London and New York: Routledge, 1997, p. 2. As Davies notes on the previous page of his book, Lewis Carroll's Humpty Dumpty memorably declares: 'When *I* use a word . . . it means just what I choose it to mean – neither more nor less.'
28 René Descartes, *Discourse on the Method of Rightly Conducting One's Reason and Seeking the Truth in the Sciences*, in *Descartes: Selected Philosophical Writings*, ed. and trans. John Cottingham, Robert Stoothoff and Dugald Murdoch, Cambridge and New York: Cambridge University Press, 1988, p. 21.
29 Ibid., p. 20.
30 Ibid., p. 36. I have modified the translation here in order to preserve the more familiar rendering of Descartes's most famous phrase. For the original French wording, see René Descartes, *Discours de la méthode pour bien conduire sa raison et chercher la vérité dans les sciences*, Paris: Bordas, 1984, p. 100.
31 The two terms, as John Cottingham has pointed out, are synonymous in Cartesian thought. John Cottingham, 'Cartesian dualism: Theology, metaphysics, and science', in John Cottingham (ed.) *The Cambridge Companion to Descartes*, Cambridge: Cambridge University Press, 1992, p. 236.
32 Descartes, *Discourse on the Method*, p. 36. Translation modified. For the original French wording, see Descartes, *Discours de la méthode*, pp. 100–2.
33 René Descartes, *Meditations on First Philosophy in which are Demonstrated the Existence of God and the Distinction Between the Human Soul and the Body*, in *Descartes: Selected Philosophical Writings*, ed. and trans. John Cottingham, Robert Stoothoff and Dugald Murdoch, Cambridge and New York: Cambridge University Press, p. 120.
34 Descartes, *Discourse on the Method*, pp. 44–5. Translation modified. For the original French wording, see Descartes, *Discours de la méthode*, pp. 134–5. I thank Jean-Jacques Lecercle for his assistance with the French text at this point.
35 'Man', of course, is a deeply problematic term, and it is for this reason that I place it within quotation marks throughout.
36 *The X-Files* was first aired in the United States on 10 September 1993. The films that make up the quartet are: *Alien* (dir. Ridley Scott, 1979), *Aliens*

(dir. James Cameron, 1986), *Alien 3* (dir. David Fincher, 1992), and *Alien Resurrection* (dir. Jean-Pierre Jeunet, 1997).

37 See, for instance, David Lavery, Angela Hague and Marla Cartwright (eds) *'Deny All Knowledge': Reading The X-Files*, London: Faber and Faber, 1996; Daniel Leonard Bernardi, *Star Trek and History: Race-ing Toward a White Future*, New Brunswick, NJ: Rutgers University Press, 1998; Barbara Creed, '*Alien* and the monstrous feminine', in Annette Kuhn (ed.) *Alien Zone: Cultural Theory and Contemporary Science Fiction Cinema*, London and New York: Verso, 1990, pp. 128–41.

38 There were two subsequent versions of the film: *The Special Edition* (1980), which, although a little shorter, took the viewer inside the spaceship, and the *Collector's Edition* (1997), which was something of a hybrid of the two earlier cuts.

39 Bob Balaban, *Close Encounters of the Third Kind Diary*, New York: Paradise Press, 1978, p. 39. Balaban's book offers a fascinating account of the making of the film, in which the author played the character of David Laughlin.

40 Matthew Arnold, *Culture and Anarchy: An Essay in Political and Social Criticism*, in *Culture and Anarchy and Other Writings*, ed. Stefan Collini, Cambridge: Cambridge University Press, 1993, p. 59. Emphasis in original.

41 See, in particular, the first chapter of Clifford Geertz, *The Interpretation of Cultures*, New York: Basic Books, 1973.

42 'Sweetness and light' is the title of chapter 1 of Arnold's *Culture and Anarchy*.

43 The most convincing account of cultural criticism that I have heard is Catherine Belsey, 'Made in Cardiff: The case for cultural criticism', a paper delivered at Cardiff University on 17 December 2003.

1 READING THE RED PLANET; OR, LITTLE GREEN MEN AT WORK

1 Van Morrison, 'Bein' green', *Hard Nose the Highway*, Warner Brothers Records, 1973.

2 For more information about the Herschel Museum, see <http://www.bath-preservation-trust.org.uk/museums/herschel> (accessed 12 December 2003).

3 Figures taken from Tim Radford, 'Red mist: Earth's neighbour passes by', *Guardian*, 28 August 2003, p. 11.

4 Fred Hoyle and Chandra Wickramasinghe, *Life on Mars? The Case for a Cosmic Heritage*, Bristol: Clinical Press, 1997, p. 8.

5 For the original novel, which was first published in 1898, see H. G. Wells, *The War of the Worlds*, New York: Berkley, 1964.

6 For a detailed account of the panic caused by the broadcast, see Hadley Cantril, *The Invasion from Mars: A Study in the Psychology of Panic*, Princeton: Princeton University Press, 1940. Cantril's fascinating book also reproduces the radio script in full.

7 Ibid., p. 4.

8 For a concise summary of these, see Simon Callow, *Orson Welles: The Road to Xanadu*, London: Jonathan Cape, 1995, pp. 401–3.

9 Ibid., p. 403.

10 Information about the aftermath of the broadcast is taken from Callow, *Orson Welles*, p. 404.

11 Ibid., p. 407.

12 Although the opening credits give a copyright date of 1952, the film was not actually released until October 1953. Since finishing this book, I have discovered that Steven Spielberg is to direct a new film version of H. G. Wells's tale. For more information, see Dan Glaister, 'Spielberg and Cruise plan new War of the Worlds', *Guardian*, 18 March 2004, p. 12.

13 I mention this fact simply because many of the B-movies of the 1950s (and not simply those that fell within the genre of science fiction) were produced at remarkable speed. As Thomas Doherty relates, Roger Corman, for one, took great pride in his rate of production, managing at one point to write, film *and* release a film about the Sputnik incident within eight weeks of the actual event (Thomas Doherty, *Teenagers and Teenpics: The Juvenilization of American Movies in the 1950s*, Boston: Unwin Hyman, 1988, p. 8). Many of the less expensive B-movies were, of course, shot in black and white.

14 See, for instance: Father Collins's slow march towards the invaders; several of the romantic scenes involving Forester and Sylvia; the ominous shot of a lone soldier silhouetted upon a tank; General Mann's revelation about the breakdown in communication that occurs whenever the Martians invade a given area; and the hero's lonely run through the devastated streets of Los Angeles. Many of these shots are also close-ups, further emphasizing their dramatic import. Parts of several shots not included in my figure of 82 briefly feature a sole human presence, before allowing other characters to enter the frame (see, for instance, the scene near the beginning of the film, in which a fire-fighter relays news about the crash site to headquarters).

15 It is not clear whether this sound is diegetic or extra-diegetic, but I am inclined to believe it to be the latter, simply because I find it hard to believe that, in the middle of the destruction of the city, a highly-polished team of campanologists would be waiting to spring into action.

16 Patrick Lucanio, *Them or Us: Archetypical Interpretations of Fifties Alien Invasion Films*, Bloomington and Indianapolis: Indiana University Press, 1987, pp. 117–18.

17 Ibid., p. 121.

18 Christopher Frayling, *Things to Come*, London: BFI Publishing, 1995, p. 28.
19 As this brief plot summary probably makes clear, Cahn's film exerts a strong influence upon Ridley Scott's *Alien*.
20 A poster produced by the studio to publicize the film promised, courtesy of a 'world-renowned insurance company', $50,000 to 'the first person who can prove "IT" is not on Mars now'. While a small colour reproduction of the poster can be found on the case of the Region 1 DVD of the film, a much clearer black and white image is printed in Lucanio, *Them or Us*, p. 80.
21 This gesture is symbolically repeated at the end of the film, when the monster has finally been defeated.
22 There is a sense in which *The War of the Worlds*, *Invaders from Mars*, and *It! The Terror from Beyond Space*, like many other alien invasion narratives of the period, are about an assertion of specifically American values, rather than those of the entire human race. In his essay, 'Monster movies', Brian Murphy offers a lucid discussion of *Them!* (dir. Gordon Douglas, 1954), in which he suggests that the film is really about the might and resilience of the United States, clearly 'the only fit adversary for such an enemy' ('Monster movies: They came from beneath the fifties', *Journal of Popular Film*, 1972, vol. 1.1, p. 41). But there is, I think, a sense in which Murphy misses the point, for while there might appear to be something exclusive about a film that, quite typically, narrates a struggle involving 'all of America *but only America*' (p. 41; emphasis added), it seems to me that the United States comes to stand for *the whole human race*. Beyond the evident parochialism lies humanism, for if the United States represents the entire human race, the entire human race is nonetheless represented. I am not for one moment supporting this metonymy, this sleight of hand; I merely wish to note its effect.
23 Henri Bergson, 'Laughter', in Wylie Sypher (ed.) *Comedy*, Baltimore and London: Johns Hopkins University Press, 1980, p. 62. Emphasis in original. I thank Martin A. Kayman for pointing me in the direction of Bergson (and for regularly making me laugh).
24 Ibid., p. 79. Emphasis in original.
25 Ibid., p. 85.
26 Ibid., p. 72.
27 Ibid., p. 73. Emphasis in original.
28 Ibid.
29 Ibid., p. 85. Emphasis in original.
30 Ray Bradbury, *The Martian Chronicles*, New York: Bantam, 1979.
31 Kim Stanley Robinson, *Red Mars*, New York: Bantam, 1993; *Green Mars*, New York: Bantam, 1994; and *Blue Mars*, New York: Bantam, 1996. For

related material, see Kim Stanley Robinson, *The Martians*, New York: Bantam, 2000.

32 For more information, see <http://www.moonestates.com> (accessed 12 December 2003). At the time of writing, one acre of Mars is available for £19.99 (the price includes the title deed, constitution, property map, mineral rights, and a declaration of ownership). The company also offers plots of land on the Moon and Venus.

33 The laws, articulated with particular clarity in a short story published in 1942, are as follows: (1) A robot may not injure a human being, or, through inaction, allow a human being to come to harm; (2) A robot must obey the orders given it by human beings except where such orders would conflict with the First Law; (3) A robot must protect its own existence as long as such protection does not conflict with the First or Second Laws (Isaac Asimov, 'Runaround', in *The Complete Robot*, London: Granada, 1982, pp. 257–79).

34 Robert A. Heinlein, *Starship Troopers*, New York: Ace, 1987. Heinlein's novel, first published in 1959, was released as a film, under the same title and the direction of Paul Verhoeven, in 1997. I shall return to the latter in the following chapter.

35 It would be impossible to catalogue exhaustively De Palma's recycling here. I will, therefore, limit myself to the following examples: *Obsession* (1976), *Dressed to Kill* (1980) and *Body Double* (1984) recall Alfred Hitchcock's *Vertigo* (1958), *Psycho* (1960) and *Rear Window* (1954), respectively; *Blow Out* (1981) reworks both *Blow-Up* (dir. Michelangelo Antonioni, 1966) and *The Conversation* (dir. Francis Ford Coppola, 1974) in the wake of Watergate and Chappaquiddick; and, perhaps most infamously, *The Untouchables* (1987) features an audacious homage to the Odessa Steps sequence of *Battleship Potemkin* (dir. Sergei Eisenstein, 1925).

36 Kubrick's film, of course, has very little to do with Mars, for the destination of the *Discovery I* is Jupiter.

37 For more information about the 'Mars rock', including photographic evidence, see <http://www-curator.jsc.nasa.gov/curator/antmet/marsmets/alh84001/sample.htm> (accessed 17 October 2003).

38 The opening continuous meander through the barbecue gathering is the most extreme example of this tendency.

39 The effect of transformation of the human into information is one of the principal themes of N. Katherine Hayles, *How We Became Posthuman: Virtual Bodies in Cybernetics, Literature, and Informatics*, Chicago and London: University of Chicago Press, 1999.

40 Elaine L. Graham, *Representations of the Post/Human: Monsters, Aliens and Others in Popular Culture*, Manchester: Manchester University Press, 2002, p. 118.

41 *Mission to Mars* premiered in the United States on 6 March 2000. I should like to thank Richard Vine for providing me with this piece of information. Subsequently, in April 2003, it was announced that the entire human gene had finally been mapped to an accuracy of 99.999 per cent. See Tim Radford, 'Human code fully cracked', *Guardian*, 14 April 2003, p. 8.
42 Jean Baudrillard, 'The final solution: Cloning beyond the human and inhuman', in *The Vital Illusion*, New York: Columbia University Press, 2000, pp. 22–3. Emphases in original.
43 Ibid., p. 16.
44 I am alluding to Sigmund Freud, 'The dissection of the psychical personality', in *New Introductory Lectures on Psychoanalysis*, ed. James Strachey and Angela Richards, trans. James Strachey, Penguin Freud Library, vol. 2, Harmondsworth: Penguin, 1973, p. 112: 'Where id was, there ego shall be.'

2 IT LIVES; OR, THE PERSISTENCE OF HUMANISM

1 Paul Auster, *In the Country of Last Things*, London: Faber and Faber, 1989, p. 28.
2 Kate Soper, *Humanism and Anti-Humanism*, London: Hutchinson, 1986, p. 99. Soper's book offers a fine overview of what was at stake, and also what was not always addressed, in anti-humanist thinking.
3 Roland Barthes, 'Preface', in *Mythologies*, ed. and trans. Annette Lavers, London: Vintage, 1993, p. 11. Translation modified. For the original French wording, see Roland Barthes, 'Avant-propos', in *Mythologies*, Paris: Seuil, 1957, p. 9. The English text is a substantial abridgment of the original French edition. For unspecified reasons, Annette Lavers selected just 29 of the original 55 pieces for her translation, which first appeared in 1972. With one exception, the remaining pieces can be found in Roland Barthes, *The Eiffel Tower and Other Mythologies*, trans. Richard Howard, Berkeley, Los Angeles and London: University of California Press, 1979. To the best of my knowledge, 'Astrologie' (*Mythologies*, French edition, pp. 165–8), a delightful critique of horoscopes, remains unavailable in English.
4 Between November 2002 and March 2003, visitors to the Centre Georges Pompidou in Paris could see and touch many of the objects scrutinized by Barthes in *Mythologies* (including a Citroën DS, somehow transported to the fifth floor of the museum), as part of an exhibition devoted to his life and work.
5 Edward Steichen, quoted in Penelope Niven, *Steichen: A Biography*, New York: Clarkson Potter, 1997, p. 633.

6 Eric J. Sandeen, *Picturing an Exhibition: The Family of Man and 1950s America*, Albuquerque, NM: University of New Mexico Press, 1995, p. 41.
7 Edward Steichen, quoted in Sandeen, *Picturing an Exhibition*, p. 41.
8 Edward Steichen, 'Introduction', in *The Family of Man*, New York: Museum of Modern Art, 1986, p. 3.
9 Niven, *Steichen*, p. 650.
10 Ibid., p. 654. By 1978, the book of the exhibition had sold in excess of 4 million copies. Sandeen, *Picturing an Exhibition*, p. 386.
11 Barthes, 'The Great Family of Man', in *Mythologies*, p. 101. Translation modified. For the original wording, see Roland Barthes, 'La Grande Famille des hommes', in *Mythologies*, p. 174.
12 Barthes, 'The Great Family of Man', p. 100.
13 Barthes, 'Myth today', in *Mythologies*, p. 143.
14 Barthes, 'The Great Family of Man', p. 102.
15 Barthes, 'Martians', in *The Eiffel Tower and Other Mythologies*, p. 28. Translation modified. For the original wording, see Barthes, 'Martiens', in *Mythologies*, p. 43.
16 Barthes, 'Martians', p. 29. Emphasis in original. Translation modified. For the original wording, see Barthes, 'Martiens', p. 44.
17 Barthes, 'The Great Family of Man', p. 101.
18 Roland Barthes, *Writing Degree Zero*, trans. Annette Lavers and Colin Smith, New York: Hill and Wang, 1968, p. 2.
19 Barthes, 'The Great Family of Man', p. 101.
20 *Mythologies* dates from near the beginning of Barthes's career, and some of his later texts are implicitly more willing to distance themselves from all forms of humanism. I am thinking of works such as *S/Z*, trans. Richard Miller, London: Jonathan Cape, 1975; *The Pleasure of the Text*, trans. Richard Miller, Oxford: Blackwell, 1990; and *Empire of Signs*, trans. Richard Howard, New York: Hill and Wang, 1982.
21 Translated into English as: *The Raw and the Cooked*, trans. John and Doreen Weightman, London: Jonathan Cape, 1970; *From Honey to Ashes*, trans. John and Doreen Weightman, London: Jonathan Cape, 1973; *The Origin of Table Manners*, trans. John and Doreen Weightman, London: Jonathan Cape, 1978; and *The Naked Man*, trans. John and Doreen Weightman, London: Jonathan Cape, 1981.
22 Ferdinand de Saussure, *Course in General Linguistics*, ed. Charles Bally, Albert Sechehaye and Albert Reidlinger, trans. Wade Baskin, London: Fontana, 1974.
23 Roland Barthes, 'Preface to the 1970 edition (Collection "Points", Le Seuil, Paris)', in *Mythologies*, p. 9.
24 Claude Lévi-Strauss, *Tristes Tropiques*, trans. John and Doreen Weightman, New York: Penguin, 1992, p. 55.

25 The description of existentialism as a humanism belongs to Sartre himself. See, in particular, *L'Existentialisme est un humanisme*, Paris: Nagel, 1946. For some inexplicable reason, the English translation was given the title *Existentialism and Humanism* (trans. Philip Mairet, London: Methuen, 1997).
26 Jean-Paul Sartre, *What is Literature?*, trans. Bernard Frechtman, London: Methuen, 1950.
27 *Writing Degree Zero* contains just three explicit (yet passing) references to Sartre, none of which concerns *What is Literature?* The first (p. 26) alludes to the style of writing found in Sartre's journal, *Les Temps modernes*; the second (p. 61) merely lists Sartre's name alongside various other authors; and the third (p. 85) consists of approximately half of a paragraph devoted to Sartre's fiction.
28 Claude Lévi-Strauss, *The Savage Mind*, trans. unnamed, London: Weidenfeld and Nicolson, 1972, p. 245.
29 Ibid., p. 247.
30 Lévi-Strauss, *Tristes Tropiques*, p. 58. Once again, Lévi-Strauss is attacking existentialism at this point in the text.
31 Althusser discusses Marx's relationship to Hegel at more length in 'On Marx's relation to Hegel', in *Politics and History: Rousseau, Hegel and Marx*, trans. Ben Brewster, London: New Left Books, 1972, pp. 161–86.
32 Louis Althusser, 'Marxism and humanism', in *For Marx*, trans. Ben Brewster, London and New York: Verso, 1996, p. 227. Emphases in original. Translation modified. For the original French, see Louis Althusser, 'Marxisme et humanisme', in *Pour Marx*, Paris: La Découverte, 1996, pp. 233–4. For some reason, Brewster casts this passage in the past tense, when Althusser actually writes in the present. In time, Althusser would back away a little from understanding the break of 1845 as clean and absolute. See, for instance, Louis Althusser, 'The humanist controversy', in *The Humanist Controversy and Other Writings (1966–67)*, ed. François Matheron, trans. G. M. Goshgarian, London and New York: Verso, 2003, pp. 267–70.
33 Althusser, 'Marxism and humanism', p. 229.
34 Ibid. Emphases in original. Translation modified. For the original French wording, see Althusser, 'Marxisme et humanisme', p. 236. For an echo of the final sentence here, see Althusser, 'The humanist controversy', p. 259: 'Man is an irrational, derisory, hollow notion, which, because it is ideological, is by its very nature incapable of explaining anything whatsoever, but has itself to be explained.'
35 Althusser, 'Marxism and humanism', p. 227.
36 Ibid., p. 236: 'We are now in a position to return to the theme of socialist humanism and to give an account of the theoretical disparity we noted

between a scientific term (socialism) and an ideological term (humanism).' Translation modified. For the original French wording, see Althusser, 'Marxisme et humanisme', p. 243.

37 Althusser, 'The humanist controversy', p. 266.

38 Louis Althusser, 'Reply to John Lewis (self-criticism)', in *Essays in Self-Criticism*, trans. Grahame Lock, London: New Left Books, 1976, pp. 52–3. Emphases in original.

39 Jean Baudrillard, *Cool Memories*, trans. Chris Turner, London and New York: Verso, 1990, p. 160.

40 For an abridged translation, see *Madness and Civilization: A History of Insanity in the Age of Reason*, trans. Richard Howard, London: Routledge and Kegan Paul, 1971. At the time of writing, no complete English translation of *Folie et déraison* exists.

41 Jacques Derrida, 'Cogito and the history of madness', in *Writing and Difference*, trans. Alan Bass, London: Routledge and Kegan Paul, 1978, p. 31. Derrida has returned to Foucault's book in the more recent essay, '"To do justice to Freud": The history of madness in the age of psychoanalysis', in *Resistances of Psychoanalysis*, trans Peggy Kamuf, Pascale-Anne Brault and Michael Naas, Stanford: Stanford University Press, 1998, pp. 70–118.

42 David Macey, *The Lives of Michel Foucault*, London: Vintage, 1994, p. 144.

43 Ibid., p. 143.

44 Derrida, 'Cogito and the history of madness', pp. 33–4. Emphases in original.

45 Ibid., p. 34. Emphasis in original.

46 Ibid., p. 35. Emphasis in original.

47 Ibid., p. 36.

48 Macey, *The Lives of Michel Foucault*, p. 144.

49 Ibid., pp. 144–5.

50 Michel Foucault, 'My body, this paper, this fire', trans. Geoffrey Bennington, *Oxford Literary Review*, 1979, vol. 4.1, pp. 9–28.

51 Foucault, 'My body', p. 27.

52 Ibid., p. 18.

53 Ibid., p. 26.

54 Ibid., p. 27. Emphasis in original. Translation slightly modified. For the original French wording, see Michel Foucault, 'Mon corps, ce papier, ce feu', in *Dits et Écrits 1954–1988*, 4 vols, ed. Daniel Defert, François Ewald and Jacques Lagrange, Paris: Gallimard, 1994, vol. 2, p. 267. I thank Laurent Milesi for his assistance with the French text here.

55 Foucault, incidentally, returns the 'compliment' in 'My body', p. 23: 'Derrida's hypothesis is a seductive one.'

56 It is also, perhaps, undesirable, for, as Derrida has more recently noted, '[t]eleology is, at bottom, the negation of the future, a way of knowing beforehand the form that will have to be taken by what is still to come' (Jacques Derrida, '"I have a taste for the secret"', in Jacques Derrida and Maurizio Ferraris, *A Taste for the Secret*, ed. Giacomo Donis and David Webb, trans. Giacomo Donis, Cambridge: Polity, 2001, p. 20). To claim the past to be a closed book is, precisely, to adopt a decidedly closed view of things. The decision has been made, the break has occurred, the Truth has been spoken.

57 Jacques Derrida, 'Implications: Interview with Henri Ronse', in *Positions*, trans. Alan Bass, Chicago: University of Chicago Press, 1981, p. 12.

58 Michel Foucault, *The Order of Things: An Archaeology of the Human Sciences*, trans. unnamed, London: Tavistock, 1970, p. 387.

59 Sigmund Freud, 'A note upon the "Mystic writing-pad"', in *On Metapsychology: The Theory of Psychoanalysis*, ed. Angela Richards, trans. James Strachey, Penguin Freud Library, vol. 11, Harmondsworth: Penguin, 1991, pp. 427–34.

60 Shyamalan's film recycles more than just *The War of the Worlds*, in fact: there are clear allusions to *The Birds* (dir. Alfred Hitchcock, 1963) and *Night of the Living Dead* (dir. George A. Romero, 1968) scattered throughout the narrative. But it is Haskin's film, I think, that casts the longest shadow of all.

61 This, I think, is one of the moments at which the debt to *Night of the Living Dead* is particularly clear, for, in Romero's film, a small group of humans is eventually forced to take refuge from the invading zombies in the basement of a farmhouse.

62 Information taken from Michael Rogin, *Independence Day, or How I Learned to Stop Worrying and Love the Enola Gay*, London: BFI Publishing 1998, p. 12.

63 Ibid.

64 Bill Clinton, quoted in Rogin, *Independence Day*, p. 9.

65 Bob Dole, quoted in Rogin, *Independence Day*, p. 12.

66 Vivian Sobchack, 'Cities on the edge of time: The urban science-fiction film', in Annette Kuhn (ed.) *Alien Zone II: The Spaces of Science-Fiction Cinema*, London and New York: Verso, 1999, p. 139. As the date of publication of this essay makes clear, Sobchack's allusion to urban terrorism in New York is not a reference to the events of 11 September 2001. She is, rather, probably thinking of the attack upon the World Trade Center that took place in February 1993.

67 Ibid., p. 139.

68 *Independence Day* opened in Canada on 2 July 1996, and in the United States, Jamaica, and Puerto Rico on the following day. *Mars Attacks!* was

first released in the United States and Canada on 13 December 1996. Information taken from The Internet Movie Database. Available <http://us.imdb.com> (accessed 13 December 2003).

69 This wonderful piece of information is revealed by Dean Devlin, the film's producer, in the audio commentary that he and Roland Emmerich provide for the Region 2 DVD version of the film.

70 There have been two previous incidents of alien hostility, in which American military aircraft were shot from the sky, but this is the first terrestrial attack.

71 Dean Devlin, quoted in Rogin, *Independence Day*, p. 28.

72 Ibid., pp. 54–6 (p. 55 is a colour plate). There is also, I would add, a certain visual fidelity to William Cameron Menzies's film in both of these moments, for the shield that protects the invaders is an identical shade of green.

73 Ibid., p. 57. In the Region 2 DVD audio commentary, Dean Devlin openly acknowledges the debt: 'This, of course, is our allusion to the ending of *War of the Worlds*, when the alien invaders were killed by the common cold. And Roland [Emmerich] and I, when we were writing [*Independence Day*], we thought, "Well, what would be the modern equivalent?" And we thought the modern equivalent would be the computer virus.' Michael Rogin's reference to 'Jewish hypochondria' might seem a little strange when this particular passage is read out of context, but his book is elsewhere concerned (particularly in chapter 4, which is entitled 'Multiculturalism') with David Levinson's status as a Jew in the narrative.

74 Ibid., p. 57.

75 Jodi Dean, *Aliens in America: Conspiracy Cultures from Outerspace to Cyberspace*, Ithaca and London: Cornell University Press, 1998, p. 29.

76 Rogin, *Independence Day*, p. 39.

77 For a useful overview of the incident and its aftermath, see Tim Shawcross, *The Roswell File*, London: Bloomsbury, 1997.

78 First aired in the United States on 21 September 1996.

79 First aired in the United States on 2 December 2002. For a brief discussion of the place of *Taken* in a culture of Alien Chic, see my 'Come on down!', *Guardian*, 11 January 2003, 'The Guide' section, pp. 4–6.

80 Information taken from the audio commentary to the Region 2 DVD of *Independence Day*.

81 Rogin, *Independence Day*, p. 38.

82 Ibid., p. 40.

83 William V. Spanos, *The End of Education: Toward Posthumanism*, Minneapolis and London: University of Minnesota Press, 1993, p. 3.

84 Jean-François Lyotard, *The Differend: Phrases in Dispute*, trans. Georges Van Den Abbeele, Manchester: Manchester University Press, 1988, p. 98. Ellipsis and emphases in original.

85 In Heinlein's novel, however, Major Reid perversely insists that the Federation operates a version of democracy: 'Superficially, our system is only slightly different [from that of an unlimited democracy]; we have democracy unlimited by race, color, creed, birth, wealth, sex, or conviction, and anyone may win sovereign power by a usually short and not too arduous term of service – nothing more than a light workout to our caveman ancestors' (Robert A. Heinlein, *Starship Troopers*, New York: Ace, 1987, p. 183).
86 Ibid., p. 26.
87 Heinlein's novel names this particular class History and Moral Philosophy.
88 Ibid., p. 92. Somewhat confusingly, Verhoeven's film renders as one what are actually two separate characters in the novel. In Heinlein's original tale, the teacher is named Mr Dubois, while the leader of Rico's platoon is Lieutenant Rasczak.
89 Walter Benjamin, 'The work of art in the age of mechanical reproduction', in *Illuminations*, ed. Hannah Arendt, trans. Harry Zohn, New York: Schocken, 1969, p. 242.
90 See, in particular, Louis Althusser, 'Ideology and ideological state apparatuses (Notes towards an investigation)', in *Lenin and Philosophy and Other Essays*, trans. Ben Brewster, New York: Monthly Review Press, 1971, pp. 127–86.
91 Heinlein, *Starship Troopers*, pp. 1, 13, 239.
92 Ibid., p. 1.
93 For a detailed description of these suits, see Heinlein, *Starship Troopers*, pp. 99–104.
94 Ibid., pp. 14–15.
95 See Manfred E. Clynes and Nathan S. Kline, 'Cyborgs and space', *Astronautics*, September 1960, pp. 26–7, 74–6.
96 Heinlein, *Starship Troopers*, p. 101.
97 Ibid., p. 100.
98 I take the concept of cyborg citizenship from Chris Hables Gray, *Cyborg Citizen: Politics in the Posthuman Age*, New York and London: Routledge, 2001.
99 Needless to say, as one critic has pointed out, this was one of the film's main selling points (Barry Keith Grant, '"Sensuous elaboration": Reason and the visible in the science-fiction film', in Annette Kuhn (ed.) *Alien Zone II: The Spaces of Science-Fiction Cinema*, London and New York: Verso, 1999, p. 27).
100 In the film, the questioner is Dizzy, one of the main characters. In Heinlein's novel, however, the dissenting voice belongs to an unidentified female student.
101 Heinlein, *Starship Troopers*, p. 26.

102 In Ted Post's film, the line – spoken by Ursus, one of the apes – is: 'The only good human is a dead human.'

103 I have not included the fourth film in the *Alien* series, *Alien Resurrection*, because it seems to me that, by placing a human-alien hybrid at the centre of the narrative, Jeunet's movie unsettles the binary opposition upon which the previous three *Alien* films rely.

104 See, in particular, Raymond Williams, 'Base and superstructure in Marxist cultural theory', in *Problems in Materialism and Culture: Selected Essays*, London: Verso, 1980, pp. 31–49.

3 I WANT TO BE LEAVING; OR, TRACKING ALIEN ABDUCTION

1 Patti Smith, 'Birdland', *Horses*, Arista Records, 1975.

2 For a novel that consistently refuses to take the phenomenon seriously, see Christopher Buckley, *Little Green Men*, London: Allison and Busby, 2001. In Buckley's book, 'alien' abductions are actually staged by MJ-12, a shadowy branch of the American government, in order to 'kee[p] the taxpaying U.S. citizenry alarmed about the possibility of invasion from outer space, and therefore happy to fund expansion of the military-aerospace complex. A country convinced that little green men were hovering over the rooftops was inclined to vote yea for big weapons and space programs' (p. 39). There are some delightfully playful moments: one character edits a magazine called *Cosmospolitan* – 'for women who've been abducted by aliens' (p. 109) – while a 'Grammy-winning sci fi/country-western singer' named Darth Brooks serenades audiences with his hit song, 'Momma don't go with little green men' (p. 227).

3 For a more detailed discussion of the relationship between alien abduction and conspiracy theory, see Jodi Dean, *Aliens in America: Conspiracy Cultures from Outerspace to Cyberspace*, Ithaca and London: Cornell University Press, 1998. Dean revisits some of the questions raised in her book in 'If anything is possible', in Peter Knight (ed.) *Conspiracy Nation: The Politics of Paranoia in Postwar America*, New York and London: New York University Press, 2002, pp. 85–106.

4 As one prominent researcher has pointed out, there is always the possibility that a person who claims to have been abducted really is psychotic. David M. Jacobs, *Alien Encounters: First-Hand Accounts of UFO Abductions*, London: Virgin Books, 1994, pp. 293–4. Jacobs's book was originally published under the title *Secret Life: First-Hand Accounts of UFO Abductions*, New York: Simon and Schuster, 1992. All subsequent references will be to the former edition.

5 Whitley Strieber, *Confirmation: The Hard Evidence of Aliens Among Us*, New York: Pocket Books, 1999, p. 200.
6 Whitley Strieber, *Communion: A True Story: Encounters with the Unknown*, London: Arrow, 1988, p. 13. I should explain at this point why Strieber's book is not more central to the present chapter. *Communion*, as its very first sentence insists, is a long and extremely detailed account of one man's attempt to deal with the implications of his encounters with extraterrestrial beings. I am more interested in the work of John E. Mack because it brings together a host of different narratives of abduction, and, moreover, asks how the phenomenon might call centuries of humanist thinking into question. Strieber has continued his study of aliens in *Transformation: The Breakthrough*, London: Century, 1988; *The Secret School: Preparation for Contact*, New York: HarperCollins, 1996; and *Confirmation*.
7 John E. Mack, *Abduction: Human Encounters with Aliens*, New York: Scribners, 1994, p. 15. Furthermore, Whitley Strieber has noted that in the decade following the publication of *Communion* he received 'nearly a quarter of a million letters claiming contact, with more than thirty thousand of them offering detailed descriptions of the encounters' (Strieber, *Confirmation*, p. 86).
8 Dean, *Aliens in America*, p. 30.
9 Elaine Showalter, *Hystories: Hysterical Epidemics and Modern Culture*, rev. edn, London: Picador, 1998, p. 194.
10 Ibid., p. 199.
11 Jacobs, *Alien Encounters*, p. 46.
12 Ibid., p. 34.
13 Ibid., p. 39. Ellipsis in original. I have restored the circumflex which Jacobs consistently omits from Villas-Boas's first name. For a transcription of Villas-Boas's deposition, which was given to Dr Olava Fontes in the presence of a journalist named João Martins, see Gordon Creighton, 'The amazing case of Antônio Villas-Boas', in D. Scott Rogo (ed.) *UFO Abductions: True Cases of Alien Kidnappings*, New York: Signet, 1980, pp. 51–85.
14 Jacobs, *Alien Encounters*, p. 39.
15 John G. Fuller, *The Interrupted Journey: Two Lost Hours Aboard a Flying Saucer*, new edn, London: Corgi, 1981, p. 36. For this revised edition, Fuller added a foreword and an important epilogue of some 50 pages to the original text of 1966.
16 Ibid., p. 37.
17 Ibid., p. 38.
18 Jacobs notes (*Alien Encounters*, p. 40) that the original edition of *The Interrupted Journey* deliberately omitted details of the sperm sample taken

from Barney Hill. There is, however, a brief, somewhat guarded allusion to the event in the new edition of Fuller's book (p. 369).

19 Fuller, *The Interrupted Journey*, p. 297.
20 See, for instance, Mack, *Abduction*, p. 13; Dean, *Aliens in America*, p. 49; Budd Hopkins, *Witnessed: The True Story of the Brooklyn Bridge UFO Abductions*, London: Bloomsbury, 1997, p. 398.
21 Budd Hopkins, *Missing Time: A Documented Study of UFO Abductions*, New York: Marek/Putnam, 1981.
22 Jacobs, *Alien Encounters*, p. 44.
23 Dean, *Aliens in America*, p. 52.
24 See, for instance, Jacobs, *Alien Encounters*, pp. 335–6; Mack, *Abduction*, pp. 1–3 (the entire book, in fact, is dedicated to Hopkins); Strieber, *Communion*, p. 17; C. D. B. Bryan, *Close Encounters of the Fourth Kind: Alien Abduction and UFOs – Witnesses and Scientists Report*, London: Orion, 1996, p. 17. Christopher Buckley's *Little Green Men* even features a UFO expert called Bart Hupkin, who is 'author of the best-selling abduction study *Plucked* . . .' (p. 105).
25 Dean, *Aliens in America*, pp. 29–30.
26 Michael Marshall Smith, *One of Us*, London: HarperCollins, 1998. I owe thanks to Robert Thomas for bringing this text to my attention.
27 Dean, *Aliens in America*, p. 18. Emphasis in original.
28 It is widely believed that the term 'flying saucer' was used for the first time in 1947. According to Jacques Vallee, however, the phrase was actually coined half a century earlier, but did not enter general circulation until 1947. Jacques Vallee, quoted in J. Allen Hynek, *The Hynek UFO Report*, London: Sphere, 1978, p. 12.
29 J. Allen Hynek, *The UFO Experience: A Scientific Inquiry*, London: Corgi, 1974, p. 117.
30 Ibid., p. 144.
31 Ibid., p. 177.
32 Ibid.
33 A close encounter of the fourth kind involves the abduction of a human subject by alien beings. For more on this, see Bryan, *Close Encounters of the Fourth Kind*. A close encounter of the fifth kind is one in which deliberate and direct communication between aliens and humans occurs. For further information about this category, see Richard F. Haines, *CE-5: The Chronicle of Human-Initiated Contact*, Naperville, IL: Sourcebooks, 1998. Christopher Buckley offers his own mischievous definition of close encounters of the fifth kind ('rough sex with aliens'), and even adds close encounters of the sixth kind (being assassinated by the American government for knowing too much about the other five types of close encounters) (Buckley, *Little Green Men*, p. 173).

34 Bryan, *Close Encounters of the Fourth Kind*, pp. 69–78, 270–311.
35 Showalter, *Hystories*, p. 199. As C. D. B. Bryan has noted, Mack's struggle against academia was actually predated by the case of Leo Sprinkle, a professor in the University of Wyoming's Counseling-Psychology Department, who, in 1989, 'was forced to resign his tenure when it became public knowledge that he claimed to have been abducted by aliens as a child' (Bryan, *Close Encounters of the Fourth Kind*, p. 193).
36 Anne Taylor, quoted in Jim Marrs, *Alien Agenda: The Untold Story of the Extraterrestrials Among Us*, London: HarperCollins, 1997, p. 229.
37 Mack was awarded a Pulitzer Prize for his book, *A Prince of Our Disorder: The Life of T. E. Lawrence*, London: Weidenfeld and Nicolson, 1976.
38 John E. Mack, *Passport to the Cosmos: Human Transformation and Alien Encounters*, London: Thorsons, 2000, p. 6. According to Clare Birchall, a young television producer named Chris Carter was so taken with Mack's work on abduction that he decided to develop a new series. This would eventually be known as *The X-Files* (Clare Birchall, 'The commodification of conspiracy theory', in Peter Knight (ed.) *Conspiracy Nation: The Politics of Paranoia in Postwar America*, New York and London: New York University Press, 2002, p. 239).
39 Mack, *Passport to the Cosmos*, p. xi.
40 Ibid., pp. 272–3.
41 Ibid., p. 103.
42 Ibid., p. 267.
43 See the final chapter of Mack, *Abduction* ('Alien intervention and human evolution'). See also Mack, *Passport to the Cosmos*, p. 275.
44 Ibid., p. 280.
45 Jacobs, *Alien Encounters*, p. 310.
46 Mack, *Abduction*, p. 39.
47 Ibid., p. 261. Emphasis in original.
48 Mack, *Passport to the Cosmos*, p. 252.
49 Mack, *Abduction*, p. 374.
50 Showalter, *Hystories*, p. 196.
51 Mack, *Abduction*, p. 404.
52 Ibid., p. 389.
53 Sigmund Freud, 'Fixation to traumas: The unconscious', in *Introductory Lectures on Psychoanalysis*, ed. James Strachey and Angela Richards, trans. James Strachey, Penguin Freud Library, vol. 1, Harmondsworth: Penguin, 1973, p. 326. Emphasis in original.
54 Charles Darwin, quoted in John Bowlby, *Charles Darwin: A Biography*, London: Hutchinson, 1990, p. 349.
55 Ernest Jones, *Sigmund Freud: Life and Work*, 3 vols, London: Hogarth Press, 1953–7, vol. 2, p. 120.

56 Ibid., p. 122.
57 Mack, *Abduction*, p. 390.
58 Ibid., p. 420. Whitley Strieber, to whom Mack refers on several occasions, also describes his encounters with extraterrestrials as 'shattering' in the opening sentence of *Communion* (p. 13). Similarly, David M. Jacobs notes that '[g]oing from a normal environment into a UFO can be a shattering experience' (Jacobs, *Alien Encounters*, p. 49).
59 Mack, *Passport to the Cosmos*, pp. 34–5.
60 Ibid., p. 277.
61 Ibid., p. 279.
62 Quoted in Jones, *Sigmund Freud: Life and Work*, vol. 3, p. 42.
63 Sigmund Freud, *Beyond the Pleasure Principle*, in *On Metapsychology: The Theory of Psychoanalysis*, ed. Angela Richards, trans. James Strachey, Penguin Freud Library, vol. 11, Harmondsworth: Penguin, 1991, pp. 269–338.
64 Jacques Derrida, 'To speculate – on "Freud"', in *The Post Card: From Socrates to Freud and Beyond*, trans. Alan Bass, Chicago and London: University of Chicago Press, 1987, p. 261. Emphasis in original.
65 Ibid., pp. 293–4.
66 'Paralysis', in fact, is the title of the third section of 'To speculate' (pp. 338–86).
67 Derrida, 'To speculate', p. 338.
68 Ibid., pp. 262 n. 6, 336 n. 48, 401 n. 9. For 'Pas' itself, see Jacques Derrida, 'Pas', in *Parages*, Paris: Galilée, 1986, pp. 19–116. I should like to thank Laurent Milesi for providing me with a copy of 'Pas'.
69 Maurice Blanchot, *Le Pas au-delà*, Paris: Gallimard, 1973. Translated into English as *The Step Not Beyond*, trans. Lycette Nelson, Albany, NY: State University of New York Press, 1992.
70 See, for instance, pp. 260, 323, 338, 344, 362.
71 The latter *faux pas* is somewhat strange. While Derrida's passing allusion to Blanchot's *Arrêt de mort* is glossed by Alan Bass in one of his translator's footnotes (p. 285 n. 17), no step is taken to treat the many echoes of *Le pas au-delà* in the same manner.
72 Maurice Blanchot, *The Writing of the Disaster*, trans. Ann Smock, Lincoln, NE: University of Nebraska Press, 1986.
73 Roger Laporte, 'Maurice Blanchot today', in Carolyn Bailey Gill (ed.) *Maurice Blanchot: The Demand of Writing*, London and New York: Routledge, 1996, p. 25.
74 Paul de Man, 'Impersonality in the criticism of Maurice Blanchot', in *Blindness and Insight: Essays in the Rhetoric of Contemporary Criticism*, 2nd edn, Minneapolis: University of Minnesota Press, 1983, p. 62.
75 Derrida, 'Pas', p. 51. I have left the titles of Blanchot's texts in French in order to preserve the '*pas*'. For English translations, see *Faux Pas*, trans.

Charlotte Mandell, Stanford: Stanford University Press, 2001; *The Work of Fire*, trans. Charlotte Mandell, Stanford: Stanford University Press, 1995; *The Space of Literature*, trans. Ann Smock, Lincoln, NE: University of Nebraska Press, 1982.

76 Translated into English as *The One Who Was Standing Apart from Me*, trans. Lydia Davis, Barrytown, NY: Station Hill Press, 1992.

77 Derrida, 'Pas', p. 52. As ever, Derrida's text is working on many levels here. The '*o*', I think, is a step back towards an earlier moment in 'Pas', where '*eau*' becomes '*o*', a homonym that flows into a zero, a nothingness (p. 41). Beyond that, it is possible to hear an echo of Alan Bass's remark about *au-delà* being 'the homonym of *aux-deux-là*, "to those two", those two being, for example, Plato and Socrates, or Freud and Heidegger, or any of the "odd couples" to be found throughout the "Envois"' (Derrida, *The Post Card*, p. xvi).

78 Budd Hopkins, *Intruders: The Incredible Visitations at Copley Woods*, New York: Random House, 1987.

79 Mack, *Passport to the Cosmos*, p. 112. Emphasis in original. See also Jacobs, *Alien Encounters*, particularly chapter 5; Bryan, *Close Encounters of the Fourth Kind*, *passim*. The phenomenon also lay at the heart of *Taken*, the successful television mini-series, and has featured in many episodes of *The X-Files*. To travel back a little further in time, I have a vivid memory of encountering my first fictional human-alien hybrid in '*V*', the popular television series that offered a welcome escape from coverage of the Olympic Games in 1984.

80 Octavia E. Butler, *Dawn*, New York: Warner Books, 1987; *Adulthood Rites*, New York: Warner Books, 1988; *Imago*, New York: Warner Books, 1989.

81 See, for instance, Donna J. Haraway, 'A cyborg manifesto: Science, technology, and socialist-feminism in the late twentieth century', in *Simians, Cyborgs, and Women: The Reinvention of Nature*, London: Free Association Books, 1991, pp. 149–81; Gloria Anzaldúa, *Borderlands/La Frontera: The New Mestiza*, San Francisco: Aunt Lute Books, 1987; Paul Gilroy, *The Black Atlantic: Modernity and Double Consciousness*, London and New York: Verso, 1993.

82 Mack, *Passport to the Cosmos*, p. 129.

83 Jacobs, *Alien Encounters*, p. 305. Emphasis in original.

84 Mack, *Passport to the Cosmos*, pp. 128–9.

85 Ibid., p. 128.

86 Strieber, *Communion*, p. 76. Emphasis in original.

87 Ibid., p. 276.

88 Ibid., p. 225.

89 Mack, *Passport to the Cosmos*, p. 128. The choice of title is probably deliberate, as Mack's earlier book confirms Eva's knowledge of Strieber's text (Mack, *Abduction*, pp. 242–3).

90 Mack, *Abduction*, p. 293.
91 Ibid., p. 303.
92 Ibid., p. 328.
93 Ibid., p. 332.
94 Jacques Derrida, *Of Spirit: Heidegger and the Question*, trans. Geoffrey Bennington and Rachel Bowlby, Chicago and London: University of Chicago Press, 1989.
95 The English language used to contain a transitive form of the verb 'to oblique', but this seems to have become obsolete towards the end of the nineteenth century. For more on this, see Neil Badmington, 'Post, oblique, human', *Theology and Sexuality*, 2004, vol. 10.2, pp. 56–64.
96 Tom Wolfe, 'Radical Chic', in *Radical Chic and Mau-Mauing the Flak Catchers*, London: Cardinal, 1989, p. 91.
97 Ibid., pp. 34–5.
98 Ibid., p. 32–3.
99 Ibid., p. 33.
100 H. P. Blavatsky, *The Secret Doctrine: The Synthesis of Science, Religion, and Philosophy*, 2 vols, Pasadena, CA: Theosophical University Press, 1952, vol. 2, p. 684. Emphasis in original.
101 Ihab Hassan, 'Prometheus as performer: Toward a posthumanist culture? A university masque in five scenes', *The Georgia Review*, 1977, vol. 31, pp. 830–50.
102 See, for instance, Donna J. Haraway, 'Ecce homo, ain't (ar'n't) I a woman, and inappropriate/d others: The human in a post-humanist landscape', in Judith Butler and Joan W. Scott (eds) *Feminists Theorize the Political*, New York and London: Routledge, 1992, pp. 86–100; K. Michael Hays, *Modernism and the Posthumanist Subject: The Architecture of Hannes Meyer and Ludwig Hilberseimer*, Cambridge, MA and London: MIT Press, 1992; William V. Spanos, *The End of Education: Toward Posthumanism*, Minneapolis and London: University of Minnesota Press, 1993; Judith Halberstam and Ira Livingston (eds) *Posthuman Bodies*, Bloomington and Indianapolis: Indiana University Press, 1995; Thomas Foster, '"The sex appeal of the inorganic": Posthuman narratives and the construction of desire', in Robert Newman (ed.) *Centuries' Ends, Narrative Means*, Stanford: Stanford University Press, 1996, pp. 276–301; Scott McCracken, 'Cyborg fictions: The cultural logic of posthumanism', in Leo Panitch (ed.) *Socialist Register 1997*, London: Merlin, 1997, pp. 288–301; Keith Ansell Pearson, 'Life becoming body: On the "meaning" of post human evolution', *Cultural Values*, 1997, vol. 1.2, pp. 219–40; Robert Pepperell, *The Post-Human Condition*, 2nd edn, Exeter: Intellect Books, 1997; Ross Farnell, 'Posthuman topologies: William Gibson's "architexture" in *Virtual Light* and *Idoru*', *Science-Fiction Studies*, 1998, vol. 25.3, pp. 459–80;

N. Katherine Hayles, *How We Became Posthuman: Virtual Bodies in Cybernetics, Literature, and Informatics*, Chicago and London: University of Chicago Press, 1999; R. L. Rutsky, *High Technē: Art and Technology from the Machine Aesthetic to the Posthuman*, Minneapolis and London: University of Minnesota Press, 1999; Neil Badmington (ed.) *Posthumanism*, Basingstoke and New York: Palgrave, 2000; Cathy Waldby, *The Visible Human Project: Informatic Bodies and Posthuman Medicine*, London and New York: Routledge, 2000; Chris Hables Gray, *Cyborg Citizen: Politics in the Posthuman Age*, New York and London: Routledge, 2001; Elaine L. Graham, *Representations of the Post/Human: Monsters, Aliens and Others in Popular Culture*, Manchester: Manchester University Press, 2002; Amanda Fernbach, *Fantasies of Fetishism: From Decadence to the Post-Human*, Edinburgh: Edinburgh University Press, 2002; Francis Fukuyama, *Our Posthuman Future: Consequences of the Biotechnology Revolution*, London: Profile, 2002; Dominique Lecourt, *Humain, posthumain: La technique et la vie*, Paris: Presses Universitaires de France, 2003; Cary Wolfe, *Animal Rites: American Culture, the Discourse of Species, and Posthumanist Theory*, Chicago and London: University of Chicago Press, 2003.

103 Gregory M. Grazevich, 'Emerging terminology in the *MLA International Bibliography*', *MLA Newsletter*, 2002, vol. 34.1, p. 6. I owe this reference to Claire Connolly.

104 The programme was first broadcast on 27 May 2002, and was largely concerned with the publication of Fukuyama's *Our Posthuman Future*.

105 Haraway, 'A cyborg manifesto', p. 150.

106 Ibid., p. 173.

107 Donna J. Haraway, *The Companion Species Manifesto: Dogs, People, and Significant Otherness*, Chicago: Prickly Paradigm Press, 2003, p. 4.

108 Ibid., pp. 9–10.

109 Ibid., p. 11.

110 Wolfe, *Animal Rites*, p. 1.

111 Ibid., pp. 1–2. Emphases in original.

112 Ibid., p. 9.

113 Roland Barthes, *A Lover's Discourse: Fragments*, trans. Richard Howard, Harmondsworth: Penguin, 1990, p. 73.

114 Wolfe, 'Radical Chic', p. 4.

115 Philip Roth, *The Human Stain*, London: Vintage, 2001, p. 242.

4 ALIEN OBJECTS, HUMAN SUBJECTS

1 Bob Dylan, 'Masters of war', *The Freewheelin' Bob Dylan*, Columbia Records, 1963.

2 See G. W. Leibniz, 'Principles of nature and of grace, founded on reason', in *Philosophical Writings*, trans. Mary Morris, London: J. M. Dent, 1934, p. 26: '*Why is there something rather than nothing?*' Emphasis in original. I owe thanks to Andrew Belsey for answering my questions about Leibniz.
3 Michel Foucault, 'Preface to *Anti-Oedipus*', in *Power: Essential Works of Foucault 1954–1984, Volume Three*, ed. James D. Faubion, trans. Robert Hurley et al., Harmondsworth: Penguin, 2002, p. 107.
4 Marshall Berman, *All That is Solid Melts into Air: The Experience of Modernity*, London and New York: Verso, 1983, p. 146.
5 Ibid.
6 Walter Benjamin, *The Arcades Project*, trans. Howard Eiland and Kevin McLaughlin, Cambridge, MA and London: The Belknap Press of Harvard University Press, 1999. Walter Benjamin, *Moscow Diary*, ed. Gary Smith, trans. Richard Sieburth, Cambridge, MA and London: MIT Press, 1986. One particular moment in the latter text (pp. 38–40) has always stayed with me: Benjamin ends the entry for 22 December 1926 by recording his unhappiness at the state of his relationship with Asja Lacis, but opens the following day's account with a joyous celebration of the 'very beautiful toys' that he has discovered in the Kustuaray Museum of Arts and Crafts. Toys, in fact, seemed to be one of the few things that brought Benjamin happiness during his difficult trip to Moscow.
7 Benjamin, *The Arcades Project*, p. 37.
8 Ibid., p. 866.
9 See, for instance, Walter Benjamin, 'Unpacking my library: A talk about book collecting', in *Illuminations*, ed. Hannah Arendt, trans. Harry Zohn, New York: Schocken, 1969, pp. 59–67.
10 Benjamin, *The Arcades Project*, pp. 203–11.
11 Ibid., p. 204.
12 Jean Baudrillard, *The System of Objects*, trans. James Benedict, London and New York: Verso, 1996, p. 3. Baudrillard's text was first published in French in 1968.
13 Ibid., p. 3. Translation modified. For the original wording, see Jean Baudrillard, *Le Système des objets*, Paris: Gallimard, 1968, p. 7.
14 Baudrillard, *The System of Objects*, p. 3.
15 Ibid., p. 4.
16 *The System of Objects* does, however, briefly refer to several of Barthes's other works, on pp. 11 n. 7, 25 n. 7, and 165 n. 19. And, in a section of the more recent *Passwords* devoted to objects, Baudrillard names Barthes as one of his main influences at the time of *The System of Objects* (Jean Baudrillard, *Passwords*, trans. Chris Turner, London and New York: Verso, 2003, p. 4).

17 *The System of Objects*, p. 199. Translation modified. For the original wording, see Baudrillard, *Le Système des objets*, p. 275.
18 Baudrillard, *The System of Objects*, p. 199. Translation modified. For the original wording, see Baudrillard, *Le Système des objets*, p. 275.
19 Baudrillard, *The System of Objects*, p. 86.
20 Ibid. Translation modified. For the original wording, see Baudrillard, *Le Système des objets*, p. 121.
21 Baudrillard, *The System of Objects*, p. 94. Emphasis in original.
22 Ibid., p. 90. Translation modified. For the original wording, see Baudrillard, *Le Système des objets*, p. 127.
23 Baudrillard, *The System of Objects*, p. 96. Emphasis in original.
24 Sigmund Freud, *Beyond the Pleasure Principle*, in *On Metapsychology: The Theory of Psychoanalysis*, ed. Angela Richards, trans. James Strachey, Penguin Freud Library, vol. 11, Harmondsworth: Penguin, 1991, p. 283.
25 The boy remains unidentified in *Beyond the Pleasure Principle*, however. For confirmation of his identity, see Ernest Jones, *Sigmund Freud: Life and Work*, 3 vols, London: Hogarth Press, 1953–7, vol. 3, p. 288. Jones suggests that Freud's original observation of the *fort/da* game took place in September 1915, when he visited his daughter at her home in Hamburg for several weeks.
26 Freud, *Beyond the Pleasure Principle*, p. 284. The parentheses here are the work of the translator and/or editor. Baudrillard mistakenly refers to Ernst's toy as a 'ball' (*System of Objects*, p. 97). This is not an error of translation, for the original French text describes a '*balle*' (*Le Système des objets*, p. 136).
27 Sigmund Freud, 'Parapraxes', in *Introductory Lectures on Psychoanalysis*, ed. James Strachey and Angela Richards, trans. James Strachey, Penguin Freud Library, vol. 1, Harmondsworth: Penguin, 1973, p. 52.
28 Freud, *Beyond the Pleasure Principle*, p. 285.
29 Ibid. Emphases in original.
30 Baudrillard, *The System of Objects*, p. 91.
31 The English translation, I should point out, allows for a shade of meaning that is not to be found in the original French, where the phrase 'Car on se collectionne toujours soi-même' (*Le Système des objets*, p. 128), although something of a *forçage de la langue*, does not suggest collecting oneself in the sense of *composing* oneself. I thank Claire Joubert for explaining Baudrillard's French (and much more) to me.
32 Jean Baudrillard, *Fatal Strategies*, trans. Philip Beitchman and W. G. J. Niesluchowki, New York: Semiotext(e)/London: Pluto, 1990, p. 111. In *Passwords*, Baudrillard explains that his fascination with objects began with a desire 'to break with the problematic of the subject. The question of the object represented the alternative to that problematic, and it has remained

the horizon of my thinking' (p. 3). Contrary to the claims of humanism, the object, he insists, can 'have a life of its own' (p. 3). It can, that is to say, be released from its traditional passivity, and understood instead as 'a fully fledged actor' (p. 5). It falls beyond the limits of the present project to examine the way in which Baudrillard, here as elsewhere, merely inverts the binary opposition to which he objects, thus remaining somewhat trapped within the orbit of structuralism. Once the subject was dominant; now it is the object; there seem to be only two distinct possibilities.

33 Charles Baudelaire, 'On wine and hashish compared as means of augmenting the individuality', in *Artificial Paradises*, trans. Stacy Diamond, New York: Citadel Press, 1996, p. 14.

34 Charles Baudelaire, 'The soul of wine', in *The Flowers of Evil*, trans. James McGowan, Oxford and New York: Oxford University Press, 1993, p. 215.

35 Baudelaire, 'On wine and hashish', p. 6.

36 Ibid., pp. 24–5.

37 Charles Baudelaire, 'The poem of hashish', in *Artificial Paradises*, 1996, pp. 31–76.

38 This effect is not only to be found in the writings of Baudelaire. Texts by Thomas De Quincey, Samuel Taylor Coleridge, Aldous Huxley, William Burroughs, Carlos Castaneda, Jack Kerouac, Hubert Selby Jr., Hunter S. Thompson and Irvine Welsh, for instance, also examine – often in different ways – the effect that intoxicants have upon the partaking subject. Walter Benjamin, with whom I began this chapter, discussed his experiences with hashish in 'Hashish in Marseilles', in *One-Way Street*, trans. Edmund Jephcott and Kingsley Shorter, London and New York: Verso, 1997, pp. 215–22.

39 Baudelaire, 'On wine and hashish', p. 20. See also 'The poem of hashish', p. 51.

40 Baudelaire, 'On wine and hashish', p. 15.

41 Baudelaire, 'The poem of hashish', p. 51. Emphasis in original. A similar scene is described in 'On wine and hashish', p. 20.

42 Baudelaire, 'On wine and hashish', p. 22. I have corrected a minor typographical error in the translation at this point.

43 Baudelaire, 'On wine and hashish', pp. 22–3.

44 Baudelaire, 'The poem of hashish', p. 61.

45 Baudrillard, *Fatal Strategies*, p. 111.

46 Claude Lévi-Strauss, *The Way of the Masks*, trans. Sylvia Modelski, Seattle and London: University of Washington Press/Vancouver and Toronto: UBC Press, 1988, p. 144. Emphasis in original.

47 Ibid., p. 228.

48 Ibid., p. 12.

49 I cannot help wondering, however, exactly what an alien would sound like when speaking through the voice changer.

50 Jacques Derrida, *Of Grammatology*, trans. Gayatri Chakravorty Spivak, Baltimore and London: Johns Hopkins University Press, 1976; *'Speech and Phenomena' and Other Essays on Husserl's Theory of Signs*, trans. David B. Allison, Evanston, IL: Northwestern University Press, 1973.
51 Derrida, *Of Grammatology*, p. 3.
52 Benjamin, 'Unpacking my library', p. 64.
53 There is a significant homogenization at work here: English is but one terrestrial language, but all extraterrestrials appear simply to speak 'Alien'. The other is simply evoked for its absolute difference, its utter alien-ness.
54 Gene Brewer, *K-PAX*, London: Bloomsbury, 1996; *K-PAX II: On a Beam of Light*, London: Bloomsbury, 2001; *K-PAX III: The Worlds of Prot*, London: Bloomsbury, 2002. The first novel in the trilogy was filmed under the direction of Iain Softley in 2001.
55 Steve Beard, *Logic Bomb: Transmissions from the Edge of Style Culture*, London and New York: Serpent's Tail, 1998, p. 114.
56 Jacques Derrida, 'Of an apocalyptic tone recently adopted in philosophy', trans. John P. Leavey, Jr., *The Oxford Literary Review*, 1984, vol. 6.2, pp. 3–37. For a related discussion of the problems of apocalypse, see Jacques Derrida, 'No apocalypse, not now (full speed ahead, seven missiles, seven missives)', trans. Catherine Porter, *Diacritics*, 1984, vol. 14, pp. 20–31.
57 Friedrich Nietzsche, *Human, All Too Human: A Book for Free Spirits*, trans. R. J. Hollingdale, Cambridge: Cambridge University Press, 1996, p. 15.
58 Ovid, *Metamorphoses*, trans. Mary M. Innes, Harmondsworth: Penguin, 1955, p. 203.
59 I take the latter to be the counterpart, the terrible twin, of what Jill Didur usefully names 'critical posthumanism' in her fine essay, 'Re-embodying technoscientific fantasies: Posthumanism, genetically modified foods, and the colonization of life', *Cultural Critique*, 2003, vol. 53, pp. 98–115.
60 N. Katherine Hayles, *How We Became Posthuman: Virtual Bodies in Cybernetics, Literature and Informatics*, Chicago and London: University of Chicago Press, 1999, p. 1.
61 Ibid., p. 287.
62 Ibid., p. 283.
63 Ibid., pp. 286–7.
64 For a somewhat different approach to the problem of what remains in the apparently posthumanist moment, see Fred Botting, *Sex, Machines and Navels: Fiction, Fantasy and History in the Future Present*, Manchester: Manchester University Press, 1999. While I will in what follows call principally upon Derrida and Lyotard, Botting enlists Jacques Lacan to tell a fascinating story about the return or the resilience of the real in these allegedly hyper-real times.

65 I take the question of what desists from Philippe Lacoue-Labarthe, *Typography: Mimesis, Philosophy, Politics*, ed. Christopher Fynsk, Stanford: Stanford University Press, 1998.
66 Neil Badmington, 'Introduction: Approaching posthumanism', in Neil Badmington (ed.) *Posthumanism*, Basingstoke and New York: Palgrave, 2000, p. 1.
67 *Time*, 3 January 1983, p. 3.
68 Well, almost. Deep within the issue in question (pp. 26–7), in what was surely a desperate attempt to shore up humanism, the editors listed several human 'runners-up': Menachem Begin, Paul A. Volcker, and Margaret Thatcher. I am tempted to interpret the choice of the latter as yet another instance of humanism merrily siding with the monstrously inhuman.
69 Letters page, *Time*, 24 January 1983.
70 I should like to thank Marjorie Garber and Rainer Emig for pushing me, in a seminar on posthumanism at Cardiff University in 1999, to think further about the strange presence of this figure.
71 Jacques Derrida, 'The ends of Man', in *Margins of Philosophy*, trans. Alan Bass, Hemel Hempstead: Harvester Wheatsheaf, 1982, p. 117.
72 Ibid., p. 135. Translation modified. For the original French wording, see Jacques Derrida, 'Les fins de l'homme', in *Marges de la philosophie*, Paris: Minuit, 1972, p. 162.
73 Derrida, 'The ends of Man', p. 135.
74 Jacques Derrida, 'Structure, sign, and play in the discourse of the human sciences', in Richard Mackey and Eugenio Donato (eds) *The Structuralist Controversy: The Languages of Criticism and the Sciences of Man*, Baltimore and London: Johns Hopkins University Press, 1972, p. 271. This remark is made during the discussion that follows Derrida's presentation, and is in response to a question posed by Serge Doubrovksy. The version of the essay published in *Writing and Difference* does not, unfortunately, reproduce the discussion.
75 Derrida, 'The ends of Man', p. 135. Emphasis in original. Translation modified. For the French wording, see Derrida, 'Les fins de l'homme', p. 162.
76 Derrida, 'The ends of Man', p. 135.
77 Ibid. Translation modified. For the original French wording, see Derrida 'Les fins de l'homme', p. 163.
78 Derrida, 'The ends of Man', p. 135. Translation modified. For the original French wording, see Derrida 'Les fins de l'homme', p. 163.
79 Or, more precisely, upon what Bill Readings describes as the ruins of the university. See his *The University in Ruins*, Cambridge, MA and London: Harvard University Press, 1996.
80 See Constance Penley and Andrew Ross, 'Cyborgs at large: Interview with Donna Haraway', in Constance Penley and Andrew Ross (eds) *Technoculture*,

Minneapolis and Oxford: University of Minnesota Press, 1991, p. 18: 'I would rather go to bed with a cyborg than a sensitive man, I'll tell you that much.'

81 My turn of phrase here is an allusion to the description that Ernesto Laclau and Chantal Mouffe provide of their own work in *Hegemony and Socialist Strategy: Towards a Radical Democratic Politics*, London and New York: Verso, 1985, p. 4: 'But if our intellectual project in this book is *post*-Marxist, it is evidently also post-*Marxist*.'

82 This crucial phrase features in a particularly memorable paragraph in *Of Grammatology*, where Derrida writes: 'The movements of deconstruction do not destroy structures from the outside. They are not possible and effective, nor can they take accurate aim, except by inhabiting those structures. Inhabiting them *in a certain way*, because one always inhabits, and all the more when one does not suspect it' (Derrida, *Of Grammatology*, p. 24. Emphasis in original).

83 Jacques Derrida, *Mémoires for Paul de Man*, rev. edn, trans. Cecile Lindsay, Jonathan Culler and Eduardo Cadava, New York: Columbia University Press, 1989, p. 73. Emphases in original.

84 Don DeLillo, *Valparaiso*, New York: Scribner, 1999, p. 45. This is not to say that Derrida is only concerned with the marginal, and that his gaze never travels beyond the outskirts. 'Demeure: Fiction and testimony', for example, not only offers a remarkable reading of Blanchot's 'The instant of my death', but also manages – as it negotiates the twists and turns of Blanchot's haunting story – to quote 'The instant of my death' *in its entirety*. No sentence of a tale about the escape from a sentence is allowed to escape (Maurice Blanchot and Jacques Derrida, *The Instant of My Death/Demeure: Fiction and Testimony*, trans. Elizabeth Rottenberg, Stanford: Stanford University Press, 2000).

85 Derrida, *Dissemination*, trans. Barbara Johnson, London: Athlone, 1981, p. 99.

86 Ibid., p. 67. Emphasis in original.

87 Derrida, 'Violence and metaphysics: An essay on the thought of Emmanuel Lévinas', in *Writing and Difference*, trans. Alan Bass, London: Routledge and Kegan Paul, 1978, p. 111.

88 For an analysis of this tendency, see Frank Furedi, *Culture of Fear: Risk-Taking and the Morality of Low Expectation*, rev. edn, London and New York: Continuum, 2002.

89 I briefly alluded to this particular moment in the *Discourse on the Method* in my 'Introduction: Approaching posthumanism' (pp. 3–4), but lacked the space in that context to work through the complexities of Descartes's position. It seems that a ten-hour lecture given in 1997 by Jacques Derrida at the 'L'Animal autobiographique' conference in Cérisy-la-Salle also touched

upon the passage in question. But as, at the time of writing (December 2003), only selected sections of Derrida's talk have been published, I cannot engage with his reading of Descartes here. Derrida briefly alludes to his analysis of the relevant moment in the *Discourse on the Method* in 'And say the animal responded?', in Cary Wolfe (ed.) *Zoontologies: The Question of the Animal*, Minneapolis and London: University of Minnesota Press, 2003, p. 143 n. 1. This essay originally formed part of the Cérisy lecture. For another fragment, see Jacques Derrida, 'The animal that therefore I am (more to follow)', trans. David Wills, *Critical Inquiry*, 2002, vol. 28.2, pp. 369–418.

90 The phrase in question occurs at various moments in Elaine L. Graham, *Representations of the Post/Human: Monsters, Aliens and Others in Popular Culture*, Manchester: Manchester University Press, 2002.

91 Donna J. Haraway, *The Companion Species Manifesto: Dogs, People, and Significant Otherness*, Chicago: Prickly Paradigm Press, 2003, p. 51.

92 This wonderful phrase was suggested to me by Catherine Belsey.

93 Philip K. Dick, *A Scanner Darkly*, London: HarperCollins, 1996, p. 223. Emphasis in original.

94 I am by no means the first person to play on this virtual homonym. See, for instance, Slavoj Žižek, *Tarrying with the Negative: Kant, Hegel, and the Critique of Ideology*, Durham, NC: Duke University Press, 1993, p. 12; Kevin McCarron, 'Corpses, animals, machines and mannequins: The body and cyberpunk', in Mike Featherstone and Roger Burrows (eds) *Cyberspace/Cyberbodies/Cyberpunk: Cultures of Technological Embodiment*, London: Sage, 1995, p. 264.

95 Philip K. Dick, *Do Androids Dream of Electric Sheep?*, London: Panther, 1972. Some later editions are published under the title *Blade Runner*, even though there are many substantial differences between the novel and the film.

96 Derrida, 'Structure, sign, and play', p. 254.

97 Donna J. Haraway, 'Situated knowledges: The science question in feminism and the privilege of partial perspective', in *Simians, Cyborgs, and Women: The Reinvention of Nature*, London: Free Association Books, 1991, p. 189.

98 Mark Z. Danielewski, *House of Leaves*, London: Anchor, 2000. Jacques Derrida makes several appearances – some 'real', some 'fake' – in Danielewski's fascinating (and terrifying) novel. For a reading of *House of Leaves* that takes into account the question of posthumanism, see the final chapter of N. Katherine Hayles, *Writing Machines*, Cambridge, MA, and London: MIT Press, 2002.

99 Jean-François Lyotard, *The Postmodern Condition: A Report on Knowledge*, trans. Geoffrey Bennington and Brian Massumi, Manchester: Manchester University Press, 1984.

100 Jean-François Lyotard, 'Answer to the question: What is the postmodern?', in *The Postmodern Explained to Children: Correspondence 1982–1985*, trans. Don Barry et al., ed. Julian Pefanis and Morgan Thomas, London: Turnaround, 1992, pp. 87–93; 'Note on the meaning of "post-"', in *The Postmodern Explained to Children*, pp. 9–25.
101 Jean-François Lyotard, 'Rewriting modernity', in *The Inhuman: Reflections on Time*, trans. Geoffrey Bennington and Rachel Bowlby, Cambridge: Polity Press, 1991, p. 24.
102 Jean-François Lyotard, 'Rules and paradoxes and svelte appendix', trans. Brian Massumi, *Cultural Critique* 1986/7, vol. 5, p. 209.
103 Lyotard, 'Rewriting modernity', p. 34.
104 Ibid., p. 25.
105 See, for instance, Jürgen Habermas, 'Modernity versus postmodernity', trans. Seyla Ben-Habib, *New German Critique*, 1981, vol. 22, pp. 3–14.
106 Lyotard, 'Rewriting modernity', p. 26.
107 Sigmund Freud, 'Remembering, repeating and working-through (Further recommendations on the technique of psycho-analysis II)', in *The Standard Edition of the Complete Psychological Works of Sigmund Freud*, 24 vols, ed. and trans. James Strachey, with Anna Freud, Alix Strachey and Alan Tyson, London: Hogarth Press and the Institute of Psychoanalysis, 1953–74, vol. 12, p. 155. Emphasis in original.
108 Ibid., p. 155.
109 Lyotard, 'Rewriting modernity', p. 33.
110 For a wonderful book that also works with (and through) Freud's theory of 'working-through' to tell a slightly different story about the difficult relationship between humanism and posthumanism, see Iain Chambers, *Culture After Humanism: History, Culture, Subjectivity*, London and New York: Routledge, 2001. If Chambers's project is to examine how modernity 'remains irretrievably undone by the questions it can no longer contain' (p. 17), mine involves a more localized attention to the same type of undoing in the realm of humanism.
111 I take this beautiful phrase from Michel de Certeau, *The Writing of History*, trans. Tom Conley, New York: Columbia University Press, 1988, p. 2.
112 Antonio Gramsci, *Selections from the Prison Notebooks of Antonio Gramsci*, ed. and trans. Quintin Hoare and Geoffrey Nowell Smith, London: Lawrence and Wishart, 1971, p. 276.
113 Ted Mooney, *Easy Travel to Other Planets*, New York: Vintage, 1992, p. 186.
114 Ibid., p. 103. Ellipsis in original.
115 I owe something like this point to Malcolm Bull.

116 I am thinking here of the now archaic use of the term to mean, in phrases such as 'Send me good speed', prosperity or success. Posthumanist cultural criticism needs, I think, to remember and repeat this very obsolescence.
117 Paul Celan, 'Fadensonnen', in *Gesammelte Werke*, 5 vols, Frankfurt am Main: Suhrkamp Verlag, 1983, vol. 2, p. 26.
118 Martin Heidegger, 'The question concerning technology', in *The Question Concerning Technology and Other Essays*, trans. William Lovitt, New York: Harper & Row, 1977, p. 3.

5 A CRISIS OF *VERSUS*: REREADING THE ALIEN

1 Don DeLillo, *Americana*, Harmondsworth: Penguin, 1990, p. 364.
2 Although the series has always been known in the United States as *Roswell*, it was first transmitted in Britain under the title *Roswell High*.
3 Richard Vine, 'Home and away', *Guardian*, 7 September 2000, section G2, p. 17.
4 Available: <http://www.yearbox.com/roswell/roswell.html> (accessed 18 November 2003).
5 Available: <http://www.bbc.co.uk/cult/roswell/characters/index.shtml> (accessed 18 November 2003).
6 A list of titles drawn from the filmography of Thomas Doherty's fine history of 'teenpics' will suffice here: *Diary of a High School Bride* (dir. Burt Topper, 1959), *High School Big Shot* (dir. Joel Rapp, 1958), *High School Confidential* (dir. Jack Arnold, 1958), *High School Hellcats* (dir. Edward Bernds, 1958), *Platinum High School* (dir. Charles Hass, 1960), and *Reform School Girl* (dir. Edward Bernds, 1957) (Thomas Doherty, *Teenagers and Teenpics: The Juvenilization of American Movies in the 1950s*, Boston: Unwin Hyman, 1988, pp. 245–61). To this it would be possible to add more recent examples such as: *Fast Times at Ridgemont High* (dir. Amy Heckerling, 1982), *High School High* (dir. Hart Bochner, 1996), *The Faculty* (dir. Robert Rodriguez, 1998), *Massacre at Central High* (dir. Renee Daalder, 1976), and, of course, *Class of Nuke 'Em High* (dir. Richard W. Haines, 1986).
7 Martin Heidegger, 'What is metaphysics?', in *Basic Writings*, ed. David Farrell Krell, rev. edn, London: Routledge, 1993, p. 98.
8 The incident in question occurred in an episode entitled '101 damnations', in which the night clerk of a somewhat seedy hotel was clearly seen to be reading a copy of *Libidinal Economy*. This wonderfully bizarre moment was the work of the GALA Committee – a group consisting largely of students and faculty at the University of Georgia and CalArts – which collaborated with the makers of *Melrose Place* over a period of two

years. Constance Penley gave a fascinating account of her involvement in the project in 'Melrose space: Art, politics and identity in the age of global media', a paper presented as a plenary lecture at the Third International Crossroads in Cultural Studies conference, University of Birmingham, 23 June 2000. For the GALA Committee homepage, see <http://www.arts.ucsb.edu/projects/mpart/core/core.html> (accessed on 19 November 2003).

9 Jean-François Lyotard, 'A podium without a podium: Television according to J.-F. Lyotard', in *Political Writings*, trans. Bill Readings and Kevin Paul Geiman, Minneapolis: University of Minnesota Press, 1993, p. 91. Ellipses in original. The subject of the sentences is, of course, Lyotard himself.

10 Jean-François Lyotard, 'Introduction: About the human', in *The Inhuman: Reflections on Time*, trans. Geoffrey Bennington and Rachel Bowlby, Cambridge: Polity Press, 1991, p. 3. Ellipsis in original.

11 Raymond Williams, 'Culture is ordinary', in *Resources of Hope: Culture, Democracy, Socialism*, ed. Robin Gable, London and New York: Verso, 1989, pp. 3–18.

12 Louis Althusser, 'Ideology and ideological state apparatuses (Notes towards an investigation)', in *Lenin and Philosophy and Other Essays*, trans. Ben Brewster, New York: Monthly Review Press, 1971, pp. 156–7: 'But no other ideological State apparatus has the obligatory (and not least, free) audience of the totality of the children in the capitalist social formation, eight hours a day for five or six days out of seven . . . In fact, the Church has been replaced today *in its role as the dominant Ideological State Apparatus* by the School.' Emphasis in original.

13 The link between posthumanism and a resistance to compulsory education became apparent to me at an early age. In my native South Wales, it is not unusual (even for speakers of English) to refer to the fine art of truancy as 'mitching' or 'mooching' (both spellings are assumed; I have only ever come across the term in conversation). In this, I cannot help hearing an echo of *mochyn*, the Welsh word for 'pig'. To 'mitch' or 'mooch', then, is to become an animal, an inhuman thing.

14 Judith Butler, *Gender Trouble: Feminism and the Subversion of Identity*, New York and London: Routledge, 1990, p. vii.

15 Higher education continues the trend. As an undergraduate at the University of California in the early 1990s, I was amazed to see regular television coverage of, and huge crowds at, college football games. While sport is an unmistakable part of university life in Britain – it is traditional, for instance, to leave Wednesday afternoons free from teaching in order to allow sporting fixtures to take place – its profile is considerably lower.

16 I take this concept from Jean-François Lyotard, *The Differend: Phrases in Dispute*, trans. Georges Van Den Abbeele, Manchester: Manchester University Press, 1988. In Lyotard's account, a differend exists when a conflict between two or more parties cannot be settled or even phrased in a language that would do justice to all sides. To bear witness to a differend is, as he puts it, to acknowledge that 'a universal rule of judgment between heterogeneous genres is lacking in general' (p. xi). By the same token, to ignore a differend is to deny difference and justice. A section entitled 'Differend' in the posthumous book on Augustine adds the following warning: 'Who can take the common measure of something incommensurable? A form of knowledge that vaunts that it can do so, in bestriding the abyss, forgets the abyss and relapses. The cut is primal' (Jean-François Lyotard, *The Confession of Augustine*, trans. Richard Beardsworth, Stanford: Stanford University Press, 2000, p. 36).

17 Don DeLillo, *End Zone*, Harmondsworth: Penguin, 1986, p. 118. Emphasis added.

18 The specificities of the latter event only really become apparent in the novelization: 'Then he *nudged* the molecules. That's the only way he could describe it. He nudged them, and they broke apart. The bullet dissolving into microscopic particles. Harmless now as they were swept away in Liz's bloodstream' (Melinda Metz, *Roswell High: The Outsider*, New York: Pocket Books, 1998, p. 13. Emphasis in original).

19 Similar situations arise in 'Skin and bones', when Max is unable to save Nasedo, and the later 'Cry your name', in which attempts to revive Alex are unsuccessful.

20 Frank Sinatra, 'Young at heart', *The Very Best of Frank Sinatra*, Warner Brothers Records, 1997.

21 Frank Sinatra, 'Love and marriage', *The Very Best of Frank Sinatra*, Warner Brothers Records, 1997.

22 In the novelization, however, Max's love for Liz is clearly established as early as the scene in which he heals her gunshot wound: 'He knelt beside Liz and placed his hands over her wound. In an instant his fingers were slick with blood. I love her. The thought exploded in his mind. It was true. He'd been keeping it a secret, even from himself. Loving a human wasn't smart. It wasn't safe. But he couldn't help it. He loved Liz, and he would not let her die' (Metz, *Roswell High: The Outsider*, pp. 11–12).

23 Friendship does not always, of course, call for silence. In the pilot episode, for instance, Liz reveals Max's secret and her innermost feelings to Maria, even when she knows that this risks placing him and the other aliens in a position of danger. Moreover, she knows in advance that such a revelation will be disturbing to her friend. On this occasion, that is to say, Liz wants to confide when common sense and logic would dictate silence.

24 The friendship does falter a little in the later 'Heatwave', but remains intact at the moment of crisis in 'Blood brother'. And Alex's subsequent hostility soon disappears when Liz tells him the truth about the aliens.
25 This is particularly evident in 'Heatwave', where the soaring temperature prompts a veritable epidemic of lust.
26 Jacques Derrida, 'Ellipsis', in *Writing and Difference*, trans. Alan Bass, London: Routledge and Kegan Paul, 1978, p. 296.
27 My reading is not framed in terms of authorial intention. I have no way of knowing whether or not the creators of *Roswell* are deliberately putting posthumanist theories into practice. What matters, rather, is the movement of meaning, the undecidability that invades the text at every turn.
28 Vladimir Nabokov, *Pnin*, Harmondsworth: Penguin, 1960, p. 14.
29 Brian Murphy, 'Monster movies: They came from beneath the fifties', *Journal of Popular Film*, 1972, vol. 1.1, p. 43.
30 Vivian Sobchack, *Screening Space: The American Science Fiction Film*, 2nd edn, New York: Ungar, 1987, p. 125. Emphasis in original.
31 This is not to say that feelings *alone* are satisfactory, for it seems to me that in the marginal figure of Teddy Bellicec, the film warns that an excess of emotion leads to hysteria. Teddy, in fact, does little but exhibit her emotions, a condition which renders her dependent upon her husband and unable truly to contribute to the resistance. And yet, while unchecked feeling is problematic, Danny Kaufman would appear to represent the perils of abandoning emotion in the name of scientific reason. Indeed, Kaufman's alien conversion leads to no apparent change in his behaviour: he continues to act exactly as he has always done, appealing to science and reason in calm, measured tones. Two possible conclusions may be drawn from this: either Kaufman was inhuman all along (which is to say that the viewer never sees the 'real' character), or there is no detectable difference between a man of pure reason and an emotionless alien. What the film seems to propose, therefore, is an ideal state in which reason and emotion exist in harmonious equilibrium. David Lavery's suggestion that *Invasion of the Body Snatchers* stages a simple binary opposition between feeling humans and reasoning aliens is, from this perspective, somewhat misguided (David Lavery, 'Departure of the body snatchers, or the confessions of a carbon chauvinist', *The Hudson Review*, 1986, vol. 39.3, pp. 383–404)
32 Because the pod lies at the very margin of the frame, its presence is lost in some pan-and-scan presentations of the film.
33 By this stage in the proceedings, Miles has already called upon Shakespeare in a playful attempt to win Becky's heart, (mis)quoting from *A Midsummer Night's Dream* as he arranges a date for the evening. Little wonder, then, that he now chooses, as the film begins its descent into tragedy, to mimic Hamlet's hesitation before the kneeling Claudius.

34 The response to the gap between what a text *declares* and what it subsequently *describes* is one of the hallmarks of deconstruction, and is explicitly identified as such by Derrida in *Of Grammatology*: 'We must measure this gap [in Rousseau's work] between the description and the declaration' (Jacques Derrida, *Of Grammatology*, trans. Gayatri Chakravorty Spivak, Baltimore and London: Johns Hopkins University Press, 1976, p. 217).

35 This is perhaps because the double clearly looks like Becky (the close-up, after all, focuses on her face). Indeed, not long after the scene in question, Miles happily destroys an inchoate pod which had been concealed in the boot of his car, and which would have eventually produced another fake Becky. The crucial difference at this later moment is that there is no visual resemblance: Miles is simply destroying a large vegetable that looks nothing like his lover. Vegetables, in fact, mark a key difference between Siegel's film and *The Thing from Another World*. In the latter movie, the troublesome alien looks nothing like a human being; it is, in fact, described at one point as 'an intellectual carrot'. The humans, accordingly, have no doubts about destroying the creature.

36 Cyndy Hendershot, 'The invaded body: Paranoia and radiation anxiety in *Invaders from Mars*, *It Came from Outer Space*, and *Invasion of the Body Snatchers*', *Extrapolation: A Journal of Science Fiction and Fantasy*, 1998, vol. 39.1, p. 34. Emphasis in original.

37 Al LaValley (ed.), *Invasion of the Body Snatchers: Don Siegel, Director*, New Brunswick, NJ and London: Rutgers University Press, 1989, p. 25.

38 Jacques Lacan, *The Seminar of Jacques Lacan, Book II: The Ego in Freud's Theory and in the Technique of Psychoanalysis 1954–1955*, ed. Jacques-Alain Miller, trans. Sylvana Tomaselli, New York and London: W. W. Norton, 1988, p. 175.

39 Jacques Lacan, 'The subversion of the subject and the dialectic of desire in the Freudian unconscious', in *Écrits: A Selection*, trans. Alan Sheridan, London: Tavistock, 1977, p. 324.

40 Jacques Lacan, 'The mirror stage as formative of the function of the I as revealed in psychoanalytic experience', in *Écrits: A Selection*, p. 1. I have slightly modified Sheridan's translation here, giving 'all' for '*toute*' in order to bring out what I see as the fundamental aggression of the sentence. For the original French wording, see Jacques Lacan, 'Le Stade du miroir comme formateur de la fonction du Je telle qu'elle nous est révélée dans l'expérience psychanalytique', in *Écrits*, Paris: Seuil, 1966, p. 93.

41 Jacques Lacan, *The Seminar of Jacques Lacan, Book III: The Psychoses 1955–1956*, ed. Jacques-Alain Miller, trans. Russell Grigg, New York and London: W. W. Norton, 1993, p. 82.

42 I should like to thank Jean-Jacques Lecercle for providing me with the French title of the film and for waxing lyrical about *Them!* (or, as he would have it, *Les Monstres attaquent la ville*).
43 Jacques Lacan, *The Four Fundamental Concepts of Psycho-analysis*, ed. Jacques-Alain Miller, trans. Alan Sheridan, Harmondsworth: Penguin, 1994, p. 205. I have substantially modified Sheridan's translation in this instance. For the original French wording, see Jacques Lacan, *Le Séminaire de Jacques Lacan, livre XI: Les quatres concepts fondamenteux de la psych-analyse*, ed. Jacques-Alain Miller, Paris: Seuil, 1973, p. 187.
44 Jacques Lacan, *The Seminar of Jacques Lacan, Book XX: Encore: On Feminine Sexuality, The Limits of Love and Knowledge 1972–1973*, ed. Jacques-Alain Miller, trans. Bruce Fink, London and New York: W. W. Norton, 1998.
45 Catherine Belsey, *Desire: Love Stories in Western Culture*, Oxford: Blackwell, 1994, p. 61. Emphases in original.
46 Jacques Lacan, 'The agency of the letter in the unconscious or reason since Freud', in *Écrits: A Selection*, p. 167. Emphasis in original.
47 Even if this is seen as a reactionary example of mindless male promiscuity – the man does not care with whom he has sex as long as she is a she; the women have no say in the matter – I would still insist that the film at once tells a more challenging story about desire's unruliness. I do not know whether or not Buñuel was aware of Lacan's work; the latter, as one critic has pointed out, was certainly an admirer of Buñuel's films (David Macey, *Lacan in Contexts*, London and New York: Verso, 1988, p. 49).
48 Jacques Derrida, 'The almost nothing of the unpresentable', in *Points . . . Interviews, 1974–1994*, ed. Elisabeth Weber, trans. Peggy Kamuf et al., Stanford: Stanford University Press, 1995, p. 83.
49 I owe thanks to another Miles, Miles Thompson, for pointing out to me that one of the possible meanings of the name in question is 'dear' or 'beloved' (the precise origin of 'Miles' would appear to be undecidable). And, quite by chance, a recent reading of one of Paul Virilio's books made me realize that Miles's position in the narrative as some kind of warrior fighting for the preservation of the human is also implied in his name, for a '*miles*' was an 'ancient [Roman] "citizen-soldier" who defended his possessions, his family and the entire city, as well as his own person' (Paul Virilio, *Desert Screen: War at the Speed of Light*, trans. Michael Degener, London and New York: Continuum, 2002, p. 9).
50 Antony Easthope, *The Unconscious*, London and New York: Routledge, 1999, p. 166.
51 Nancy Steffen-Fluhr, 'Women and the inner game of Don Siegel's *Invasion of the Body Snatchers*', *Science Fiction Studies*, 1984, vol. 11.2, p. 141.
52 Ibid.

53 Sumiko Higashi, 'Invasion of the body snatchers: Pods then and now', *Jump Cut*, 1981, vols 24/25, p. 3.
54 Probably because of the Hays Code, Miles and Becky simply mention recent visits to Reno, where divorces could (and still can) be obtained quickly and easily. As Al LaValley has noted, earlier drafts of the screenplay opened with a chance meeting between Miles and Becky at the railway station, where she informs him that she has just returned from Reno, having thrown her wedding ring into the Truckee River. This scene was dropped when the Hays Office objected to a reference to divorce at such an early stage in proceedings (LaValley, *Invasion of the Body Snatchers*, pp. 112–13).
55 Tracing the text's evolution from Jack Finney's serial and novel to Don Siegel's film, Glen M. Johnson observes that, whereas the movie attributes Miles's divorce to his work schedule, Finney's texts intimate that marriage itself is a form of invasion and dehumanization, and that the emotionally unstable protagonist is incapable of romantic commitment. Glen M. Johnson, '"We'd fight . . . we had to": *The Body Snatchers* as novel and film', *Journal of Popular Culture*, 1979, vol. 13, p. 8. For the original three-part serial, see Jack Finney, 'The body snatchers', *Collier's*, 26 November 1954, pp. 26–7, 90–4, 96–9; 10 December 1954, pp. 114, 116–25; and 24 December 1954, pp. 62, 64–5, 68–9, 71–3. For the novelization, see Jack Finney, *The Body Snatchers*, London: Eyre and Spottiswoode, 1955. In order to tie in with Philip Kaufman's remake of the film, Finney's novel was revised and republished as *Invasion of the Body Snatchers*, London: Sphere, 1978. I should like to thank Emma Mason for tracking down a copy of the original serial.
56 Jacques Derrida, 'Positions: Interview with Jean-Louis Houdebine and Guy Scarpetta', in *Positions*, trans. Alan Bass, Chicago: University of Chicago Press, 1981, p. 52.
57 Jacques Derrida, 'The Villanova roundtable: A conversation with Jacques Derrida', in John D. Caputo (ed.) *Deconstruction in a Nutshell: A Conversation with Jacques Derrida*, New York: Fordham University Press, 1997, p. 9.
58 Samuel Beckett, *Worstward Ho*, London: John Calder, 1983, p. 11.
59 N. Katherine Hayles, *How We Became Posthuman: Virtual Bodies in Cybernetics, Literature, and Informatics*, Chicago and London: University of Chicago Press, 1999, p. 6.
60 See, for instance: Stuart Rosenthal and Judith M. Kass, *Tod Browning/Don Siegel*, New York: A. S. Barnes, 1975, p. 119; Lavery, 'Departure of the body snatchers', p. 387; Johnson, '*The Body Snatchers* as novel and film', pp. 11, 12–13; Charles T. Gregory, 'The pod society versus the rugged individualists', *Journal of Popular Film*, 1972, vol. 1.1, p. 8; Cyndy Hendershot,

'Vampire and replicant: The one-sex body in a two-sex world', *Science-Fiction Studies*, 1995, vol. 22.3, p. 395 n. 26; Higashi, 'Pods then and now', p. 4; Stuart Samuels, 'The age of conspiracy and conformity: *Invasion of the Body Snatchers*', in John E. O'Connor and Martin A. Jackson (eds) *American History/American Film: Interpreting the Hollywood Image*, New York: Ungar, 1979, p. 214; John Brosnan, *The Primal Screen: A History of Science Fiction Film*, London: Orbit, 1991, p. 78; J. Hoberman, 'Paranoia and the pods', *Sight and Sound*, May 1994, p. 29; Mark Jancovich, *Horror*, London: B. T. Batsford, 1992, p. 68; Arthur Le Gacy, '*The Invasion of the Body Snatchers*: A metaphor for the fifties', *Literature/Film Quarterly*, 1978, vol. 1, p. 286.

61 Don Siegel, *A Siegel Film: An Autobiography*, London and Boston: Faber and Faber, 1993, p. 178.

62 I take this idea from Shoshana Felman, 'Turning the screw of interpretation', *Yale French Studies*, 1977, vols 55/56, pp. 94–207. In her fascinating essay, Felman points out that criticism of *The Turn of the Screw* frequently repeats and restages key features of Henry James's text.

63 Philip Kaufman, 'Are we pods . . . yet?', interview with Ralph Appelbaum, *Films and Filming*, April 1979, p. 11.

64 Although it is never mentioned, it seems to me that Kaufman's movie is a particularly fine example of the 'incoherent' film identified by Robin Wood in his fine book, *Hollywood from Vietnam to Reagan*, New York: Columbia University Press, 1986.

65 I am not for one moment suggesting that Nancy, *as a woman*, is incapable of saving the world. The text does not disclose her fate, but she has been constructed throughout the narrative as a weak, hysterical figure, and I think that the viewer is intended to conclude that the end of the male protagonist – the centre, the hope – is the end of humanity.

66 Kaufman, 'Are we pods . . . yet?', p. 13.

67 Lavery, 'Departure of the body snatchers', p. 389.

68 Hoberman, 'Paranoia and the pods', p. 31.

CONCLUSION: FROM DIFFERENCE TO DIFFERANCE (WITH AN 'A')

1 Philip Roth, *The Human Stain*, London: Vintage, 2001, p. 52.

2 Stuart Hall, 'Cultural identity and diaspora', in Jonathan Rutherford (ed.) *Identity: Community, Culture, Difference*, London: Lawrence and Wishart, 1990, p. 229.

3 Ferdinand de Saussure, *Course in General Linguistics*, ed. Charles Bally, Albert Sechehaye and Albert Reidlinger, trans. Wade Baskin, London: Fontana, 1974, p. 65.

4 Ibid., p. 116.
5 Ibid., p. 14.
6 Ibid., p. 67.
7 Ibid., p. 120. Emphasis in original.
8 Ibid., p. 66.
9 Ibid., p. 113.
10 Ibid., p. 13.
11 Jacques Derrida, *Of Grammatology*, trans. Gayatri Chakravorty Spivak, Baltimore and London: Johns Hopkins University Press, 1976, p. 43. Emphasis in original.
12 Ibid., p. 62.
13 Ibid., p. 65. Emphasis in original.
14 Jacques Derrida, 'Differance', in *'Speech and Phenomena' and Other Essays on Husserl's Theory of Signs*, trans. David B. Allison, Evanston, IL: Northwestern University Press, 1973, pp. 129–30. Emphases in original.
15 Ibid., p. 142.
16 Ibid., p. 134.
17 Ibid., p. 130. Emphases in original. See also p. 131.
18 R. L. Rutsky, *High Technē: Art and Technology from the Machine Aesthetic to the Posthuman*, Minneapolis and London: University of Minnesota Press, 1999, p. 21.

Index

An environmentally friendly book printed and bound in England by www.printondemand-worldwide.com

This book is made entirely of sustainable materials; FSC paper for the cover and PEFC paper for the text pages.

#0022 - 191016 - C0 - 234/156/12 - PB